THEODORA FITZGIBBON

TRADITIONAL SCOTTISH COOKERY

'We were astonished at its elegance in so
desert a place . . . Our supper consisted of
two dishes of fine game, the one of heathcock,
the other of woodcock, a creamy fresh butter,
cheese of the country, a pot of *vaccinium*
(blaeberries), a wild fruit which grows on the
mountains, and port wine – all served up together.
It was a luxurious repast for the country.'

> Faujas de St Fond (the King of France's
> Commissioner for Wines) *c.* 1780, writing
> of an inn at Dalmally, Argyll.

SOUVENIR PRESS

For my many Scottish friends and
particularly Kitty Forbes for the loan of
family papers and practical help

First published by Fontana Paperbacks 1980
Copyright © Theodora FitzGibbon 1980
Copyright © 1991 George Morrison

This edition first published 1991 by
Souvenir Press Ltd,
43 Great Russell Street, London WC1B 3PA
and simultaneously in Canada

ISBN 0 285 63065 2

Printed and bound in Great Britain by
Mackays of Chatham PLC, Chatham, Kent

TRADITIONAL
SCOTTISH COOKERY

CONTENTS

INTRODUCTION

It is remarkable that a small country such as Scotland should have so many traditional dishes, not only dishes which are served in Scotland today, but many which are famous all over the English-speaking world. She has contributed many original daily foods, such as bitter orange marmalade, porridge, smoked fish of several kinds, grouse, the king of game birds, which doesn't exist in such fine form anywhere else, despite many attempts to acclimatize him, and at least two original sauces (often thought of as English), bread sauce and egg sauce. Everyone has heard of haggis, even if they haven't tasted it, and this is only a very short list of Scottish foods which have entered into the *cuisine* of Britain and Ireland, and still thrive in many foreign countries where they have been taken by Scottish expatriates.

Scottish food derives from several cultures. First the Celtic culture, which makes good use of oatmeal and the griddle or girdle, the very name of which is thought to come from the Gaelic word *greadeal*, the name for the hot stones used for cooking by the early Gaels. Griddle cakes exist in many forms from Ireland, Wales, the Isle of Man and Brittany, and the latter country makes a *Pain d'avoine*, an oat bread, and also a creamy oatmeal soup similar to that served in Scotland.

These countries, too, were 'visited' by the Norsemen and this led to Scandinavian methods of curing and salting fish and also pork. Salted and smoked mutton is a traditional food both in Scotland and Scandinavia. It is probable that the original Aberdeen Angus cattle were of Viking stock.

Scotland's links with France go back to the Emperor Charlemagne in the ninth century and the many French queens have left many traces of their influence, not only in the *cuisine*, but also in the language. Gigot is still common to both countries for a leg of lamb or mutton; ashet, from the French *assiette*, for a flat serving dish; gean, for a wild cherry, from the French *guigne* and rizzared, meaning dried in the sun, from *ressoré*. These are only a fraction of French words which have entered the Scots vocabulary and are firmly entrenched there.

This book could not have been written as it is without recourse to Miss F. Marian McNeill's superb and scholarly book *The Scots Kitchen* (Blackie & Son Ltd., 1929 and 1963). Those of you who wish to know more of Scotland's culinary history should consult it forthwith.

This is not my first venture into Scotland's magnificent larder (*A Taste of Scotland*, 1970), though once again it has been a delight to test and sample further – a delight which I hope will be passed on to my readers all over the world.

Theodora FitzGibbon
Atlanta, Dalkey, Co. Dublin, 1979

SOUPS

Scotland is rightly famous for her excellent soups, broses and pottages, the latter having been the staple diet of both English and Scottish people for many centuries. It was eaten at every level of society and Andrew Boorde, who had travelled extensively in Europe, wrote in *A Compendyous Regyment, or A Dyetary of Helth* (1542): 'Pottage is not so much used in all Christendom as it is used in Britain. Pottage is made of the liquor in the which flesh is sodden in, with putting-to chopped herbs, and oatmeal and salt.' It is thought that the word 'pottage' comes from the Latin *porrus*, a leek, for the leek was one of the most important of pot-herbs from earliest times and figures in many traditional recipes of Celtic countries.

Some traditional Scottish soups such as Scotch Broth and Cock-a-Leekie are well known all over the English-speaking world and are served in countless homes, not only in Scotland but over the border and the seas. Some attribute this excellence of soup-making to the long connection with France, the Auld Alliance, and the influence of the three French queens, particularly Mary of Lorraine or Guise, wife of James V and mother of Mary Stuart, who did so much for the Scottish kitchen; others say that it is due to the thriftiness and ingenuity of the Scottish housewife and maybe it is a combination of the two.

Dr Redgill in *The Annals of the Cleikum Club* (1826) writes: '... I yield the Scots the superiority in all soups – save turtle and mulligatawny.' So let us put his edict to the test.

ARTICHOKE SOUP

Also known as Palestine soup, for the botanical name of the artichoke is *Girasole* (turning to the sun) which was corrupted into Jerusalem. Recipe from Lady Forbes's manuscript book, *c.* 1900.

1½ lb. (700 g.) Jerusalem artichokes
1 teaspoon vinegar
2 medium onions
2 oz. (50 g.) butter or margarine
1 pint (600 ml.) water
salt and pepper
1 pint (600 ml.) boiling milk

1 level tablespoon cornflour
2 tablespoons milk or water
2 dozen hazel-nuts, grilled, crushed and pounded, optional

Wash, peel and slice the artichokes and put into salted water with a teaspoon of vinegar to prevent discoloration. Peel and slice the onions, then melt half the butter until foaming and soften the onions in it. Then add the drained and dried artichokes and shake over a low heat until they soften a little. Season, pour over the water, cover and simmer for 20 minutes.

Put through a sieve or liquidize, then add the boiling milk. Mix the cornflour with the 2 tablespoons of milk or water and stir until creamed, then add to the artichoke mixture stirring all the time with a whisk until it has boiled and thickened slightly. Taste for seasoning, then add the remaining butter cut into small pieces. Serve with the hazel-nuts sprinkled over as a garnish. If not using the hazel-nuts then garnish with chopped chives or parsley.

Serves 6.

VARIATION: salsify, also known as the 'oyster plant', was a popular vegetable in the nineteenth century and can be used instead of artichoke for this soup.

BARLEY BROTH

Also known as Scotch Broth.

Meg Dods called it 'the bland, balsamic barley-broth of Scotland'.

This is the pot-au-feu of Scotland and enough is usually made for two days, the second day's broth being known as 'cock-crown kail'. It was well known in the eighteenth century and Faujas de St Fond, the King of France's Commissioner for Wines, who visited Scotland in the 1780s, commented on its excellence: '. . . a large dish of Scots Soup, composed of broth of beef, mutton and sometimes fowl, mixed with a little oatmeal, onions, parsley and a considerable quantity of peas. Instead of slices of bread, as in France, small slices of mutton and giblets of fowl are thrown into this soup.'

2 lb. (900 g.) neck of mutton or lamb trimmed of fat OR half mutton and half shin beef, called hough in Scotland

3 oz. (75 g.) pot barley

4 oz. (125 g.) shelled peas OR 3 oz. (75 g.) soaked dried split peas according to season

5 pints (2 litres approx.) water

salt and pepper

3–4 diced turnips

3 medium grated or diced carrots

1 large onion, sliced

white part of 2 large leeks

1 small white cabbage, shredded

2 tablespoons chopped parsley

Soak the dried peas if using, for not less than three hours. Then trim the meat well and put into a large saucepan with the water, bring to the boil and skim the top. Season to taste, then add the dried peas and the pot barley. Simmer gently for about 20–30 minutes, then add the turnip, carrots, onion and leek, and bring back to the boil and simmer covered for about 1½ hours or until the meat is tender. Then put in the shredded cabbage and fresh peas and simmer for not longer than 20–30 minutes. A few minutes before serving, taste for seasoning and add the

3

parsley and serve with a cutlet of lamb per person in the soup. Some cooks serve the broth first and then the meat afterwards with a caper sauce (see page 196).

The vegetables can be varied according to season, or to hand, and if using beef, kail, celery or artichoke can be used instead of cabbage. Hodgils (page 188) or dumplings are also sometimes cooked with the beef.

Serves about 8.

VARIATION: soaked dried beans can also be added if liked, using about 2 oz. (50 g.). Leftover pieces or joints of chicken can be added with the cabbage, or it can be made with a boiling fowl instead of meat, when it is known as 'Hen Broth'.

BAWD BREE

Bree is a Gaelic word for broth, but this rich traditional soup is not what we would style a broth nowadays. In Scotland there are two kinds of hare: the English brown hare (*Lepus europaeus*) and the blue or mountain hare (*Lepus timidus*) which changes its coat to white in the winter and is fairly common in the highlands of Scotland. It is smaller and thinner than the brown hare and the one most often used for this magnificent hare soup. However the brown hare *can* be used, but keep the saddle for roasting or braising and use only the legs, ribs, neck etc. If possible ask the game merchant to reserve a 4 fl. oz. (125 ml.) pot of the hare's blood to use as a thickening agent.

1 white hare jointed, or the legs, ribs etc. of a brown hare
1 teaspoon vinegar
1 lb. (450 g.) shin or chuck beef, diced
3 quarts (3½ litres) water
2 oz. (50 g.) butter, margarine or dripping
1 large onion, sliced
2 carrots, sliced
1 medium turnip, sliced

4

2–3 stalks celery
bouquet garni of: parsley,
  thyme and bayleaf
1 small blade mace or a
  pinch ground
10 peppercorns, whole
2 tablespoons fine oatmeal,
  optional
1 tablespoon mushroom
  ketchup

pinch of brown sugar
salt and cayenne pepper
4 fl. oz. (125 ml.) hare
  blood if available
$\frac{1}{2}$ pint (300 ml.) port wine
1 tablespoon rowan or
  redcurrant jelly

It is best to prepare the hare the day before by soaking it in cold water with a teaspoon of vinegar. The next day, strain the water into a large saucepan, trim and chop the beef into small dice and put both the beef and the hare joints into the saucepan, making up the water to the required amount. Bring to the boil and when boiling add about 1 rounded teaspoon of salt and take off any scum. Meanwhile heat the butter and lightly soften the vegetables in it; do not let them brown, but just soften, then pour off any excess fat. Add these to the hare, together with the herbs and spices, cover and simmer for about 2–3 hours, very slowly.

When the hare is tender, strain with the vegetables into a large basin and remove the better pieces of hare from the bones and liquidize them with about half a pint (300 ml.) of hare stock and reserve. Heat up the strained stock, add the oatmeal (if using) and cook for about half an hour, taste for seasoning and see that it is quite spicy. Add some of this stock gradually to the hare purée, stirring well after each addition, then turn it into the stock and stir again until it reaches boiling point, add the sugar, mushroom ketchup and port wine and taste again. Bring to boiling point, then draw the saucepan to the side of the burner, salt the blood and strain a little at a time, stirring well, into the soup until it thickens. Stir only one way and do not let it reboil.

Traditionally a tablespoon of rowan or redcurrant jelly is put into the tureen and the hot soup poured over it, but if not using a tureen then stir it into the soup just before serving.

Enough for about 8–10.

GARNISH OF FORCEMEAT BALLS

This soup can be served with croûtons or cubes of fried bread, or traditionally with little forcemeat balls made from the boiled, mashed hare liver, mixed with 1 oz. (25 g.) shredded suet, butter or margarine, 2 oz. (50 g.) dry breadcrumbs, 1 oz. (25 g.) flour, salt and pepper, all mixed, then bound with an egg. This mixture is shaped into walnut-sized balls with floured hands and poached in boiling, salted water for about 5–7 minutes. They are strained and added to the soup just before serving.

It will be realized, however, that this makes a very substantial dish which could be served as a main course.

MEG DODS'S BROWN SOUP

An extravagant soup with a delicious flavour.

Meg Dods was the pseudonym of Mrs Isobel Christian Johnston (born in Fife 1781, died in 1857), a great friend of Sir Walter Scott and the author of *The Cook and Housewife's Manual* (1826). It went into at least eleven editions and is a much treasured Scottish cookery book.

This recipe in its original form has double the quantities.

4 lb. (2 kg.) shin beef
1 small knuckle bone of
   veal or ham
2 oz. (50 g.) butter
1 small carrot, sliced
2 stalks celery, chopped
white part 2 leeks, chopped
Garnish: sippets of dry
   toast

1 small sliced turnip
2 quarts (2½ litres) water
salt, pepper and cayenne
   pepper
1 lb. (450 g.) rump steak,
   cubed
1 tablespoon mushroom
   ketchup

First cut the shin beef into large pieces and if possible chop the veal or ham bone. Heat up the butter and soften the chopped vegetables in it, then add the meat and brown it well, adding a little more butter if necessary. Pour off any excess fat and add the water, bring to the boil, then skim off the scum.

When skimmed add a cup of cold water, bring back to the boil, cover and simmer very gently for about 3–4 hours without stirring so that all the goodness can be extracted from the meat. (Nowadays, the slow crockery pot electric cooker would be ideal for this.) Take from the heat, let it get quite cold, then remove any fat from the top and strain well.

Cut the rumpsteak very small and brown quickly without fat in the frying-pan, then add to the soup. Simmer for 1 hour, then season to taste, add the mushroom ketchup and the cayenne pepper and serve with sippets (small triangles) of dry toast. It is a very fine consommé indeed. Originally it was strained again before serving; however with the price of meat today I do not think this is feasible and the small pieces of rump steak are very delicious. A glass of port or sherry added at the last minute is very good.

Serves about 8.

COCK-A-LEEKIE

One of the most famous Scottish 'soup-stews' which was mentioned as early as 1598 by Fynes Morrison in his book *An Itinerary*: '. . . had a Pullet with some prunes in the broth'. Two well-known Frenchmen renowned for their knowledge of food commented on it. Talleyrand the diplomatist thought it very good, but that the prunes should be removed before serving. The famous chef Alexis Soyer said: 'I will always give preference in the way of soup to their Cock-a-Leekie, even before their inimitable Hotch-Potch!' It is often served for banquets or large dinners.

1 boiling fowl about 4lb. (2 kg.) jointed or carcase, leg and wings of a bird
3 chopped rashers streaky bacon
water or stock to cover

mixed bouquet garni of: parsley, thyme and bayleaf
salt and pepper
12 medium-sized leeks
¼ lb. (125 g.) cooked, stoned prunes

Put the jointed bird, or carcase, legs and wings, and the bacon into a large saucepan and cover with water. Bring to the boil and remove any scum. Add about 8 of the leeks, which have been well washed and chopped, the green as well as the white part, the herbs tied into a faggot, salt and pepper. Return to the boil, then simmer very gently for about 2–3 hours or until the chicken is cooked. Add a little more water if necessary but do not weaken the stock too much. Taste for seasoning, then strain, picking out the chicken, taking the meat from the bones and cutting it into small pieces. Add to the soup, together with the stoned prunes and the remaining chopped leeks and simmer very gently for not more than 15 minutes. It can be garnished with a very little cream and chopped parsley, but do not disguise the pure flavour too much.

Serves 8 if a whole bird is used, and at least 6 with the carcase etc.

CRAB SOUP

See *Partan Bree*, page 19.

CULLEN SKINK

Skink comes from the Gaelic and originally meant 'essence'; today it usually means a stew-soup. It is traditional to the shores of the Moray Firth.

1 large smoked haddock
   (preferably Finnan)
   approx. 2 lb. (1 kg.)
water to cover
1 medium finely sliced
   onion

1½ pints (900 ml.) milk
2 tablespoons butter
8 oz. (225 g.) mashed
   potato, approx.
salt and pepper
triangles of dry toast

Put the haddock in a shallow pan skin side down, cover with water, bring to the boil and simmer for 4–5 minutes, turning once. Take from the pan, remove the skin and bones, then flake it and put back in the stock with the sliced onion and pepper to taste and simmer for 15 minutes. Strain but reserve the stock and fish and add the milk to the fish stock and bring to boiling point, then add enough mashed potato to make it the consistency you like. Put the fish back and reheat, then taste for seasoning.

Add the butter cut into very small pieces: it should hardly melt but run in rivulets through the creamy soup. Serve with the triangles of dry toast.

Serves 4.

FEATHER FOWLIE

Recipe from Lady Clark of Tillypronie, *c.* 1880s.

Lady Clark thinks the name of this delicious soup is a corruption of *oeufs filés*, but F. Marian McNeill suggests that *fowlie* is a corruption of *volaille* as it is very like the French *velouté de volaille*, and might be an inheritance from the Auld Alliance.

1 chicken approx. 3 lb.
   (1½ kg.) jointed
salt
4 oz. (125 g.) bacon or ham
2 stalks celery, chopped
small blade mace
1 medium onion, sliced

stock or water to cover
bouquet garni of: parsley,
   thyme, tarragon
1 tablespoon fresh,
   chopped parsley
2–3 egg yolks beaten with
   2 tablespoons cream

9

Soak the jointed bird in salted water to cover for half an hour, then strain and wash well. Put into a large saucepan with the chopped ham or bacon, vegetables, herbs, mace and the stock or water to cover. Bring to the boil, cover and simmer gently for about 1½ hours or until the bird is cooked. Strain, but reserve both stock and chicken, let the stock get cold and remove any fat from the top.

Put back into a clean saucepan and add the finely chopped or minced chicken meat. (If liked the chicken meat and soup can be liquidized for 1 minute.) Heat up, add the parsley, beat the egg yolks with the cream and add to the hot soup. Heat gently whisking all the time, but do not let it reboil for if it does the eggs will curdle.

Serves 6–8.

NOTE: this soup can be made with the carcase and leftover pieces of a cooked bird, but in this case add two stock cubes to the soup, if using water.

FISH SOUP

There are many variations of fish soup in Scotland, but this nineteenth-century recipe adapted from a manuscript book is particularly delicious.

2 lb. (1 kg.) fillets of haddock or other white fish
2 pints (1¼ litres) milk
teaspoon salt
2 sliced carrots
2 stalks celery, chopped
1 medium onion
2 tablespoons chopped parsley
For garnish: croûtons of fried bread

1 teaspoon chopped fennel
½ pint (300 ml.) dry white wine
2 oz. (50 g.) butter or margarine
1 oz. (25 g.) flour
1 pint (600 ml.) fish stock
pinch nutmeg or mace
¼ pint (150 ml.) cream
cayenne pepper

Take one fillet of fish, cut it up and cook with the milk and salt for 5 minutes, then add the sliced vegetables and half the parsley. Cover and simmer gently for 30 minutes or until the carrot is cooked, then strain.

Meanwhile skin the remaining fillets and add to the stock above, then put the fillets into a fireproof dish with the wine, cover with foil and poach for about 15 minutes allowing the wine to reduce slightly. When cooked, liquidize or sieve them with half the butter until very smooth.

Heat the remaining butter, stir in the flour, cook for 1 minute then add the strained stock stirring until it is smooth and creamy. Whisk in the fish and wine purée, taste for seasoning, add the chopped parsley and nutmeg. Add the cream (with a little more milk if it is too thick), heat but do not reboil. Garnish with the remaining parsley, and cayenne pepper and serve with the chopped croûtons.

Serves 6–8.

MEG DODS'S FISH-IN-SAUCE

Despite its name this is a simple fish soup, easy to make and with a pure and good flavour.

1 lb. (450 g.) white fish such as haddock, whiting, cod etc. filleted and skinned

Head, skeletons and skin of 2 white fish

2 quarts (2 litres) water

4 spring onions or green onion tops

4 sprigs parsley with stalks

1 tablespoon chives

10 whole white peppercorns

1 oz. (25 g.) butter

1 oz. (25 g.) flour

juice of 1 lemon or 2 teaspoons mushroom ketchup

salt and pepper

See that the fish is well filleted and skinned, then cut into convenient serving pieces. If fish is plentiful then allow a little more and use some in the court bouillon. Sprinkle over the juice of half a lemon and some salt and leave for about half an hour.

Put the skeletons (and a fish if plentiful) into a large saucepan, cover with the water and add the onions, parsley and chives with the peppercorns. Bring to the boil, cover and simmer for about 1 hour, then strain it. Knead the flour (which has been heated slightly) with the butter in a saucepan over a low heat and cook for about 1–2 minutes until it is well amalgamated, then work it into a ball. Remove and break it into pieces, heat up the stock and add these pieces gradually, stirring all the time until the stock has thickened. Put the filleted and chopped fish into the stock and boil for no longer than 10 minutes. Add the remaining lemon juice or mushroom ketchup and serve.

Enough for 4–6.

VARIATION: this soup is very good if 4 cleaned and chopped leeks are cooked in the strained stock with 2 medium sliced potatoes for about 20 minutes. This is then liquidized, the fish added and cooked for 15 minutes. The top is garnished with chopped parsley and a small nut of butter.

FRIAR'S CHICKEN

This soup is very good made with rabbit fillets.

Recipe adapted from *The Practice of Cookery* by Mrs Dalgairns (Edinburgh, 1829).

1 large, chopped knuckle of veal or ham
1 young chicken about 3 lb. (1½ kg.) jointed or fillets of rabbit
4 pints (2¼ litres) chicken stock or water

pinch of mace or 1 small blade
pinch of dried tarragon
salt and pepper
1 tablespoon chopped parsley
3 well-beaten eggs

Boil the chopped knuckle bone in the stock for at least two hours. Then strain and take off any pieces of meat that are not gristly and chop them. Put the skinned and boned chicken or rabbit into the boiling stock, add the tarragon, salt, mace and pepper and simmer gently for about 1 hour or until the bird or rabbit is quite tender. Then add the parsley, and taste for seasoning.

Well beat the eggs, take the saucepan from the heat and stir in the well-beaten eggs and serve at once. Allow one portion of chicken per person in the soup.

Serves 6–8.

GAME SOUP

This recipe comes from Lady Forbes, *c.* 1910.

Scotland still has a good quantity of game, although the price has risen steeply since these traditional recipes were formed. However, trimmings or carcases of birds such as pheasant, blackcock, grouse and ptarmigan, as well as the elderly birds which are no good for roasting, can be used; also odd joints from a hare, venison and so on.

2 cooked or uncooked carcases of game plus 1 lb. (450 g.) mixed game meat
2 sliced carrots
3 leeks, white and green, chopped
1 celery heart, chopped
1 large onion, stuck with cloves
1 bayleaf, parsley, pinch of rosemary

4 oz. (125 g.) lean chopped beef
2 quarts (2½ litres) beef stock (2 stock cubes will do)
1 sherry glass medium sherry
¼ pint (150 ml.) port or red wine

Break up the carcases, chop the meat and put into a large sauce-pan with the chopped vegetables and stock, bring to the boil and simmer slowly for about 2 hours, then strain and remove any pieces of game which can be chopped and added to the stock. Let it get cold and remove any fat from the top. Put into a clean saucepan, add the finely chopped beef and the sherry and taste for seasoning. Bring back to the boil, cook for 40 minutes, then strain. Pour the port or red wine into the reinforced stock and simmer for 5 minutes, then serve.

A little cream can be added but in my opinion it is not needed; however some game quenelles (see Fish Quenelles page 81) are delicious floating in this strong, clear game consommé.

Serves about 8.

HAIRST BREE

Meaning Harvest Broth; it is also known as Hotch-Potch.

> 'Then here's to ilka kindly Scot:
> Wi' mony gude broths he boils his pot,
> But rare hotch-potch beats a' the lot,
> It smells and smacks sae brawly.'   Sheriff Bell.

This traditional soup-stew should be made when all the vegetables are young. The varieties can be mixed or inter-changed, for instance if small cabbage is better than cauliflower then it should be used instead. On some of the islands young nettle tops, wild spinach, wild carrot and garlic are all included or used when fresh vegetables are scarce.

2 lb. (1 kg.) neck of lamb chops	6 Spring onions, with green
1 teaspoon salt	1 lb. (450 g.) young broad beans
2 quarts (1½ litres) water	
4 young turnips, chopped	1 medium cauliflower, cut into flowerlets
6 young carrots	

1 lettuce heart, chopped
1 teaspoon sugar
2 teaspoons chopped fresh
  mint

1–2 tablespoons chopped
  parsley
pepper

Boil the lamb with the salt in the water and remove any scum from the top, then simmer gently for about 40 minutes. Lift the meat from the stock and remove the bones and any lumps of fat, then put back. Add the turnips, carrots, onions, half the broad beans and half the peas, cover again, bring to the boil and simmer for a further hour. Then add the cauliflower, shredded lettuce and the rest of the beans and peas, sugar, mint and season again to taste. Cook until these vegetables are just tender but not mushy. Add the chopped parsley and pepper and taste before serving for seasoning.

Serves 6–8.

KAIL BROSE

Kail or kale is a hardy green vegetable (*Brassica oleracea*) which withstands severe frost and is said to taste even better during very cold weather. The word has two meanings in Scotland: it refers to the curly, green-leafed vegetable, while 'to be asked to kail' is an invitation to dinner, not one at which kail is necessarily served. In a cold country like Scotland this hardy vegetable was and still is used in many ways, but especially for soups. It was also the basis for *Colcannon* both in Scotland and Ireland, the *col* deriving from kail and not from cabbage, although they are both members of the same family.

Brose or *Brochain* are Gaelic words which mean broth and this can be made with many foods, sometimes simply boiling liquid poured over oatmeal, but the Green Brose is often made in the spring with young nettle tops, spring onions or whatever is available. Ingredients for these traditional recipes are very fluid and can be altered according to choice or what is available.

1 lb. (450 g.) bullock's cheek, beefskirt, hough etc.	2 lb. (1 kg.) kale
	4 oz. (112 g.) oatmeal
	salt and pepper
6 pints (3½ litres) water	

Boil the trimmed meat in the water for about 1½–2 hours. Meanwhile take the leaves from the kail stock, remove any hard stalk and chop the green finely. Take the meat from the stock, trim and cut into convenient serving pieces, then put back with the kail, salt and pepper and continue cooking for about half an hour or until the kail is quite tender. Toast or grill the oatmeal lightly, put it into a basin with a pinch of salt and add a ladle-full of the stock, stirring it into knots, then add this to the brose, stir well and serve hot.

Enough for 8.

VARIATION: rabbit or pickled pork can be used instead of the beef, or even good meaty marrow bones, in the latter case remove the bones before serving.

In Aberdeenshire, Neep Brose is made with Swede turnips and a marrow-bone, with a nut of butter added to the oatmeal. Barley can be used instead of oatmeal. On special occasions a little cream is added before serving. Sometimes the kail was removed and eaten separately with butter on it.

LORRAINE SOUP

or Soupe à la Reine.

This soup is thought to have been named after Mary of Lorraine, wife of James V and mother of Mary Stuart, but some authorities think it is named after Margot (Marguerite de Valois), and to confuse things even further, the classical French soup Crème Marie-Stuart is similar in style. Whichever is the right answer makes little difference to this excellent white soup which has been served for centuries in Scotland. There are many recipes but this one is suited to modern taste.

10 oz. (275 g.) cooked
    chicken, either the
    breast or thigh
8 oz. (225 g.) boiled veal
2 oz. (50 g.) blanched
    almonds
2 oz. (50 g.) ground
    almonds
2–3 hard-boiled egg yolks
1 oz. (25 g.) breadcrumbs
2 tablespoons boiling milk

salt and pepper
4 pints (2 litres) chicken
    stock
squeeze lemon juice and a
    little grated rind
pinch of ground mace or
    nutmeg
$\frac{1}{4}$ pint (150 ml.) cream
2 tablespoons chopped
    parsley

Pound the skinned chicken and veal, or grind in a food processor with the almonds, then add the ground almonds and the
mashed egg yolks. Cover the breadcrumbs with the boiling milk
and let them absorb the liquid. When cold add to the meat
mixture and season. Gradually stir in the stock (using the veal
stock as well) and when it is all absorbed taste for seasoning
again and add the lemon juice, finely grated lemon rind and
mace. Heat, stirring all the time until it is hot, then add the
cream, but after this do not let it boil. Garnish with the chopped
parsley before serving.

Serves 8.

MUSSEL AND ONION SOUP

From the Open Arms, Dirleton, East Lothian. Musselburgh
was once the site of a Roman Camp and owes its name to the
mussel-bed found there at the mouth of the River Esk. It has
always been a great mussel-eating centre and this soup-stew
can be served as a main course.

50 mussels
$\frac{1}{2}$ bottle dry white wine

1 large onion, finely
    chopped

1 oz. (25 g.) butter
1 oz. (25 g.) flour
1 pint (600 ml.) warm
  milk

salt and pepper
2 tablespoons chopped
  parsley
½ pint (300 ml.) cream

Wash and scrub the mussels well and discard any that are open. Then put them into a large saucepan with the wine, put the lid on and bring them to the boil. Shake the pan and cook for about 5 minutes or until all the shells are open. Strain off the liquid and let the mussels cool, then take from the shells and remove the beards.

Heat the butter in another pan, stir in the flour and let it cook for 1 minute and then add the hot milk gradually, stirring all the time so that it is smooth and creamy. Now add the mussel liquor. Add the onion, finely chopped, and simmer gently until it is cooked. Season to taste, add the mussels, parsley and cream, reheat, but do not reboil once the cream is in. If the mussels are allowed to boil they will become rubbery, and the cream could curdle.

Serves 4.

VARIATION: use a mixture of mussels, scallops, cockles or periwinkles.

MUSSEL BROSE

40 mussels
1 pint (600 ml.) water
1 oz. (25 g.) lightly toasted
  oatmeal

1 pint (600 ml.) hot milk
salt and pepper

Wash the mussels as above, and put into a large saucepan with the water, cover and heat until they open (about 5 minutes). Strain the liquor into a basin, then shell and beard the mussels. Lightly grill the oatmeal and reserve. Add the milk to the finely strained mussel juice, taste for seasoning, heat up, then add a cupful to the oatmeal stirring it quickly so that it forms knots. Add to the soup, and finally put back the mussels, reheat but do not let them boil.

Serves 6.

OATMEAL SOUP

Recipe from Miss Kitty Forbes, House of Newe, Newe, Aberdeenshire.

It is a delicious soup, easy to make, with a delicate flavour.

1 tablespoon butter or margarine	1 pint (600 ml.) chicken stock
1 large onion, finely chopped	$\frac{1}{2}$ pint (300 ml.) milk
2 tablespoons oatmeal	$\frac{1}{4}$ pint (150 ml.) cream
salt and pepper	1 tablespoon chopped parsley

Heat the butter and when foaming add the finely chopped onion and soften, but do not colour. Then add the oatmeal and seasonings and cook for a few minutes. Add the stock, stirring all the time, bring to the boil and simmer, covered, for half an hour. Then liquidize or sieve, return to the pan, reheat with the milk, and serve with a little cream in each dish and a sprinkle of chopped parsley.

Serves 4.

PARTAN BREE

Crab Soup; Partan is the Gaelic for crab.

2 large boiled crabs or a 2 × 8 oz. (225 g.) tins of crab	3 tablespoons long-grained rice
	1 pint (600 ml.) milk

1 pint (600 ml.) chicken stock	½ teaspoon anchovy essence
salt and white pepper	½ pint (300 ml.) cream

Take the meat from the crabs, and put aside the claw meat. Cook the rice in the milk for about 15 minutes or until it is soft but not mushy, then add it to the crab meat (not the claws) and either sieve or liquidize for 1 minute. Put into a clean saucepan then gradually stir in the stock over a low heat. Continue stirring as it boils and season to taste after adding the anchovy essence.

Finally add the claw meat and stir until reheated. Add the cream just before serving in heated soup bowls.

Serves 4–6.

RED POTTAGE

This is a delicious soup worthy of the fame of some good French or Russian *potages.**

10 oz. (275 g.) dried haricot beans, soaked overnight	1 small celery heart, finely chopped
1 medium cooked beetroot, cut in 4	2 oz. (50 g.) butter or margarine
2 medium onions, sliced	4 pints (2½ litres) stock or water
6 ripe tomatoes or 1 × 7 oz. (220 g.) can tomatoes	2 tablespoons chopped parsley

Drain the soaked beans and prepare all the vegetables, then heat the butter and soften the vegetables in it for a few minutes. Put into a large saucepan with the beans, add the stock and some pepper, bring to the boil and simmer gently, covered for about 2½–3 hours, stirring from time to time and adding a little more stock if necessary. Add the salt and some more pepper if needed, and when the beans are quite soft, take out the beetroot

SOUPS

pieces and sieve or liquidize the soup. Reheat and serve with the
chopped parsley scattered over the top.

VARIATION: use brown lentils instead of the beans: also
parsnip or turnip can be used instead of the celery.

* Pressure cooking time is 25 minutes after 15 lb. pressure
has been reached.

SALMON SOUP

Salmon holds a very high place in the Scottish cuisine and is
used in many ways. Scotch salmon, like Scotch beef, is famous
in many places and needs little introduction from me. The
thrifty Scottish housewife uses even quite small amounts of the
'King of Fish' to make a superb soup.

1 salmon head, and if
available, 1 small salmon
steak or tail-end
skeletons and skin of 4–6
plaice or soles which
most fishmongers will be
glad to give you
1 medium-sized leek; 2
medium carrots; 1 stalk
celery; 1 medium onion
3 large, ripe tomatoes
small bunch of parsley
with the stalks

sprig of lemon thyme
sprig of fennel
1 tablespoon sea-salt
12 white peppercorns
pinch grated nutmeg
3 pints (1·8 litres) water
2–3 tablespoons medium
sherry, whisky or
brandy
4 tablespoons double
cream

Put the salmon head with the skeletons into a large pan with the
chopped vegetables, the salt, peppercorns, herbs and spices and
cover with the water. Bring to the boil and after about half an
hour simmering add the skinned and coarsely chopped tomatoes
and continue cooking for a further 25 minutes. Then strain it
and in the clear stock poach the salmon steak if using for about
15 minutes.

Meanwhile take any flakes of salmon from the head and also a little of the cooked vegetables. Lift out the salmon steak, and take the flesh from the bone and peel off the skin, flake it and reserve. Put about half a pint of the stock into a liquidizer with the vegetables and fish from the head and blend for about 1 minute. Put into the remaining stock with the flesh from the steak and reheat adding the grated nutmeg and taste for seasoning. Let it simmer until it has reduced a little, but do not make it too thick. Add the sherry, whisky or brandy and if using the latter two put into a ladle, warm it and flame before adding. Finally add the cream, reheat, but do not reboil.

Serves at least 6.

This can be made with canned salmon, or a small can could be incorporated if you are not using the salmon steak, but mix it first with a little creamy milk until it is a paste and remove the small back bones.

NOTE: in Scotland in the old days this soup was thickened with toasted brown breadcrumbs and served with a garnish of chopped parsley.

FISH

Fish has always played a great part both in the economy and the *cuisine* of Scotland. The famous salmon rivers and the many lochs and streams packed with trout have not only been the hunting-ground for anglers from all over the world, but also the sustenance of the Scottish people. The vast herring shoals from Stornoway to Eyemouth provided the sturdy fishermen with fish of good quality, not forgetting the white fish such as cod, haddock, plaice, halibut, whiting and so on which gave nutritional food not only to Scotland but also to Britain.

Aberdeen has been known since the thirteenth century for her cured fish, an art possibly acquired from the Norsemen, and at an early time the curing of herrings and salmon was an important part of Glasgow's trade. Many foreign ships fished these waters, particularly the Dutch, and in the eighteenth century much was done to develop the Scottish industry and an attempt was made, unsuccessfully, to keep the fishing rights for Scottish fishermen. 'Caller Herring', fresh herring, was the cry of the Newhaven fisherwives in their picturesque clothes. Loch Fyne herring are considered the finest and they were often jokingly referred to as 'Glasgow Magistrates'. It is sad that today many of our waters are being over-fished, but is good that conservation is also getting a hearing and attempts are being made to build up the stocks again.

Shellfish of all kinds from the now luxurious oyster to the humble winkle were staple items of the Scottish diet. The 'native' oysters bred in the renowned oyster-beds of the Firth of Forth were commented on in the eighteenth century by the King of France's Commissioner for Wines, Faujas de St Fond, as to their succulence and flavour. 'Such is their reputation,' he said, 'that they are sent to all the principal towns in England and Wales, and are exported in barrels to all quarters.'

Unlike the English and the Irish whose favourite meal is probably of roast beef, the Scots have always favoured fish as their prime ingredient of food. It is almost certain that most of the good Highland beef was exported to England, mutton was certainly used, pork seldom, but game and fish were always and are still held in high esteem.

ARBROATH SMOKIES

These delicious delicacies are quite unlike any other smoked fish in the world. Small haddocks are cleaned but not split open, salted, then tied in twos by the tails, and hung high on little wooden spits or over halved whisky barrels above a fire which should be made of oak or silver birch chips. This method of smoking haddock originated at Auchmithie but, by the beginning of the nineteenth century, the fisher-folk settled at Arbroath had taken it up and by the end of the century the smokies prepared in this way had become so popular that the name became Arbroath smokies. It is difficult to obtain them outside Scotland, but they are so excellent that it is well worth making strenuous efforts to do so and, if you are lucky enough to have been successful, the traditional method of serving them is as follows: either steam them or heat them in a gentle oven or under a moderate grill, then split them and remove the backbone. Dust with black pepper, add a knob of butter, close them up and heat through again. The long smoking has cooked them already so be sure not to dry them out by further cooking once they are hot.

BLAWN FISH

This is a Scottish method of preparing fish by salting and drying overnight in the wind, used for whiting, haddock or speldings (a small fish of the cod family). The fish should be really fresh, skinned and thoroughly cleaned and the eyes removed. Rub them all over with salt, particularly the body cavity, shake off the surplus salt that does not cling to the moist flesh and thread them by passing a string through the eye-sockets, then hang them in a stream of cool air in a shady place and leave them overnight. In the morning, roll them lightly in flour and grill them on both sides (for the best possible flavour do this over a peat fire on a brander) and serve with a knob of butter on top and a sprinkling of freshly ground black pepper. They can also be lightly poached and served with a jug of melted butter.

The ordinary whiting, when thus prepared and eaten with hot barley bannocks, is hardly recognizable! Alexis Soyer, the great chef of the Reform club, preferred this method of preparing whiting for breakfast to any other.

BLOATERS

See *Kippers*, pages 45–7.

CABBIE-CLAW

This dish takes its name from the French word *cabillaud*, a codling, as can be seen from the Shetland dialect form *kabbi-low*.

1 whole young codling
about 2½ lb. (1 kg.)
2 tablespoons coarse sea-
salt
1 sprig parsley
2 teaspoons grated
horseradish

water
1 lb. (450 g.) hot mashed
potatoes
parsley and cayenne
pepper to garnish

The fish needs to be very fresh. Clean it and skin it at once, removing the eyes and split it lengthwise. Wipe it with a clean cloth and rub the coarse salt into it both inside and out and leave it in a cool current of air in a shady place for twenty-four hours, hanging on a string through the eye-sockets. Take it down, cover it with boiling water, add the parsley and horseradish and simmer very gently until it is cooked (about twenty-five minutes depending upon the size). Very gently lift it out, and having removed all the bones, break it into large pieces with a fork and keep hot on a warmed dish.

For the sauce

2 tablespoons butter
2 tablespoons flour
½ pint (¾ litre) milk
½ pint (¼ litre) of the water
the fish was cooked in

a pinch of nutmeg, salt
and pepper
2 hard-boiled eggs

Melt the butter, stir in the flour, then gradually add the hot stock and the milk, stirring all the while to avoid lumps forming.

Separately chop the whites and yolks of the hard-boiled eggs, then stir the whites into the sauce with the seasoning. Pour this over the fish and garnish the top with the coarsely shredded yolks. Arrange the finely mashed potatoes around the outside and, finally, sprinkle a little cayenne pepper and chopped parsley over all.

Serves 4.

CASSEROLE OF FISH

This can be made with almost any white fish but is particularly good when halibut, a very popular fish in Scotland, is used.

2 medium-sized carrots
1 medium celery heart
2 medium onions
2 lb. (900 g.) halibut, hake
  or cod
seasoned flour
3 oz. (75 g.) butter

1 teaspoon chopped
  fennel
2 tablespoons chopped
  parsley
1 tablespoon lemon juice
salt and pepper

Scrape the carrots and chop them *en paysanne*, chop the celery and onions likewise and put all three into a saucepan covering with boiling water. Add salt to taste and simmer very slowly for 15 to 20 minutes, until the vegetables are just soft. Skin and bone the fish and cut into convenient sized pieces, coat with seasoned flour, then melt the butter in a pan and fry the halibut sprinkled with the chopped fennel until it is golden on both sides, then transfer the fish portions to a casserole without breaking them and pour over the pan juices and the lemon juice. Add the strained vegetables and a half pint ($\frac{1}{4}$ litre) of the stock from their cooking and season. Bake at 325°F. (170°C.) or gas mark 4 for half an hour, then transfer the fish and vegetables to a heated dish with the latter arranged around the outside. Pour the casserole juices into a saucepan and boil rapidly to reduce a little, then, at the last moment, add the chopped parsley, pour over the fish and serve.

Serves 4.

COD WITH MUSTARD SAUCE

The serving of a special mustard sauce with cod is a reminder of the many culinary influences upon Scottish cookery left by the Vikings and such a sauce for cod is very prevalent in contemporary Scandinavian cookery.

3 lb. (1·4 kg.) fresh cod
½ pint (¼ litre) milk
½ pint (¼ litre) water
a pinch of salt
freshly ground pepper
2 tablespoons butter or
    margarine

1½ tablespoons flour
1 heaped teaspoon made
    English mustard (or
    more if the sauce is
    preferred hot)
4 sprigs of parsley, left
    whole

If you put the fish on top of the parsley sprigs in a pan, it will help to stop it sticking, then add the milk and water, mixed, and a little salt. Cover and simmer gently for about ten minutes (depending upon the size of the piece) turning the fish once to ensure that it is evenly cooked through. Gently lift the fish on to a warmed dish and remove any remaining bones and skin and keep the fish hot in a warm oven with foil over the top to prevent drying. Melt the butter or margarine in a saucepan and stir in the flour and the mustard and blend in the warm fish liquor from the pan, stirring all the time to ensure that no lumps form and continuing the gentle heat until the sauce thickens to a creamy consistency, taste for flavour and add a little salt, if needed, and the pepper. Pour the sauce over the fish and serve.

Serves 4–6.

This dish is often accompanied by *Skirlie* (see page 189), *Mealie Pudding* (page 189) and *Clapshot* (see page 170).

CREAMED COD WITH
EGG AND SULTANA SAUCE

This delicious way of treating cod is also excellent for hake and halibut and can be varied by using seedless white grapes instead of the sultanas.

1½ lb. (700 g.) filleted cod
1 bay leaf
1 pint (½ litre) milk
2 hard-boiled eggs
3 oz. (75 g.) sultanas or
  seedless white grapes

1 oz. (25 g.) butter or
  margarine
1 tablespoon flour
juice of half a lemon
salt and pepper

In a pan gently cook the cod fillets with the bay leaf in the milk for about ten minutes. Lift the fillets carefully out of the milk and put them into an oven-proof dish. Melt the butter in a saucepan, stir in the flour and blend in the milk from the pan stirring continuously until the sauce thickens. Remove the bay leaf and add the chopped hard-boiled eggs, the sultanas (or the peeled and stoned grapes), the lemon juice, the salt and the pepper. Let all simmer for a few minutes then pour the sauce over the fish and bake at 350°F. (180°C.) or gas mark 4 for about twenty minutes.

Serves 4.

GLASGOW COD

Though the traditional form of this recipe calls for suet, tastes are changing and some may now prefer to use butter or margarine in its place.

1 lb. (450 g.) skinned and
  filleted cod

3 oz. (75 g.) medium
  oatmeal

1 oz. (25 g.) finely
shredded suet OR 1 oz.
(25 g.) butter or
margarine (2 oz. (50 g.)
if not using suet)

½ teaspoon finely chopped
chives

salt and pepper

½ pint (¼ litre) hot but not
boiling milk

1 teaspoon finely chopped
onion

½ teaspoon finely chopped
parsley

Using absorbent kitchen paper, pat the fish dry and put into a
greased fireproof dish, seasoning with salt and pepper, then dot
the top of the fish with the ounce of butter or margarine and
pour the hot milk around it. Mix the oatmeal, suet (or the
remaining butter or margarine), onion, chives and parsley to a
firm paste, seasoning to taste and using a little of the hot milk
if it is too dry, then form into small balls about 1–1½ inches
across, place around the fish and bake the whole at 350°F.
(180°C.) or gas mark 4 for around half an hour, depending upon
the size of the fillets.

Serves 4.

Crab

TO PREPARE AND DRESS CRAB

Always choose a crab that is heavy for its size, for these contain
the most meat. The most humane way to cook them is to put
them into cold sea-water in a pot whose top will lock on (otherwise, when the water becomes tepid they will lift the lid, an
appeal difficult to resist) and bring them very gradually to the
boil on a very low heat. When they have boiled for twelve to
fifteen minutes (depending on size) they should be removed
from the stove and allowed to grow cold in the sea-water. If you
live away from the sea, make up a brine with sea-salt or ordinary
salt until it tastes as salty as sea-water. Lobsters and crabs
cooked in this way are much more tender and better flavoured

and laboratory tests have shown that this is because when plunged into boiling water, the agony makes them contract all their muscles thus rendering them tough, whereas those brought very slowly to the boil in saline water simply faint away as one would in too hot a turkish bath.

When cold, remove from the brine and take off the large claws and their adjacent joints, putting them aside. The smaller legs also contain meat but are only worth the trouble of extraction if the crab is a reasonably large one. Turn the body of the crab on its back and, inserting the point of a strong, stiff, filleting knife between the body and the shell, mid-way between where the front pair of large claws were attached, lever upwards, separating the body from the shell. You can then draw the body and shell apart with your hands.

The section which comes away from the shell is known as the apron, and, apart from a small hollow filled with soft flesh in the middle which can be extracted with a teaspoon, should be discarded. Also to be discarded are the 'dead men's fingers' the grey, pointed, spongy masses found immediately under the apron (sometimes some of them come away with it), a small sack in the upper part of the shell which is often not present and the tough thin membrane covering the body meat and any green slime near it or adhering to it. All the rest of the crab-meat, both brown and white, is edible. When all the meat has been removed from the shell, push with your thumbs against the edges of the open shell where they are marked with a wavy line and these sections will break off, leaving the open half shell, when washed, as a natural receptacle for cold dressed crab. Electricians' side-cutters are the best device for getting the meat out of the claws, but a nutcracker can also be used.

BUTTERED CRAB

2 good-sized cooked
crabs, approximately
12 oz. (340 g.) or the
equivalent in frozen or
tinned crab meat
2 anchovy fillets
½ pint (¼ litre) white wine
a pinch of grated nutmeg
or mace

slices of buttered toast
3 oz. (75 g.) butter or
margarine
3 heaped tablespoons
breadcrumbs
salt and pepper

Pound the anchovy fillets in the wine, add the nutmeg or mace
and the breadcrumbs, then season to taste. Bring gently to the
boil and simmer for 5 minutes. Meanwhile mix the flaked crab-
meat with the butter and add to the hot wine mixture. Cook
gently for a further four minutes, then serve on a hot dish surrounded with the buttered toast.

Serves 2.

DRESSED CRAB

1 large crab, approximately
6 oz. (150 g.) crab-meat
2 tablespoons fresh white
breadcrumbs or cottage
cheese

a few drops of Tabasco or
Worcestershire sauce
2 tablespoons cream or
plain yoghurt
salt and pepper

Mash the brown crab-meat and half of the white meat from the
claws together in a bowl and mix in the breadcrumbs or cottage
cheese and the cream or plain yoghurt, then add the Tabasco or
Worcestershire sauce and finally season to taste with the pepper
and salt. Put the whole back into the half shell and decorate the

top with the remaining meat from the claws. Arrange wedges of lemon around and serve.

Serves 1.

POTTED CRAB

2 large crabs or the equivalent in frozen or tinned crab-meat, approximately 14 oz. (400 g.)	1 dessertspoon anchovy essence
	salt and cayenne pepper
	3 tablespoons melted butter
4 oz. (113 g.) butter or margarine	a pinch of mace

Take all the edible meat from the crabs, both the brown and the white. Mash it finely and then pound it well in a mortar with the solid butter or margarine, the anchovy essence, the mace and the salt and cayenne pepper to taste. Pack it into a pot leaving no air spaces and cover it with the melted butter or margarine. If kept in a cold place it will be good for some days as long as the butter seal is intact. Serve with hot toast.

Serves 2–4.

CRAB CUTLETS

This recipe uses the white crab-meat only.

12 oz. (340 g.) cooked, flaked, white crab-meat or the same amount of frozen or tinned	1 oz. (25 g.) flour
	½ pint (¼ litre) milk
	1 egg
	1 pint (½ litre) frying oil
1 oz. (25 g.) butter or margarine	dry white breadcrumbs

Melt the butter in a saucepan and stir in the flour. When the roux is hot again add the milk, blending well, and heat gently until it begins to simmer, continuing to stir for a couple of minutes while the flour cooks, then add the crab-meat and salt and pepper to taste.

Spread the mixture evenly a half inch thick on to a marble slab or cold plate to cool and when cold cut into cutlet shapes. Dip the cutlets in egg and breadcrumbs and deep fry in hot oil until they are golden brown, drain them well and serve them on a hot dish, surrounded by lemon wedges and strewn with coarsely chopped parsley.

Serves 2.

SEE ALSO: *Partan Bree*, page 19.

CRAPPIT HEIDS

4 haddock heads
oatmeal
salt and pepper
4 haddock livers (or
   haddock or cod roes)

3–4 tablespoons milk
fish stock to cover

Only very fresh livers or roes should be used. Chop them finely, weigh, and mix with an equal quantity of oatmeal. With this mixture stuff the cleaned heads sufficiently loosely to allow for the swelling of the oatmeal on cooking, cover with the fish stock and simmer very gently for around 30 minutes, depending on the size of the heads.

Serves 4.

Elizabeth Craig, in *The Scottish Cookery Book* (André Deutsch), says: 'This dish, which is also popular in Shetland, is sometimes served alone, but the heads are more generally cooked with the fish from which they are taken and served with the fish.'

FINNAN HADDIE POACHED

1 large haddock, approx.	½ pint (¼ litre) milk
1 lb. (450 g.)	1 oz. (25 g.) butter
1 tablespoon cornflour	salt and pepper
parsley	

'At tea last night and at breakfast we had Findon haddocks, which Mr Telford would not allow us to taste at Dundee, nor until we reached Stonehaven, lest this boasted dainty should be disparaged by a bad specimen . . . They are broiled or toasted, I know not which; and are as good as any fish can be when cured . . .' Robert Southey, *Journal of a Tour in Scotland*, 1819.

To enjoy this Scottish speciality it is extremely important to obtain the true Finnan Haddie as it used to be traditionally prepared in the vicinity of Findon in Kincardineshire, originally in the smoke of burning seaweed, but more recently in the smoke of peat or wood. Avoid carefully all haddock having a uniform yellow appearance; these have not been, properly speaking, smoked at all but sprayed with a 'smoke substitute' containing a yellow dye, a practice similar to that employed in the production of ersatz kippers. The true Finnan Haddie has a golden sheen, more noticeable on some parts of the fish than on others. Depending upon the amount of smokiness liked in the flavour, soak for up to an hour in either fresh water or preferably fresh whey or buttermilk and then poach in milk to cover, skin side down, for three minutes, after which turn the fish, remove the skin and continue poaching for a further three minutes. Lift carefully out, drain, remove the bones if desired and reserve on a hot dish and keep warm.

Strain the fish stock from the poaching into another saucepan and bring just to a simmer. Cream the cornflour with a little milk and add to the simmering fish stock, stirring well and raising the heat a little until the cornflour is cooked and the sauce smooth and creamy, then season with salt and pepper to taste, pour over the fish, dot with butter and strew with finely chopped parsley.

According to Lady Clark (*c.* 1884), in Scotland, Finnan Haddie were cooked unopened in a double gridiron, turning the fish frequently, having been first rubbed with olive oil, the thin side being put first to the fire and neither butter nor flour used.

> 'Roast my breist afore my back,
> And dinna burn my banes,
> An' I'll never be a stranger syne
> Fra' yure hearth stanes.'

Whether roasted thus or poached, Finnan Haddie is extremely good with a poached egg on top.

Serves 1 or 2.

CRUMBED SMOKED HADDOCK

1 large Finnan Haddie or Arbroath Smokie approximately 1 lb. (450 g.) in weight
2 eggs

salt and cayenne pepper
2 tablespoons melted melted butter or margarine
white breadcrumbs

Poach, skin and fillet the smoked haddock and flake it up, mixing the flakes with half their quantity of breadcrumbs, the melted butter and the two eggs well beaten up. Season to taste, put into a greased oven-proof dish and bake at 350°F. (180°C.) or gas mark 4 for about 20–25 minutes until the top is slightly browned.

Serves 2–3.

FINNAN HADDIE MOULD

This is similar to the Swedish Fisk-pudding, and shows the Scandinavian influence on Scottish food.

1½ lb. (700 g.) flaked
   poached Finnan Haddie
4 oz. (125 g.) dry
   breadcrumbs
2 oz. (50 g.) butter or
   margarine
1 tablespoon finely
   chopped parsley

salt and pepper
1 teaspoon of chopped
   fennel
1 small shallot, finely
   chopped
2 beaten eggs

Mix the fish and the breadcrumbs together carefully so as to avoid breaking up the fish flakes too much, then add all the other ingredients but the eggs, see that they are evenly incorporated and then stir in the beaten eggs. Fill a greased pudding basin with the mixture to within an inch of the rim, cover it tightly with grease-proof paper and steam for one hour. Alternatively, it can be baked in a similarly filled greased loaf tin with a sheet of oven-proof roasting film cut to fit the top. Bake at 375°F. (190°C.) or gas mark 5 for around 50 minutes, until the centre is firm and does not stick to a needle and the top is golden brown. When cooked, serve hot with parsley or mushroom sauce, or cold, set in aspic.

NOTE: aspic powder can be had at most good grocers. It is best to follow the directions given by the particular brand.

Serves 4–6.

HADDOCK STRACHUR

This recipe was kindly given by the Honourable Lady Veronica MacLean, who with her husband Sir Fitzroy MacLean has had a long connection with the famous and excellent Creggans Inn Strachur, Argyll.

4 large (or 8 small) Finnan haddock	1 pint (½ litre) double cream
½ oz. (15 g.) butter	black pepper

Poach the fish lightly in boiling water for 4 minutes and then drain and flake, being particularly careful to remove all bones and skin. Arrange in a buttered gratin dish and pour the double cream over, so as to completely cover the fish. Grate black pepper on top. Bake at 350°F. (180°C.) or gas mark 4 for ten minutes, then brown quickly under the grill.

Serves 6–8.

HAM AND HADDIE

1 large smoked haddock (the pale Moray Firth kind is best)	a little water 2 large slices of smoked ham
2 tablespoons butter	black pepper

The most convenient way of preparing this dish, so that there are no bones and skin left in, is first to put the haddock, skin side down, in a large flat pan and barely cover with water, bring to the boil and simmer for 2 minutes, turn the fish and simmer for a further two. Remove the fish, skin it and remove all the bones. Heat the butter in a frying-pan and lay the ham slices in it, turn them once and then put the fish on top, seasoning with freshly milled black pepper, cover and simmer gently for about 3 minutes. Covering with double cream and browning under the grill, as in Haddock Strachur, makes this dish even more delicious.

Serves 2.

HADDOCK PUFFS

From a Victorian manuscript recipe of 1880.

1 lb. (450 g.) cooked,
   boned, smoked haddock
   or cod
2 oz. (50 g.) self-raising
   flour
2 eggs, beaten

¼ teaspoon cayenne pepper
3–4 tablespoons of the
   liquor in which the fish
   was cooked
oil for frying

Flake the fish and mix with the flour and beaten eggs, then add the cayenne pepper and enough of the fish liquor to make the mixture the consistency of a sponge dough. Heat the oil but do not let it smoke and drop in a tablespoonfull at a time, cooking until they puff up and are a golden brown all over.

Serves 2 for a main course and 4 for a first course.

SEE ALSO: *Kedgeree*, page 46 and *Newhaven Creams*, page 58.

HADDOCKS IN BROWN SAUCE

Adapted from Mrs Elizabeth Cleland's recipe in *A New and Easy Method of Cookery* (Edinburgh, 1759).

For the court bouillon

Head, bones and skin of
   two fresh haddocks or
   other white fish
   approximately 2 lb.
   (1 kg.) in weight each
6 whole black peppercorns

1 small onion, finely
   chopped
1½ pints (¼ litre) water
grated peel and juice of
   one small lemon
sprig of parsley and fennel

First make the court bouillon by boiling up the fish heads, bones and skins in the water with the other ingredients for half an hour. Skim and strain.

8 skinned fillets of fresh   2 teaspoons butter
  haddock   2 teaspoons mushroom
2 teaspoons flour   ketchup

For garnish

20 cooked mussels or cockles or 12 large chopped prawns

Poach the fish fillets in the strained court bouillon, covered, for
20 minutes, then lift carefully out and put into a fireproof dish
and cook the shellfish in the court bouillon for 7 minutes,
remove from shells, then reserve them and keep them warm.
Rub the flour into the butter and add to the boiling court
bouillon in small pieces, stirring continuously until it thickens.
Add the mushroom ketchup to taste, then pour over the haddock and shellfish and cook in the oven at 400°F. (200°C.) or
gas mark 6 for 15 minutes.

Serves 4.

CREAMED FRESH HADDOCKS

2 medium-sized cleaned   1½ oz. (40 g.) butter or
  and skinned fresh   margarine
  haddocks   salt and freshly ground
flour   black pepper
10 fl. oz. (¼ litre) half milk   1 teaspoon of made English
  and half cream   mustard

Warm the butter in a frying-pan, flour the fish and season them
with salt and black pepper. Turn them in the butter until
coated all over and then add the already mixed cream and milk
to the pan, heat until it is just boiling, then reduce the heat so
that it barely simmers until the liquid is reduced and the fish
cooked and tender, finally, add the made mustard. This makes a
very good breakfast dish.

Serves 2.

HADDOCKS, RIZZARED

Cleaned but unskinned   a little flour
    fresh haddocks   salt

Rub the fish well with the salt, particularly the inside of the ribs, and leave in a cool place for another few hours. Take them down, dredge them with a little flour and grill them under a medium grill for about 8–10 minutes a side, depending upon the size of the fish, and remembering the wise advice given in the little traditional verse on page 36. When they are done, the outside 'should be a nice brown, like the outside of a toasted muffin' (Miss Brown, the Alexandra Hotel, Edinburgh, 1886). Whiting may be treated in the same way but they must not be rubbed with salt, only cleaned and dried. However, see Alexis Soyer's comment on whiting under *Blawn Fish*, page 25. Fresh haddock is said to be at its best in January, hence the old Moray proverb:

> 'A January haddock an' a February hen
> Are nae to be marrowed in ither months ten.'

SCOTCH HADDOCK PUDDING

10 oz. (275 g.) cooked,
    boned and skinned
    flaked haddock
salt and pepper
1 teaspoon finely chopped
    onion
¼ teaspoon mixed dried
    herbs
a few drops of Tabasco
    sauce

3 eggs, separated
1 lb. (450 g.) mashed
    potatoes
1 tablespoon lemon juice
¼ teaspoon celery salt
1½ tablespoons finely
    chopped parsley
1½ oz. (40 g.) butter or
    margarine

41

Mix the fish into the potato, season with the salt and pepper, then stir in the lemon juice, onion, celery salt, herbs, parsley and Tabasco sauce. Beat the egg yolks slightly and stir in, then beat the egg whites until stiff and fold carefully into the mixture. Place in a large but shallow greased oven-proof dish and bake at 350°F. (180°C.) or gas mark 4 for around half an hour until it has puffed up and become a golden brown.

Serves 6.

BAKED STUFFED FRESH HERRINGS

These admirable creatures have, in recent years, suffered so much from over-fishing in our waters that catches are now restricted and they do not appear on our tables as often as they used; nor can one today contemplate the gastronomical pleasure of herring roes without a pang of conscience. They are a fish which varies very much in condition throughout the year and the good old saying still holds true that 'Herring are no good till they smell the new-mown hay.'

8 herrings, cleaned and filleted	1 small, finely chopped onion
2 oz. (50 g.) dry white breadcrumbs	1 large, soft, herring roe
	pinch of powdered mace
2 teaspoons finely chopped parsley	1½ oz. (40 g.) butter or margarine
grated rind of 1 lemon	salt and pepper
1 egg, well beaten	¼ pint (150 ml.) white wine
1 bay leaf	

Finely chop the onion and the soft roe and add to the breadcrumbs together with the herbs, grated lemon rind, the well beaten egg, salt and pepper. When thoroughly mixed, divide the stuffing into 8 portions and spread a portion on to each herring, which is then rolled up and secured with a cocktail stick. Place the rolled herring in a greased oven-proof dish, add the bay leaf, dot with a little more butter and pour over enough white wine to come half way up the herrings. Cover with an oven-proof dish cover or oven-proof film or foil and bake for 35 minutes at 375°F. (190°C.) or gas mark 5, removing the cover or foil about 5 minutes earlier to ensure that they are slightly browned.

Serves 4.

If you live by the sea in an unpolluted area, you may like to follow the traditional practice of putting about ½ inch of sea-water into the dish instead of the white wine. Mackerel are also very good treated in this way but you will need nearly twice the quantity of stuffing, depending on the size of the mackerel.

Serves 4.

BUTE HERRINGS

6 cleaned and filleted
   herrings
water
6 boiled new potatoes
2 teaspoons finely chopped
   fennel
tablespoon finely chopped
   parsley

salt and sugar
juice of 1 lemon
2 chopped hard-boiled
   eggs
4 fl. oz. (125 ml.) sour
   cream
½ small cucumber, grated

Sprinkle the herring fillets with the salt and sugar and leave for 4 hours in a cool place, then dry them well, roll them up and place side by side in a deep oven-proof dish, pour over the lemon juice and just cover with cold water. Bake at 350°F. (180°C.) or gas mark 4 for ¾ hour to 1 hour, depending on the size of the fish, then lift the fish carefully out, drain them and place in the refrigerator to become cold. Serve with diced new potatoes and sliced hard-boiled eggs and a sauce made by mixing the chopped fennel, parsley and grated cucumber into the sour cream and adding a little salt to taste.

Serves 6.

HERRINGS FRIED IN OATMEAL

8 fresh herrings	salt and pepper
4 oz. (125 g.) coarse oatmeal	4 oz. (125 g.) dripping

Scrape the scales off the fish with a knife or fish-scaler, clean them and remove the heads and tails, then score them with a knife a few times on both sides, sprinkle them well with salt and pepper and toss them in a plastic bag with the oatmeal until they are well coated. Fry them in hot dripping, browning them on both sides, drain the fat from them on kitchen absorbent paper and serve on a hot dish with lemon wedges and a scattering of chopped parsley. Pinhead oatmeal imparts a particularly nutty and delicious character to herrings prepared in this way. F. Marian McNeill says, 'In Buchan, vinegar and oatcakes are considered the perfect accompaniment to this dish.' As a variation, herring fillets can be treated in the same way, but, before coating with the oatmeal, which should be a finer grade of pinhead and sprinkled on, both sides should be painted with made English mustard and cooking oil used in place of dripping.

Serves 4.

POTTED HERRINGS

See *Potted Trout*, page 77.

PICKLED SALTED HERRINGS

6 salted herring   water
6 thinly sliced onions   salt and pepper
3 tablespoons brown sugar   vinegar to cover

Take the herrings out of the brine and soak them in cold water overnight in a cool place. Clean them and cut them into half-inch-wide strips crosswise. Put them into a deep dish with the onion slices and sprinkle them with salt and pepper followed by the brown sugar, then pour over them enough vinegar to cover and leave in a cool place for ten to twelve hours.

Allow 1 or 2 herrings per person depending on size.

TO DRESS RED HERRING, SARDINIAS, AND BUFFED (PICKLED) HERRING

This is the original recipe given by 'Meg Dods', 1826.

Red herring   hot beer or water
oil or butter   made mustard
potatoes or parsnips
  mashed

'Skin, open and trim red herring. If old and dry, pour some hot small beer or water over them [to cover] and let them steep a half-hour, or longer if hard. Broil [grill] them over a clear fire at a considerable distance, or before the fire; rub them with good oil or fresh butter while broiling, and rub on a little more when they are served. Serve them very hot with cold butter, or with melted butter and mustard, and mashed potatoes or parsnips.' 'Steep pickled herrings from one to two days and nights, changing the water if they be very salt. Hang them up on a stick pushed through the eyes and broil them when wanted.

45

These are called *buffed* herrings in Scotland, and are used at breakfast or supper.'

(All salt fish is improved by soaking in buttermilk or the whey left over from cheese-making. The soaking should be done in a cool place or in the refrigerator.)

KEDGEREE

¾ lb. (350 g.) flaked cooked fish, such as smoked haddock or salmon
½ lb. (225 g.) cooked rice
2 oz. (50 g.) butter or margarine
2 hard-boiled eggs

1 tablespoon finely chopped parsley
¼ pint (150 ml.) cream
pinch grated nutmeg
squeeze of lemon juice
salt and cayenne pepper

Cut the hard-boiled eggs up small and combine them with the fish, rice, nutmeg, lemon juice, salt and pepper, then stir in the cream and put into a greased oven-proof dish. Dot the top with the remaining butter, cover and bake at 350°F. (180°C.) or gas mark 4 for around 20 minutes. Strew the top with the chopped parsley and serve with lemon wedges.

Serves 4.

Kippers

Many of the techniques for preserving fish, used over the centuries in Scotland, were introduced and developed by the Norsemen. Until the coming of railways and refrigeration, fish catches could only be distributed to distant markets and centres of population by being treated in such a way as to preserve the fish: chiefly salting, smoking, combined salting and smoking and pickling. Salted herrings underwent a slight fermentation in the barrels into which they were packed, giving them a characteristic flavour which was something of an acquired taste. The famous 'red herring', for so long one of the chief protein sources of the majority of Scots, was (and still is) both salted and smoked and needed lengthy soaking to make it really palatable. With the improvements in rail and road transportation, the more lightly smoked, more delicately flavoured fish, which had before then only been available in the vicinity of the fishing ports, began to be appreciated more widely and grew rapidly in popularity, the red herring gave place to the kipper and the bloater. These forms of more lightly salted herring are smoked for only around eight hours, the bloater being cleaned only before salting and smoking, the herring being both cleaned and split. Many claim that the finest kippers are those from Loch Fyne, which are, like the Manx kippers and indeed all those that have the most delicate flavour, very pale in colour. Beware particularly of the bright yellow uniformly coloured 'kippers' increasingly met with; these have almost certainly not been regularly smoked at all, but sprayed with a 'curing solution' containing a yellow dye, and heavens knows what else besides.

KIPPERS, JUGGED

| kippers | parsley butter |
| boiling water | lemon wedges |

One of the quickest and easiest ways to cook kippers, this method appeals particularly to those who like their kippers to be less oily when they come to table. Take a jug large enough to contain whatever number of kippers are required. Remove the heads and tails and put the kippers into the jug, fill it with boiling water and cover it. After 6 to 8 minutes, depending on the number and size of the kippers, drain them well and serve on very hot plates with a generous knob of parsley butter and a lemon wedge on each.

KIPPERS, GRILLED

kippers
parsley butter

whole black pepper in
mill

Take a grill pan and cover it in cooking-foil (this greatly simpli-
fies the elimination of clinging fishy flavours), remove the heads
and tails of the kippers, grind a little black pepper over them on
the inside and grill under a moderate grill for 3 to 4 minutes
starting with the skin side next the heat and turning to avoid
burning. Serve on very hot plates with a knob of butter and a
lemon wedge on each.

Allow 1–2 kippers per person.

KIPPER PASTE

6 Loch Fyne kippers
juice of 1 lemon
6 oz. (175 g.) butter or
 margarine

whole black peppercorns
in mill

Jug the kippers (as on page 47), remove the larger bones and
take the flesh off the skin and put it into a blender with the
butter and the lemon juice. Blend to the consistency desired
and grind in black pepper to taste.

KIPPER SAVOURY À LA HAMILTON

4 Loch Fyne kippers
4 eggs, well beaten
1 tablespoon finely
 chopped parsley

4 fl. oz. (100 ml.) milk
4 slices hot buttered toast
Tabasco sauce

48

Jug the kippers (as on page 47), then remove the larger bones and take the flesh off the skin. Put the flesh into a pan with the milk and heat, add the eggs and a few drops of Tabasco sauce, stir well to incorporate the whole. When the eggs are cooked but still slightly liquid, cover the slices of hot buttered toast, strew with parsley and serve on very hot plates.

LING, FRESH, BAKED

'Ling would be the beef of the sea if it had always salt enough, butter enough and boiling enough.'   Old Gaelic proverb.
This very meaty fish does not deserve the degree of neglect which it tends to receive nowadays. When given the right treatment it can be excellent but this is not helped by unscrupulous fishmongers passing it off under the names of other species. It should be eaten young, when not much longer than two foot, the older fish becoming coarse.

3 lb. (1·4 kg.) young ling, sliced
salt and whole black pepper in mill
juice and zest of half an orange
1 pint ($\frac{1}{2}$ litre) hot fish court bouillon (see page 40)

4 oz. (125 g.) flour
3 oz. (75 g.) butter or margarine
2 blades of mace
1 tablespoon finely chopped parsley

Take the ling pieces, wash them and dry them well. Put 2 oz. of the flour in a plastic bag, season with salt and black pepper and toss the ling pieces in the bag until they are well coated with the seasoned flour, then lay them in a deep oven-proof dish, pour over them the orange juice and scatter them with the zest and give another small grind of black pepper, add the mace, dot with 2 oz. of the butter and pour the hot fish court bouillon around and bake in the oven at 325°F. (170°C.) or gas mark 3 for

1 hour. Remove from oven, lift the fish pieces out carefully, draining them, reserve on a hot dish and keep warm. Pour the court bouillon into a saucepan, remove the two blades of mace and boil up until the quantity is reduced by half. Work the rest of the butter into the remaining flour and add to the sauce a small quantity at a time stirring and blending until it is all incorporated. Pour the sauce over the fish and scatter with the chopped parsley before serving.

Serves 4.

VARIATION: cod, haddock and hake can be used instead of ling.

SALT LING PIE

2 lb. (900 g.) salt ling
1 tablespoon chopped parsley
8 oz. (225 g.) short-crust pastry
3 oz. (75 g.) butter or margarine
¼ pint (150 ml.) cream, warm
1 well-beaten raw egg

2 hard-boiled eggs cut into thin slices
1 teaspoon salt
¼ teaspoon cayenne pepper
¼ teaspoon powdered mace
1 oz. (25 g.) flour
¼ pint (150 ml.) stock fish was cooked in

Leave the ling soaking in cold water overnight in a cool place, then wash it in several waters and put it into a saucepan with hot water to cover and let it simmer very gently until probing with a fork shows it to be cooked through. Lift out carefully, drain, remove the skin, if any, and layer the bottom of a greased oven-proof dish with a layer of the fish, followed by a layer of hard-boiled egg slices. Scatter the cayenne pepper and the mace over these and then make another layer with the remainder of the fish. Dot the top with 2 oz. of the butter and combine the rest with the flour to make a roux. Blend this into ¼ pint of the fish stock and bring to the boil, stirring and simmering until the flour has cooked, then add the parsley, when the sauce has thickened. Pour over the fish and cover the top with short-crust pastry. Brush the pastry with the beaten egg and make two holes for the steam to escape and put into a pre-heated oven 425°F. (220°C.) or gas mark 7. After 15 minutes turn the oven down to 375°F. (190°C.) or gas mark 5, for a further 15 minutes, then take from the oven and pour the warmed cream into the pie through the holes left in the pastry.

Serves 4.

Lobster (Homarus)

This king of shellfish, now such an expensive item on the cooks' list, deserves to be given the best and most careful treatment. Lobsters should never be plunged alive into boiling water, for research carried out at the Jersey Marine Biological Laboratory shows that when this is done they do not die instantly, as is so often claimed, but make violent attempts to emerge and live for around 58 seconds in agony. The method recommended by the laboratory is to put them into cold sea-water and put them on a very low heat. Under these conditions they show no signs of discomfort until the sea-water reaches 70°F. (21°C.) when the lobster falls over on its side in a faint, the warmth destroying the nervous system gently and painlessly. Reddening of the shell takes place before death. A confirmation of these findings is that lobsters cooked in the latter way are much more tender than those plunged into boiling water, tenderer and most digestible, so kindness to lobsters is also kindness to one's own stomach.

Never put lobsters into plain fresh water. If you do not live by the sea, stir salt into the water you will use to cook them in until it tastes as salt as the sea and then put them into that. After they have come to the boil, they should be cooked for hardly longer than one would hard-boil an egg, unless they are exceptionally large, but even the biggest should not be kept boiling for longer than about 18 minutes, to do so for longer greatly reduces the curdiness and makes the flesh dry. Likewise, if you are buying lobsters at the sea-side, select those that have not been kept for days or weeks in a 'keep', for these will have dwindled away inside their shells and will feel light for their size. Choose those that are heavy for their size and have just come out of the lobster-pots; they will not only have more flesh, but be very much more curdy if not overcooked. After boiling, allow the lobster to grow cold in the water before you take the flesh from the shell. This improves the flavour, as well as preventing drying of the flesh, a precaution necessary to the proper handling of all *crustaceae*.

Before you begin to extract the meat have the following to hand: a deep bowl big enough to hold all the flesh, a small deep bowl to hold the curd, a small but strong teaspoon, a small pointed vegetable knife, a large stiff knife, a chopping board, a small mallet and a pair of electrician's side-cutters. The latter are the key to opening a lobster easily, without the frustrating struggles with hammers and nutcrackers, to the use of which you will never return once you have used one of these inexpensive tools readily to be had at any good electrician's shop. Take the lobster out of the water and, holding it over the large bowl, break off one of the claws, together with its associated joints at the point where the first of these emerges from the body. As you do so, a large quantity of juice will pour from the body into the bowl. The same will occur each time you break one joint from another, so be sure to do this over the bowl and collect the juice, which will serve the double purpose of keeping the extracted flesh moist and contribute greatly enhanced flavour to any dressing or sauce which you may plan to use. Once broken off, each joint may easily be opened by snipping the shell, above and below, with the side-cutters, one point of which can be inserted into even quite a small opening of the shell enabling the snipping process to be done as easily as one nowadays opens a tin. As each joint is opened, remove the flesh and put it into the juice in the large bowl and, with the teaspoon, scrape up the white curd on the inside of the shell and reserve it in the small bowl, keeping it moist with a spoonful or two of the juice from the big bowl.

FISH

When you get to the claw, hold it over the bowl, take the smaller 'thumb' in your hand and bend it back until it snaps off. This releases a further quantity of juice and usually also withdraws an internal cartiliganous 'bone' from the centre of the claw meat. Snip off a few millimetres from the tip of the two parts of the claw (this often facilitates the withdrawal of the claw meat whole) then snip away the wide end of the shell of each part until you can grasp the main body of the enclosed meat and gently withdraw it. Using this technique it is possible to get whole claws nearly every time.

With the claws and their joints dealt with, take the lobster in your hands holding the head and thorax in your left hand and the curved 'tail' in your right (reversed if you are left-handed), apply a gently pulling-apart strain while bending the lobster to the right and to the left at the joint where the 'tail' meets the body. You will hear a couple of clicks and the two will come apart without damage to the soft flesh. Pull off the five petal-shaped segments at the end of the tail and working from that end snip through, above and below, each ring-shaped shell segment and remove it in turn. At the end of this quite quick process you will have a complete lobster 'tail' which only needs to have a small slit half a centimetre deep cut along its top or long outer curved surface to allow the thin black gut to be pulled out by seizing it at the 'head' end and pulling backwards gently. Put the tail into the bowl with the rest of the meat and juice.

Take the lobster's thorax and head and lay it on the chopping board so that its legs are uppermost, position the stiff large knife so that the edge of its blade runs longways exactly on the mid line between the legs and holding it steady hit the thick back of the blade a firm blow with the mallet, which will divide the lobster evenly into halves. Take one half and with the spoon scoop up the greenish liver and reserve with the curd, then take the legs in your right hand and, holding the shell in your left, pull them forwards and upwards. They will detach, bringing with them a tough rough membrane beneath which, mostly in the now empty shell, is the largest deposit of curd. Reserve this with the rest. If you have a few lobsters to deal with, do not throw away the shell fragments and legs, which can be used to make an excellent lobster court bouillon or, if you have enough of them, together with a little of the meat, an admirable lobster bisque. Remember always that the flesh of all cooked *crustaceae* very quickly becomes dry unless reserved in its own juice. External 'coral' (the red eggs) should be reserved separately as should the red internal 'coral' from the thorax, but you will find these only in lobsters that are about to reproduce, so I hope you will not find them often.

LOBSTER MORRISON

Flesh, curd, juice and coral (if present) of one cooked lobster

½ pint (¼ litre) of a classically made mayonnaise, page 193

Take the lobster curd and beat it into the mayonnaise. If the hard internal coral is present, pound it in a mortar and then beat it into the mayonnaise, or if you have the external coral (red eggs) simply beat these in without pounding. Beat half the lobster juice into the mayonnaise as well. The sauce will then be thinner (and more digestible) and have a quite exquisite flavour. Arrange lettuce on a cold dish and place the lobster meat upon it, splitting the tail in two lengthwise to achieve symmetry and reuniting each part of the claw. Sprinkle the remaining juice over the lobster meat and serve with the sauce in a sauce boat.

A medium lobster serves 2 for a first course, 1 for a main course.

LOBSTER CUTLETS VICTORIA
From Lady Forbes, 1867–1953.

The flesh of 1 cooked lobster approx. 12 oz. (350 g.) or 1 tin	½ oz. (15 g.) flour
	7 fl. oz. (200 ml.) cream
	2 teaspoons finely chopped parsley
2 oz. (50 g.) mushrooms, sliced, cooked	1 oz. (25 g.) melted butter
1 small grated onion	2 oz. (50 g.) breadcrumbs
1 oz. (25 g.) butter	salt and pepper

Remove the cooked lobster meat and cut it into small pieces. Make a white sauce by melting the butter in a pan, stirring in the flour and then adding the cream. Maintain on a low heat, making sure that it does not boil and stirring continuously until the flour cooks, then add the lobster, the chopped and cooked mushrooms, grated onion, parsley and salt and pepper to taste. Turn out on to a marble slab or large cold plate, allow to cool, chill in the refrigerator and make into cutlet shapes, dip them in the melted butter and cover them in breadcrumbs, then fry them in smoking hot cooking oil until they are golden brown and serve them with fried parsley. Almost any fish, especially salmon, can be used for these de luxe fishcakes if you do not have lobster.

Serves 4.

LOBSTER SOUFFLÉ PUDDING
From Lady Forbes, 1867–1953.

1 lb. (450 g.) cooked lobster meat	1 oz. (25 g.) butter
	1 oz. (25 g.) flour
¼ pint (150 ml.) cream	¼ pint (150 ml.) milk
1 egg, well beaten	salt and pepper

Pound the lobster in a mortar and pass through a wire sieve or mincer, or process for 30 seconds in a food processor such as a Magimix. Melt the butter in a saucepan, blend in the flour and add the milk, stirring continuously until the flour is cooked. Add the pounded lobster and pass again through a sieve (or process for ten seconds in a Magimix), then add the well-beaten egg and the cream (if using a food processor give another ten seconds). Grease a mould or individual dishes, fill it with the lobster mixture, cover tightly and steam for 1 hour.

Serves 4 for first course or 2 for main course.

Mackerel

All recipes for *Herring* are also effective for mackerel (see pages 42–5).

MACKEREL, BAKED WITH ORANGE STUFFING

4 cleaned mackerel with
  heads and tails removed
1 small onion
1 tablespoon chopped
  parsley
½ pint (¼ litre) cider or
  white wine

1 large orange
2 tablespoons fresh
  breadcrumbs
salt and pepper
1 small apple

Grate the zest of the orange on to a chopping board, then cut the orange, scoop out the flesh and chop it coarsely. Transfer the zest and chopped orange to a mixing bowl and mix in the breadcrumbs, finely chopped onion, parsley and the peeled and grated apple, season with salt and pepper and fill the fish with this stuffing. Put the fish into an oven-proof dish, pour the cider or wine around, cover, and bake for about 25–30 minutes (depending upon the size of the fish) at 350°F. (180°C.) or gas mark 4. If serving hot, pour a little of the juice over the fish, but if serving cold, drain the fish and serve with slices of fresh orange.

Serves 4.

MACKEREL PÂTÉ

4 cleaned mackerel with their heads and tails removed, either fresh or if using smoked 2 will be enough
juice of 1 lemon
2 stiffly beaten egg whites
4 rounded tablespoons dry breadcrumbs, slightly toasted

salt, pepper and a good pinch of powdered mace
2 tablespoons yoghurt or cottage cheese (crowdie)

If using fresh mackerel, brush the fish with cooking oil, wrap in cooking foil and bake at 350°F. (180°C.) or gas mark 4 for about 25 minutes (if you are using smoked mackerel, you do not need to cook them). Remove all the bones and the skin and mash the flesh up very finely (30 seconds in a food processor), then add the breadcrumbs and lemon juice, mixing well. Blend the yoghurt or cheese in thoroughly and season to taste. If you have been using a food processor, remove to an ordinary mixing bowl before gently but thoroughly folding in the stiffly beaten eggs by hand. Shape into a mound or place in a dish and chill well before serving with thin toast.

Serves 6–8.

VARIATION: smoked trout can be used instead of smoked mackerel.

SEE ALSO: *Salmon Mousse*, page 68 and *Potted Trout*, page 77·

MUSSELS WITH CREAM

60 mussels
1 dessertspoon finely
  chopped onion
½ pint (¼ litre) cream
black pepper in mill and
  salt

1 oz. (25 g.) butter or
  margarine
½ pint (¼ litre) dry white
  wine
1 tablespoon chopped
  parsley

Remove the beards from the mussels, scrub them well and rinse in several waters to remove all sand and shell fragments, then put them in a large saucepan with the chopped onion and the wine. Put on the lid and cook quickly until the shells open (5–7 minutes). Take the mussels out of their shells and keep warm. Discard the shells but keep the liquor the mussels have been cooked in and strain it, then boil it up to reduce by half. Take it off the heat, add the cream and parsley together with the butter in small pieces, stirring well. Reheat until it is hot but not boiling. Put the mussels into a deep dish, pour over the sauce and serve.

Serves 4.

SEE ALSO: *Mussel and Onion Soup*, page 17, *Mussel Brose*, page 18 and *Fried Oysters*, page 60.

NEWHAVEN CREAMS

1 lb. (450 g.) cooked,
  boned, smoked haddock
4 oz. (125 g.) breadcrumbs
4 oz. (125 g.) butter or
  margarine

¾ pint (450 ml.) milk or
  thin cream
3 eggs, well beaten
salt and pepper

For the sauce

2 oz. (50 g.) butter or margarine

2 oz. (50 g.) flour

1 pint (½ litre) milk, warm

2 tablespoons chopped parsley

salt and pepper

Mash the fish lightly, making sure that no bones remain, add the breadcrumbs and season to taste. Heat the milk or cream with the butter or margarine but do not boil and pour over the fish, mixing thoroughly, then add the beaten eggs and stir well to ensure that they are evenly incorporated.

Pour into 4 small greased bowls or moulds, cover the top and steam over boiling water for half an hour. When done, remove the covering, place a hot plate on top, invert and unmould. Serve hot, covered with the sauce.

To make the sauce, melt the butter or margarine in a saucepan and blend in the flour, allowing it to cook for a minute, then gradually add the warm milk stirring all the time until the sauce thickens, then add the parsley and season to taste.

Serves 4.

VARIATION: Salmon can be used in place of haddock in this recipe and finely chopped mushrooms instead of parsley, as can finely chopped hard-boiled egg.

OYSTER CUSTARDS

From Mrs Jamieson *c.* 1890.

24 oysters, either fresh or tinned, finely minced

4 egg yolks, well beaten

4 tablespoons cream

1 tablespoon juice from the oysters

¼ teaspoon cayenne pepper

Add the minced oysters to the well-beaten yolks, together with the cream, oyster juice and the cayenne pepper and beat well to amalgamate. Put into 8 individual soufflé dishes filling them only two-thirds full. Stand the dishes in a pan of hot water and bake at 350°F. (180°C.) or gas mark 4 for 15 minutes. Serve either hot in the dishes or allow to grow cold, unmould, chill slightly and garnish with a little lightly whipped cream containing minced oyster and lemon juice.

Serves 4.

FRIED OYSTERS

24 oysters, either fresh or
  tinned cooking oil, hot
  but not smoking
For the batter
4 oz. (125 g.) flour

10 fl. oz. (¼ litre) milk
1 egg
cayenne pepper and salt

Beat the milk carefully into the flour with an egg beater, to avoid lumps forming (if you nevertheless do get a few, simply pass the batter through a conical strainer and beat a little more). Season to taste with salt and a pinch of cayenne pepper.

Leave the batter in a cool place for 30 minutes, meanwhile open and beard the oysters and remove them from their shells, reserving the juice. Heat the cooking oil until it sizzles a breadcrumb but is not smoking, dip the oysters in the batter and deepfry them until they are golden brown, but making sure that you do not overcook them. Serve hot with the oyster juice poured over and with lemon wedges. Mussels can also be cooked in this way.

Serves 4 for a first course and 2 for a main course.

OYSTER KROMESKIES

Recipe from Lady Forbes, 1867–1953.

24 oysters, either fresh or
  tinned

1 oz. (25 g.) butter or
  margarine

1 heaped teaspoon cornflour	*For the pastry*
2 tablespoons cream	4 oz. (125 g.) flour
mace, cayenne pepper, salt, melted butter, breadcrumbs	1 egg a little water

Mix together the flour, salt and egg, then add enough water to make a good stiff dough, turn on to a marble slab and leave in a cool place until wanted. Open the oysters and remove them from their shells, reserving and straining the liquor from them. Boil it up until it is reduced by half, add the butter or margarine, a pinch of powdered mace, a pinch of cayenne pepper and a very little salt. Stir in the cornflour, blended to a cream with a little water, and continue stirring until it is cooked. Remove from the heat, stir in the cream and reheat until it is nearly boiling, add the oysters, finely chopped, and allow to come nearly to boiling point again, then remove from the heat and allow to get cold.

Roll out the pastry exceedingly thinly and with a large pastry cutter, cut into rounds. Put a spoonful of the cold mixture on to each round, damp the edges with water, place another round on top, pressing down the edges to seal them well. Dip the Kromeskies in melted butter or margarine and cover with breadcrumbs before deep-frying in hot but not smoking oil until they are a light brown.

Serves 4 for a first course, 2 for a main course.

VARIATION: crab can also be used instead of oysters (about 12 oz (325 g)).

ANGELS ON HORSEBACK

12 oysters	12 very thin slices of streaky bacon
4 slices of toast	

Roll each oyster in a strip of the thin bacon, securing the end with a cocktail stick. Grill until the bacon is crisp but do not allow it to blacken, remove the cocktail sticks and serve, three to each slice of toast, on very hot plates.

PIKE, BAKED

Recipe from Mrs Sherwood, cook to Lady Clark of Tillypronie, 1880s.

A young pike, 3–4 lb. (1·4–1·8 kilos)
salt

For the stuffing
2 oz. (50 g.) beef suet
2 oz. (50 g.) breadcrumbs
1 oz. (25 g.) chopped parsley
1 teaspoon anchovy essence
salt and pepper

For the sauce
1 oz. (25 g.) butter

1 oz. (25 g.) flour
½ pint (¼ litre) fish court bouillon (see page 40)
1 egg
1 teaspoon mushroom ketchup
1 teaspoon sherry
1 teaspoon anchovy essence
bouquet garni of thyme, parsley, half a bay leaf, marjoram, slice of carrot, onion and celery

'When the fish is cleaned rub it much with salt, and let it lie so for 2 or 3 hours before cooking; this takes away its softness and muddy taste.'

To make the stuffing, chop all the ingredients finely and, reserving a little of the parsley for scattering over the fish when it is cooked, mix together with the egg, the essence of anchovy, salt and pepper. Stuff the fish with this mixture and bake at 400°F. (200°C.) or gas mark 6 for ¾ to 1 hour.

Bring the fish court bouillon to the boil, add the bouquet garni and simmer gently for ¼ hour, skimming off any froth. Meanwhile melt the butter and combine with the flour in another saucepan. When the flour is cooked, strain the court bouillon into the roux, little by little, stirring all the while to

ensure a smooth sauce, add the mushroom ketchup, the anchovy
essence and the sherry, stir well and bring once again to the
boil. Serve in a sauce-boat with the baked fish.

Serves 4.

PLAICE, FRIED,
WITH WATERCRESS BUTTER

2 lb. (900 g.) fillets of
plaice
salt and freshly ground
black pepper
2 oz. (50 g.) flour
a pinch of fennel seeds

1 oz. (25 g.) finely
chopped watercress
3 oz. (75 g.) butter or
margarine
lemon wedges

To make the butter, pound the finely chopped watercress well
in a mortar and work into half of the butter, roll into balls and
chill in the refrigerator. Season the flour and put it into a
polythene bag, toss the fillets in this, melt the remaining butter
in the pan and when it is sizzling but before it begins to turn
brown fry the fillets lightly, scattering a small pinch of fennel
seeds over them as they cook. Dish up on to a very hot dish,
pour the pan juices over, arrange the lemon wedges around,
dot with the watercress butter and serve.

Serves 4 for a first course, 2 for a second.

Plaice is also good served with *Anchovy Cream*, page 80.

SEE ALSO: *Sole*, pages 73–6 and *Whiting*, pages 79–81.

RAY

See *Skate*, page 71.

SAITHE

Saithe or sillocks are the fry of the coalfish and a first cousin of the cod. They should not be much larger than whitebait and are a delicacy in the Shetland and Orkney Islands. They have a very marine flavour not unlike a mussel, and are really only practical to eat when freshly caught.

The tiny fish have the heads cut off, then they are rolled in salted fine oatmeal before being cooked in hot butter until crisp and golden brown.

Marian F. McNeill says: 'Sillock-eating at the kitchen table dispenses with knives and forks. You lift a sillock gently by the tail, between thumb and forefinger, . . . press the plump sides – and the backbone shoots forth! The delicious morsel is left – hot, crisp oatmeal and sweet melting fish – you eat on buttered "bere" [barley meal].'

Saithe or sillocks are also dried and used to be popular with the island school-children. They are well washed in salt water when freshly caught, then tied into bunches and hung in the open air until they are quite hard. No further cooking is needed.

Salmon

Scotch salmon has a great reputation all over and the waters of the Tay, the Tweed, the Spey, the Don and the Dee are favourite hunting-grounds for fishermen who well know the excellence of Scotch salmon. The more delicate salmon trout also abounds in these and other lesser known Scottish waters for the delight of the angler and the delectation of the eater.

All recipes for salmon can be used for salmon trout, but the cooking time is shorter.

TO POACH SALMON

Few of us today possess the large fish kettle which is needed for
perfect fish poaching, and I think that to put cut fish into water
or a court bouillon somehow dissipates the flavour. So if you
have a large fish and no pan big enough to take it, then wrap it in
a large piece of double foil which has been first rubbed with
butter, tuck a sprig of fennel or parsley in the gullet and add
about 2 tablespoons of fish stock or dry white wine, then wrap it
up well and cook it in a low oven (300°F., 150°C. or gas mark 2)
for about 12–15 minutes to the pound. Tail-ends or fish steaks
can also be done this way and if you prefer, the securely
fastened package can be poached in water for about 10–12
minutes to the pound. If it is to be eaten hot then leave it in the
unopened foil for 10 minutes, but if for eating cold let it get
cold in the foil, then open and chill slightly, but remove to room
temperature before serving.

If you do have a fish kettle complete with strainer, then as
soon as the fish is cooked, lift up the strainer, rest it across the
kettle and allow the fish to drain. Opinions vary as to whether
whole salmon should be cooked in plain salted water or in a
court bouillon (see page 40): I am of the opinion that the
strong flavour of salmon does not need the addition of vegetables
and herbs to the water if it is in prime condition, but this is a
matter of personal choice.

SAUCES for serving with hot poached salmon are varied: some
favour just melted butter, others a little of the fish stock with
lemon, and the classical French sauce with salmon is Hol-
landaise (see page 192). Mayonnaise is most often served with
cold salmon, but only home-made: Do not spoil a noble fish
with the commercially bottled variety; it is better just to serve
lemon wedges.

'. . . The more judicious gastronomes eat no other sauce than
a spoonful of the water in which the salmon has been boiled,
together with a little pepper and vinegar.' Sir Walter Scott,
St Ronan's Well.

SALMON OR SALMON TROUT STUFFED AND BAKED

1 salmon, about 3 lb. (1·4 kg.)
2 small slices crustless bread soaked in 2 tablespoons milk
2 filleted anchovies
1 hard-boiled egg
grated rind and juice of 1 lemon
2 oz. (50 g.) chopped mushrooms
salt and pepper
4 oz. (125 g.) butter
¼ pint (150 ml.) dry white wine

Wipe and dry the fish, then soak the bread in the milk and when it has absorbed it mash up with a fork. Add the finely chopped anchovies, grated lemon rind, chopped hard-boiled egg and mushrooms, season and mix very well. Stuff this into the gullet of the fish and secure with a small skewer. If any is left over, shape into small balls and reserve for frying in oil and using as a garnish with the fish.

Cover the fish all over with half the butter and a sprinkling of black pepper, then put into a fireproof dish and pour over the wine, then cover with foil and bake in a moderate oven, 350°F. (180°C.) or gas mark 4, for 45 minutes. Ten minutes before it is ready remove the foil and pour over the remaining butter which has been melted and mixed with the juice of the lemon.

Skin the fish before serving, boil up the juices to reduce slightly and serve the sauce separately with the fish portions.

Serves about 8.

SALMON FRITTERS

Adapted from a recipe of Mrs Dalgairns, 1829. It is a good way of either using up left-over salmon or a small portion.

½ lb. (225 g.) cold, boiled, salmon

2 heaped tablespoons flour

2 eggs

2 tablespoons approx. cream or top of the milk

salt and cayenne pepper

oil for frying

For the sauce

4 oz. (125 g.) melted butter

2 tablespoons cream

2 teaspoons flour

2 teaspoons soy sauce

2 teaspoons mushroom ketchup

Flake the boned and skinned fish, then add the flour, beaten eggs and enough cream or milk to make the mixture a soft consistency, like a sponge dough. Season to taste. Have the oil hot, but not smoking, then drop in tablespoons of the mixture and fry until pale brown on both sides. Drain on paper and keep warm.

To make the sauce, melt the butter, mix the cream with the flour and add to the butter, heating and stirring all the time. When it has thickened slightly add the soy sauce and mushroom ketchup mixing well into the sauce.

VARIATION: Mrs Dalgairns also serves them with quartered hard-boiled eggs and uses ½ lb. (225 g.) mashed potato instead of the flour, making them more like fishcakes than fritters, but both methods make a good dish. Crab can also be used.

GRILLED SALMON

To prevent salmon steaks drying out when grilled, first cover the grilling pan with foil, then melt a large lump of butter in it. Rub the steaks over thinly with seasoned flour, shaking them, and turn them over in the hot melted butter before grilling and cook for about 8 minutes. There is no need to turn them again if done in this way and if the pan is hot enough when the steaks are put in.

They are ready when the flesh leaves the bone *slightly*. Serve with a nut of butter worked with a little fresh parsley and some lemon juice.

SALMON STEAKS MACLEOD

4 salmon steaks
2 tablespoons seasoned
flour
1 tablespoon butter
4 tablespoons double
cream

salt and cayenne pepper
1 teaspoon chopped fennel
2 tablespoons dry sherry
1 lemon, quartered

Dip the salmon steaks in seasoned flour, then lay them in a thickly buttered shallow fireproof dish. Mix the cream with the sherry and fennel, then season with a little salt and cayenne pepper. Pour this over the steaks, cover with foil and bake in a moderate oven, 375°F. (190°C.) or gas mark 5, for about half an hour. Serve with quarters of lemon.

Serves 4.

SALMON MOUSSE

This is a very good way of using leftovers or small amounts of salmon. Smoked salmon trimmings can also be used to advantage. It is best made in a liquidizer.

$\frac{1}{2}$ lb. (225 g.) cooked or
$\frac{1}{4}$ lb. (125 g.) smoked
salmon
$\frac{1}{2}$ oz. (12 g.) gelatine
4 tablespoons water or
fish stock, boiling
12 oz. (350 g.) cottage
cheese

squeeze lemon juice
1 tablespoon medium
sherry
2 egg whites
salt and cayenne pepper

See that the fish is free from skin and bone, then flake. Put the boiling water or stock into the liquidizer, add the gelatine and blend for 1 minute. Then add the fish, lemon juice and sherry and finally the cottage cheese. Cover and blend again until well mixed. Turn out and add the stiffly beaten egg whites. Pour into a soufflé dish (or individual ones) and let it set in a cold place.

Serves 4–6.

VARIATION: lobster, crab or other smoked fish such as trout or mackerel can also be used instead of salmon.

POTTED SALMON

Recipe from a picnic luncheon at Fas-na-darroch,
Aberdeenshire, 1878.

Mix 2 cups, about 12 oz. (350 g.) cold, skinned and boned salmon with 3 pounded anchovies, ¼ lb. (125 g.) butter, a good pinch of mace, salt and cayenne pepper. Pound it well and press into a dish. Cover with melted butter, chill and serve with rolls or toast.

Serves 4–6.

TERRINE OF SALMON

2 lb. (1 kg.) salmon
1 bay leaf
2 egg yolks
salt and cayenne pepper
¼ pint (150 ml.) dry
   sherry

1½ lb. (700 g.) cod,
   haddock or other thick
   white fish
2 oz. (50 g.) fresh
   breadcrumbs
4 oz. (124 g.) butter

Cut and trim the salmon after skinning and boning, then cube into squares about 2 inches square and marinate in the sherry with salt and pepper for about 2 hours, turning occasionally. Pound the white fish and put through a mincer, or use a food processor and add the breadcrumbs, egg yolks, a little of the sherry marinade (enough to make it soft but not sloppy), salt and pepper. Butter the terrine dish thickly, then put a layer of the white fish on the bottom, then the salmon, and so on until the dish is full ending with the white fish. Add about 2–3 tablespoons of the marinade, cover and cook in a pan with water up to half way up the sides, in a moderate oven, 350°F. (170°C.) or gas mark 3, for about 1¼–1½ hours. When cool, put a sheet of foil or greaseproof paper over the top and weight overnight. If liked turn out, then cover with aspic jelly. This is obtainable in packets, and the directions can be found with it.

Or if you want to keep it for a few days, then cover the top completely with melted butter and keep in a cold place for up to 4 days.

Serves about 8–10.

TWEED KETTLE

This is also called Salmon Hash and is a nineteenth-century Edinburgh speciality.

2 lb. (1 kg.) fresh salmon tail-end is best	¼ pint (150 ml.) water
2 chopped shallots or 1 tablespoon chopped chives	¼ pint (150 ml.) dry white wine
salt and pepper	4 oz. (125 g.) chopped mushrooms
pinch of ground mace	1 tablespoon chopped parsley

Put the fish into a pan, barely cover with water, bring to the boil and simmer gently for 5 minutes. Take from the pan, but reserve the stock, remove all skin and bone, then cut the fish

into cubes about 2 inches across. Season it with salt, pepper and mace then put into a clean dish with the quarter pint of fish stock and the wine, shallot (finely chopped) or the chives. Cover and simmer gently for about 20 minutes. Meanwhile heat up the butter and just soften the mushrooms in it (do not let them colour), drain and add them to the salmon, letting them heat up for a further 5 minutes. Serve garnished with the chopped parsley.
Serves 4.

VARIATION: in the nineteenth century it was often served with chopped hard-boiled eggs added with the mushrooms and with a border of creamed potatoes if served hot, and with watercress and sliced cucumber if served cold.

SEE ALSO: *Kedgeree*, page 46, *Lobster Cutlets Victoria*, page 55, *Lobster Soufflé Pudding*, page 55, *Newhaven Creams*, page 58 and *Salmon Soup*, page 21.

Skate

Skate was formerly very popular in Scotland – especially on the islands, where it was liked quite 'high'. To achieve this it was hung up, unsalted in the open air for some days before being cooked and it was then cut into small pieces and fried in bacon fat or butter.

It was also earth dried by being placed on the damp grass and covered with earth sods for a day or so. With regard to both these methods it must be remembered that the northern climate is quite cold so decomposition would not set in very quickly. It is also thought that skate should never be boiled, but baked or fried. It makes a very good soup with onion, potato and fresh herbs.

BAKED SKATE

Adapted from *A New and Easy Method of Cookery* by
Elizabeth Cleland, 1759.

4 wings skate about 2 lb. (1 kg.)
1 pint (600 ml.) court bouillon, see page 40
small bunch parsley
3 oz. (75 g.) butter melted and mixed with 1 teaspoon dry mustard

3 oz. (75 g.) melted butter mixed with 2 teaspoons anchovy essence or 3 pounded anchovies

Put the skate into a fireproof dish, cover with the court bouillon, add parsley, then put on a lid and bake in a hot oven, 400°F. (200°C.) or gas mark 4, for about half an hour or until the flesh shrinks slightly from the bone. Lift out and put on to a warmed dish and keep warm.

Meanwhile when the fish is cooking melt the butter gently (on no account let it boil) and mix one lot with dry mustard powder before starting to heat it, and the other with the anchovy essence or the pounded anchovies. Serve with these two sauces in separate jugs.

Serves 4.

Sole

There are at least two kinds of sole commonly used: the first is black sole, known as Dover sole in the south of England, and the other is Lemon or Witch sole, sometimes known as Megrim. The latter is smaller and the flesh is softer and with less flavour, but nevertheless quite acceptable for many dishes.

The 'Black' sole is often grilled on the bone and this simple method does give the maximum of flavour. The fish is skinned, the head left on, then rubbed with butter or oil, seasoned slightly and grilled on both sides for about 8–10 minutes depending on size. It is then served with a knob of butter worked with chopped parsley and a little lemon juice.

MARINATED SOLE

Plaice of the thicker kind can also be done in this particularly nineteenth-century Scottish method. It makes an excellent first course.

2 soles or plaice, filleted not less than 1 lb. (450 g.) each in weight before filleting
¼ pint (150 ml.) milk
2 oz. seasoned flour (50 g.)
oil for frying

3 tablespoons dry sherry or dry vermouth
2 tablespoons white wine vinegar
2 whole cloves, blade of mace
salt and pepper

For garnish
mushrooms, slices of lemons and small gherkins

Dip the fillets first in milk, then in flour, heat up the oil and quickly fry the fillets on both sides until golden brown. Drain and leave to cool.

Then boil up the sherry, vinegar, cloves and seasonings and while still boiling pour over the fillets in a dish. Soak them in this for 4 days, turning every day. To serve drain the fillets and garnish with lemon, gherkins and lightly sautéed mushrooms.

Serves about 4 as a first course.

SOLE RAMEQUINS

Recipe from Auchentorlie, Aberdeenshire, 1888.

Plaice, John Dory, Bass, Salmon, Lobster or Crab etc. can all be used.

1 lb. (450 g.) fish	⅓ pint milk (200 ml.)
2 rounded tablespoons	pepper and salt
arrowroot	juice of 1 lemon
3 oz. (75 g.) butter	4 eggs, separated

Put the arrowroot, butter and milk into a saucepan and bring to the boil, stirring all the time until it thickens. Then cool. Meanwhile poach the fish in water to cover for about 10 minutes, then drain and mince or liquidize it and mix with the arrowroot mixture. Season with the salt, pepper and lemon juice. Then add the well-beaten egg yolks and finally the stiffly beaten egg whites. Put into a greased soufflé dish or 8 individual dishes and bake in a medium oven, 375°F. (190°C.) or gas mark 5, for 35 minutes for the large ramequin or for 15 minutes for the individual ones.

Serves 2 for a main course or 4 for a first course.

SOLE WITH WHITE WINE

Recipe of Lady Forbes, Newe, Aberdeenshire, *c.* 1890.

2 soles weighing approx.	salt and white pepper
1 lb. (450 g.) each	½ oz. (12 g.) butter rolled
filleted	in 2 teaspoons flour
1 shallot finely chopped	3 tablespoons double
½ pint (300 ml.) dry white	cream
wine	
4 oz. (125 g.) mushrooms,	
sliced	

Poach the sole fillets in the white wine with the shallot, mushrooms and seasonings for about 20 minutes. Then take them from the dish and keep warm. Boil up the sauce to reduce and add small pieces of the butter rolled in flour, stirring well, and gently simmering until the sauce thickens slightly. Taste for seasoning, then add the cream, stir well, heat but do not reboil. Put the fillets back in the sauce to just heat up, then glaze the top under a moderate grill until it is golden brown.

VARIATION: if liked a very little Parmesan cheese can be grated over the top before glazing. Skinned seedless green grapes can be used instead of mushrooms, but reserve a few, raw, for last minute garnish.

LEMON SOLE WITH CROWDIE

Crowdie is the Scottish word for curd or cottage cheese. It makes an excellent stuffing for the small fillets of lemon sole or plaice, but the fillets should be cut using the whole side of the fish, that is the backbone removed and also the side bones, making an almost triangular fillet.

Lay one fillet on a board or table and put on to it about 1 flat tablespoon of cottage cheese which has been seasoned with salt and pepper. Then add about 1 teaspoon finely chopped fresh herbs, such as parsley, fennel, lemon thyme or tarragon, mixed if you like. Add a squeeze of lemon, then put the other fillet on top like a sandwich.

Line the grilling pan with foil and lay on the fish 'sandwiches' dark skin side towards the heat and grill until the skin bubbles and blisters slightly, then turn over and grill the white skin side until slightly golden. Serve at once with lemon wedges.

Serve 1 fish per person.

VARIATION: this stuffing can be mixed and used to stuff the conventionally shaped oblong fillets. Put a spoonful towards one end and then roll up and put side by side, closely packed to prevent them unrolling in a fireproof dish. Dot with butter, and pour about $\frac{1}{4}$ inch of liquid around, either fish stock or white wine. Cover with buttered foil and bake for about half an hour in a moderate oven, 350°F. (180°C.) or gas mark 4. A little cheese can be scattered over the top before baking if liked. These are known as Turbans of Sole, and other fillets of white fish can be used. *Roe Krappin*, page 83, also makes a very good stuffing for the 'turbans' and 'sandwiches'. Allow at least 2 'turbans' per person.

SEE ALSO: *Plaice with Watercress Butter*, page 63.

Trout

The discerning Scot would always favour their Burn or Brown Trout in place of the trout-farm Rainbow trout and there is certainly a great difference in the texture and flavour. In Scotland they are also eaten for breakfast having been salted overnight, then wiped dry, dipped in milk and rolled in coarse oatmeal before being fried in hot butter and served with more butter and a wedge of lemon. This is a speciality at the Portsonachan Hotel, Dalmally, Argyll, where the trout come from the nearby Loch Awe.

It was a favourite dish of Queen Victoria when at Balmoral, and close by flows the Garbh Allt where John Brown fished many times. Queen Victoria recorded in her *Journal of our Life in the Highlands* (1846–61): '... Brown had caught some excellent trout and cooked them with oatmeal, which the dear Empress (Eugenie) liked extremely, and said would be her dinner.'

BUTTERED TROUT

Cut off the fins and wipe the fish, then season with salt and pepper and roll lightly in flour before cooking in foaming butter on both sides.

When cooked put on to a warmed dish and keep warm, add a nut of butter, heat to foaming and add a good squeeze of lemon juice, then pour over the fish.

POTTED TROUT (WHOLE)

From the manuscript recipe book of
Lady Theodora Forbes, 1867–1953.

8 trout, very fresh
¼ pint (150 ml.) white
   wine vinegar
salt and pepper

12 oz. (350 g.) butter
pinch each of: ground
   mace, nutmeg and clove

Clean the trout well and wash them over with a little white wine
vinegar, then slit them down the back and take out the backbone,
then sprinkle all over with salt and pepper and leave for about
2 hours.

Then put a nut of butter inside each fish and fold up as
though it was unfilleted and put them head to tail in a large
oven-proof dish in one layer only. Dot a little more butter over
the top using a little over half of the amount given. Cover and
bake in a slow to moderate oven, 325°F. (170°C.) or gas mark 3,
for about 45 minutes. Take from the oven and when cold lift
them out carefully into a clean dish. Heat up the remaining
butter with the spices and then pour this over to cover them
completely. Chill and serve cold allowing 1 to 2 per person
according to whether it is a first or main course.

If kept completely covered by the butter they will keep for at
least 5 days in the refrigerator.

NOTE: herrings and mackerel can be cooked in the same way.

SOUCHET OF TROUT

Recipe of Sir James Elphinstone of Logie Elphinstone, 1880.

The Souchet was a great favourite in the eighteenth and nineteenth centuries but seldom seen today. It is a very simple dish,
a clear fish soup, but one which needs really fresh fish to make
it well. It is full of flavour when well made. Sole or turbot can
be used instead of trout, or indeed a mixture is pleasant.

2 pints (1·4 litres) court
bouillon, page 40
4 large trout, skinned and
filleted
2 Hamburg parsley* roots
and leaves (if Hamburg
parsley, which has roots
like a small parsnip, is
not available, use plain
parsley with the stalks)

1 lemon cut in very thin
slices
12 white peppercorns,
whole
salt

* Hamburg parsley is easy to grow from seeds and has a very
fine flavour. It was used a lot in the nineteenth century both in
Scotland and Britain.

Cut the skinned and boned fish into large pieces and rub them
with salt and pepper. Heat up the strained court bouillon, add
the paper-thin lemon slices, the parsley in a bunch (and sliced
root if available) and the peppercorns and when it is hot add the
fish and poach gently for not longer than 15 minutes. Take out
the bunch of parsley and serve the soup in deep warmed plates
with slices of thin brown bread and butter.

As a main course serves 4, or 8 as a first course.

TURBOT WITH WATERCRESS SAUCE

Recipe from Lady Harriet St Clair, *c.* 1886.

4 cutlets turbot, approx.
8 oz. (225 g.) each
1 medium onion, finely
chopped
1 rounded tablespoon
flour
1 pint (600 ml.) fish stock

1 oz. (25 g.) butter
salt and pepper
1 teaspoon mushroom
ketchup
1 bunch watercress, finely
chopped

Poach the fish cutlets in about 1 pint (600 ml.) water with the
chopped onion for about 20 minutes. Drain the fish and onion,

and remove the bone and skin from the fish and keep the fillets warm.

Heat up the butter, add the flour and let it cook for 1 minute, then add the strained fish stock, heat up stirring all the time until it is smooth and creamy. Add the mushroom ketchup and taste for seasoning. Chop the watercress finely using a few of the stalks as well and add that to the sauce, stir well and let it just heat up, but do not cook the watercress for it is the crunchy contrast with the fish which makes this dish attractive. Pour over the fish fillets and serve hot or cold.

Serves 4.

Whiting

Deep-sea whiting was very popular in Scotland and was used in many ways. See *Rizzared Haddocks*, page 41. It was also used for fish forcemeat for stuffing other fish and for fish custards. Other white fish such as smoked or fresh haddock etc. can also be used.

FISH CUSTARD

1 lb. (450 g.) whiting
   fillets
½ pint (300 ml.) milk
2 tablespoons grated hard
   cheese

2 eggs
¼ pint (150 ml.) cream
salt and cayenne pepper

First poach the fish in the milk for 10 minutes, drain, then remove any skin and flake up the fish. Mix the cheese well into the fish, then beat the eggs and pour the milk over them beating well. Add the cream and seasonings. Then pour over the fish and cheese and put into an oven-proof dish, cover with a lid and stand in a pan with water to half way up the dish, then bake in a moderate oven, 350°F. 180°C. or gas mark 4, for 35–40 minutes.

Serves 4.

VARIATION: pour into a pastry case and sprinkle the top lightly with grated nutmeg then cook as above. This way it can be served hot or cold. Cook in individual dishes in which case cooking time is 15–20 minutes.

GRILLED WHITING or other white fish

Recipe from Lady Forbes, *c.* 1900.

4 large whiting fillets
approx. ¼ pint (150 ml.) milk
3 oz. (75 g.) melted butter
2 oz. (50 g.) crisp breadcrumbs
2 oz. (50 g.) seasoned flour

anchovy cream, made from ¼ pint (150 ml.) double cream, whipped and flavoured with 1½ teaspoons anchovy essence

Soak the whiting fillets in the milk for 2 hours. Drain but do not dry, dip them in the seasoned flour, then in melted butter and finally in the breadcrumbs. Grill under a moderate flame on both sides until golden brown and serve with the anchovy cream.

Serves 4.

VARIATION: from Lady Clark of Tillypronie.
'Skin and split the fish and lay them on a dish, the fleshy side uppermost and dredge with a little flour, white pepper and salt. Lay little specks of fresh butter over them, here and there, and a little chopped green of parsley or tarragon: baste with this butter and bake for about half an hour in the oven, serve dry.'

Her comment is: 'Very delicate for breakfast. The above recipe is for small haddock or whiting.'

WHITING WHITEBAIT

This was another favourite breakfast dish at Auchentorlie in the last century. 'Whiting skinned and pulled into tiny bits, floured and fried in lard (or oil) like whitebait. Serve hot and dry on a napkin. Squeeze a lemon over when dished.' This is a very good recipe for those who like whitebait, a fish not often seen today. Allow at least 12 oz. (350 g.) per person of fish for a main course portion.

FISH QUENELLES

Quenelles are part of Scotland's inheritance from France and are a really delicious way of using fish, poultry, game or meats. This recipe is from Lady Forbes's private papers. The mixture can be made into small separate quenelles or one large one if preferred.

1 lb. (450 g.) minced whiting or other fish, game etc.	salt and pepper
	½ lb. (225 g.) butter
	2 egg yolks
6 oz. (175 g.) fresh breadcrumbs	4 eggs, separated
	pinch nutmeg
¼ pint (150 ml.) milk	

Pound together the minced fish and the butter. Soak the breadcrumbs in the milk and let it absorb, then squeeze dry and add to the fish mixture with the 2 egg yolks. Add the other egg yolks, salt and pepper, nutmeg, and mix thoroughly. Beat the egg whites until stiff and fold them into the mixture very well.

Make into little oval shapes with 2 dessertspoons dipped in hot water, and either poach in boiling salted water, a few at a time, or put into a lightly buttered shallow pan, in one layer. Pour boiling stock or water over, gently to cover, lay a piece of buttered greaseproof paper or foil on top and poach very gently for about 10–15 minutes. (If 1 large quenelle is wanted then pour into a buttered basin, cover and steam for about 40 minutes, then turn out on to a warmed dish.) Lift out with a perforated spoon and serve on a bed of buttered peas mixed with mushrooms, or with a light cheese or mushroom sauce, page 196.

Some people prefer them simply served with a trickle of melted butter mixed with a squeeze of lemon juice and a scattering of grated Parmesan cheese. This is good with the fish or chicken quenelles, but the stronger game or ham can take a sauce.

Fish Roes

Fish roes of many fish have always been popular but nowadays one does feel that with many species of fish on the decline, it is perhaps wrong to eat so many future fish in one mouthful, so to speak. This applies particularly to herring roes. From January until about March cod's roes are seen in the shops and very good they are. Sometimes they are offered for sale already cooked, but if you find them raw here is the way to cook them.

TO COOK COD'S ROE

Most roes weigh about 1 pound (450 g.) give or take a few ounces: under this weight they do not have the same flavour. Put them either in a muslin or nylon bag or securely wrapped in foil and cook in boiling salted water which has had a spoonful of vinegar or lemon juice added. Cover and simmer very gently for 20–25 minutes. Let it cool, then take from the water and get cold before further preparation. Take off the outer membrane before cooking, but leave it on until you use the roe as it keeps it moist.

COD'S ROE FRITTERS

Slice the cod's roe into circles about ½ inch thick and take off the skin. Dip these slices first in seasoned flour, then in egg and fry until golden on both sides. Serve either with toast or with grilled bacon, tomatoes, mushrooms, etc. and garnish with lemon slices. These fritters also make a good garnish for fried fish.

COD'S ROE

Makes excellent omelette filling, quenelles or ramequins (see pages 73, 81) or thick slices can be heated in a Béchamel sauce with some sliced onions, covered with breadcrumbs and baked in a hot oven 425°F. (220°C.) or gas mark 7 for about 10 minutes.

It makes a very good stuffing for fish as well.

ROE KRAPPIN

Mix together ½ lb. (225 g.) cod's roe with ½ lb. (225 g.) pounded rusks or breadcrumbs. Add 2 oz. (50 g.) butter, 1 tablespoon chopped parsley and 1 beaten egg. This is enough stuffing for 12 mackerel or 1 large fish.

HERRING ROES

The 'hard' herring roes, that is the ones with the myriad tiny eggs, can be rolled in flour and fried in butter, then either eaten on toast with lemon or used as a garnish for large fish.

SOFT HERRING ROE SAVOURY

From Mrs Hart, Goodwyne's Hotel, Aberdeen, 1894.

1 lb. (450 g.) soft herring roe
4 oz. (125 g.) butter
1 rounded teaspoon made mustard

1 teaspoon Harvey's sauce (a nineteenth-century sauce, now available again made by Burgess and Co., also Watkins)
OR mushroom ketchup
salt and pepper

First make the devil paste, by mixing the butter, mustard, Harvey's sauce, salt and pepper and heat until it has liquefied. Put the herring roes into this sauce and cook for about 5 minutes. Serve on hot buttered toast.

Serves 4.

SOUSED FISH ROES

Both soft and hard herring and cod's roe can be soused as for potted or soused herrings, page 77.

SALMON ROE

This is an old Scottish recipe and I doubt whether today many of us have ever seen a whole salmon roe, but I will give the recipe for its curiosity value.

'Take the roe from the fish as nearly spawning as possible. Wash the roe well in milk and water, and then in cold water. Then drain for 15 minutes. To salt take eight ounces of salt to three pounds of spawn and let them lie in the brine for forty-

84

eight hours. Lay them on a board about three-fourths of a yard from the fire, letting them remain there about half a day. Bruise them with a roller then put them into a pot and press them well down. Put on them, in the proportion of eight drops of spirit of nitre as much saltpetre as will lie upon a six-pence to every pound of spawn. [Neither of these are recommended today! T.FG.] Cover them with a piece of writing-paper, upon which lay a coating of hog's lard as cold as it will spread, then tie over all a piece of dressed sheepskin, and keep in a warm place summer and winter.'

Meg Dods, 1826, says 'this recipe was got from Easton, Hawick, one of the best fishers in the south of Scotland, who prepared and sold salmon roe at a high price'.

POULTRY AND GAME

Poultry has long been popular with Scottish housewives, but usually served in a simple fashion with good stuffings and accompaniments. Hens and chickens were featured in early Scottish literature and were often the centrepiece of Highland rural weddings. In some of the lowland districts the keeping of hens was a condition of farm tenancy, the Laird taking eggs and poultry as part of the rent. Young birds were kept for a special occasion in many homes, but the older birds were often boiled or braised.

BOILED CHICKEN WITH EDINBURGH STUFFING

1 large chicken about 4 lb. (2 kg.)
1 lemon
1 rasher bacon
2 medium onions, 1 stuck with cloves
4 leeks
4 medium carrots
2 celery stalks
a small blade mace
salt and pepper

For the stuffing
4 oz. (125 g.) sausage-meat
liver of the bird, chopped
2 heaped tablespoons dry breadcrumbs
pinch of dried herbs
salt, pepper and pinch grated nutmeg
1 egg

Chop the liver finely and mix it into the sausage-meat with all the other ingredients adding the egg last. Then stuff the bird in the crop and body and secure well.

Put into a large saucepan after rubbing the breast of the bird with the cut lemon, then add half of it to the pan together with the chopped vegetables and seasonings. Barely cover with water (if the tip of the breast is left out it will steam which does no harm) bring to the boil and skim if necessary, then cover and simmer for 2–3 hours or until the bird is tender. Put the bird on to a heated dish and coat the top of it with either Parsley and Egg sauce; or plain parsley or Mushroom sauce. *Dumplings*, pages 184, 187, and 188 can be cooked in the stock.

Serves about 4–6.

EGG AND PARSLEY SAUCE

2 hard-boiled eggs
1 oz. (25 g.) butter
1 oz. (25 g.) flour
1 pint (600 ml.) half
   chicken stock and half
   milk

2 tablespoons fresh parsley
salt and pepper

First hard-boil the eggs for no longer than 10 minutes, then run under cold water to prevent further cooking. Heat the butter, add the flour and cook for 1 minute, then stir in and keep stirring the stock and milk mixture, until it is all smooth and creamy. Add the chopped eggs, the parsley, finely chopped and season to taste.

PARSLEY SAUCE

Make as above but omit the eggs and add 1 more tablespoon chopped parsley.

MUSHROOM SAUCE

Make as above but add 2 oz. (50 g.) thinly sliced mushrooms and cook them for about 2–3 minutes in the sauce.

OATMEAL STUFFING or SKIRLIE

This is also a popular stuffing for boiled or roasted birds, such as chicken, duck, goose or turkey.

4 oz. (125 g.) medium
  oatmeal, toasted
3 tablespoons melted butter
  or margarine
OR 2 oz. (50 g.) grated suet
1 small finely chopped
  onion

pinch of chopped herbs
2 tablespoons giblet stock
  or for special occasions,
  whisky
salt and pepper

See that the oatmeal is dry by either putting in a moderate oven for a few minutes or put under a grill, but do not let it colour. Add all the other ingredients in the order given, then stuff into the bird, crop and body and secure with skewers.

To cook: for boiling as above recipe. *To roast:* rub the bird all over with a cut lemon, then sprinkle with salt and pepper. Put into the roasting tin and rub with butter, then sprinkle some chopped tarragon over the top, and add the remainder of the giblet stock to the pan. If no giblet stock then use a dissolved chicken cube. Cover with foil and roast in the centre of a hot oven, 425°F. (220°C.) or gas mark 7, for half an hour, then lower to 400°F. (200°C.) or gas mark 6 for a further 1¼ hours. Take off the foil for the last half an hour to let the bird brown. This is for a chicken about 3½–4 lb. (1·6–1·8 kg.): reduce or increase cooking time by 20 minutes per pound (450 g.) for smaller or larger birds.

CHICKEN CREAMS

Recipe from Lady Forbes, *c.* 1910.

Chicken creams or cream of chicken was a favourite dish in Edwardian days, and used only the breast, the remainder of the birds being used for casseroles or soup. It is a useful recipe nowadays when chicken portions are available and they make an excellent first, or light main course.

1 lb. (450 g.) chicken meat, either breast or thigh, minced	salt and pepper
	½ pint (300 ml.) chicken stock
2 oz. (50 g.) butter or margarine	2 eggs
2 oz. (50 g.) flour	¼ pint (150 ml.) lightly whipped cream

Mince the chicken without any skin and reserve. Then heat up the butter, add the flour and cook for 1 minute, then add the warm chicken stock. Stir well until it boils and is quite smooth, season and then let it get cold.

When cold add the minced chicken and the eggs, one at a time (this can be done in a food processor such as the Magimix) and finally stir in the lightly whipped cream.

Put into a lightly greased dish or basin (or 8 individual ones) to within 1 inch of the top, cover and steam for 45–60 minutes if the large dish, or 20–25 minutes for the small ones. Serve hot with mushroom sauce, page 196; or cold set into aspic which has a little chopped tarragon added. Directions for using aspic are on the package.

Serves 4.

VARIATION: use turkey instead of chicken: use a mixture of half chicken and half ham. Cooked poultry can also be used, but will not have quite such a fine flavour.

HOWTOWDIE

This dish has a decidedly French influence and the name is thought to come from the Old French *hutaudeau*, meaning a pullet. In the eighteenth and nineteenth centuries it was garnished with poached eggs, known as 'Drappit Eggs'.

'This is a very nice small Scotch dish. Mushrooms, oysters, forcemeat balls, etc. may be added to enrich it; and celery may be put to the sauce . . . Slices of ham may be served around the fowl, or two young boiled or stewed fowls with a small salted tongue between them will make a nice family dinner dish.' Meg Dods, 1826.

1 roasting chicken about 4 lb. (2·8 kg.)
4 oz. (125 g.) butter or margarine
8 button onions or shallots
pinch of mace, 2 whole cloves
6 black peppercorns
salt and pepper
1 pint (600 ml.) boiling giblet stock
chicken's liver

2 lb. (1 kg.) spinach
2 tablespoons double cream

For the stuffing
2 oz. (50 g.) fresh breadcrumbs
1 small chopped shallot
1 teaspoon chopped tarragon and 1 teaspoon chopped parsley
3–4 tablespoons milk
salt and pepper

If serving with 'Drappit Eggs' allow 6 eggs, and 1 pint (600 ml.) stock. For the stuffing soak the breadcrumbs in the milk, then add all the other ingredients and put into the bird, and secure.

Heat up 3 oz. (75 g.) butter until foaming and add the onions and let them brown very slightly, then brown the chicken all over. Put into a large dish or casserole with the spices, seasoning and the hot stock. Cover and cook in a moderate oven, 350°F. (180°C.) or gas mark 4, for about 1–1½ hours. Meanwhile cook the spinach, drain it well and keep hot.

Take the bird from the oven, keep hot and strain off the

stock into a saucepan. Add the liver, chopped, and cook gently for 5 minutes, then mash it up well and add the remaining butter cut in small pieces, then pour in the cream and mix well.

Dress the strained and seasoned spinach around the edges of a large dish, put the chicken in the middle and pour the liver sauce over it, not over the spinach. If you are serving the 'drappit eggs', poach them in chicken stock and serve on the spinach.

Serves 6.

MINCE-FOWL

A well-known dish like a fricassée, from the nineteenth century in Scotland, using cooked chicken.

'There were roasted fowls, mince-fowl, apple-pie, haggis . . . and plenty of whisky.' Elizabeth Haldane, *The Scotland of our Fathers,* 1933.

12 oz. (350 g.) cooked and finely chopped chicken white meat
4 oz. (125 g.) mushrooms, sliced
4 oz. (125 g.) butter
2 oz. (50 g.) flour
1 pint (600 ml.) chicken stock
salt and pepper
1 tablespoon each of: chopped parsley and chives

pinch of grated nutmeg or mace
squeeze of lemon juice
3 tablespoons cream, optional
For Garnish: creamed potato, or rice cooked in chicken stock or scrambled eggs (4)

Take the skin and any bone from the chicken, then chop it finely and reserve. Wipe and slice the mushrooms and cook them lightly in half the butter for about 10 minutes. Season to taste. Heat up the remaining butter, stir in the flour and when smooth add the chicken stock and stir until it has thickened and is creamy. Simmer for about 5 minutes and taste for seasoning.

Add the chicken, the mushrooms and their juice, the herbs and spice and stir well. Finally add the squeeze of lemon juice and the cream. Heat, but do not reboil.

Serves 4 with creamed potatoes or rice cooked in chicken stock or with scrambled eggs around the edges.

CHICKEN QUENELLES

See *Fish Quenelles*, page 81.

SMOORED CHICKEN

This is not unlike Spatchcock, an early method of grilling or frying a young bird quickly. To 'smoor' means to smother.

1 young chicken about 2½ lb. (1 kg.) split in half down the back	salt and pepper
	1 teaspoon mustard powder
4 oz. (125 g.) melted butter	2 tablespoons milk
	2 tablespoons breadcrumbs

Beat each half of the chicken well to prevent them curling. Place either in a grilling pan without the rack, or use a heavy frying-pan. Pour half the melted butter over, salt and pepper, then either grill for about 5–6 minutes or fry. Turn over and cook the other side. Mix the mustard with the milk and paint this over the flesh side, and continue cooking under the grill, or in the pan with the lid on, but do not let it cook too quickly. It should simmer gently for about 20–30 minutes. Just before serving sprinkle the breadcrumbs over and if using the grilling method let them brown slightly, but if using the pan then let them just set on the chicken without using the lid so that they form a thin crust. Serve with a watercress salad if possible or with crisp lettuce with an oil and vinegar dressing (4 parts oil to 1 part wine vinegar ratio).

Serves 2.

STOVED CHICKEN OR CHICKEN STOVIES

The name comes from the French *étouffée*, to stew in a closed vessel. It was a favourite Highland dish, particularly popular at weddings.

1 chicken about 3½ lb. (1·6 kg.) jointed
4 oz. (125 g.) butter
2½ lb. (1·1 kg.) potatoes, sliced into medium thick circles
2 medium to large onions, or 12 shallots, sliced

salt and pepper
2 pints (1·1 litres) chicken stock or made from giblets
2–3 tablespoons chopped parsley

Wipe the chicken joints and if preferred take off the skin. Then heat 1 oz. (25 g.) of the butter and lightly brown the chicken joints all over, adding a little more butter if needed. Peel and slice the potatoes, onions or shallots and put a layer of each on the bottom of a greased casserole, then a layer of chicken, seasoning each one, and also dotting with butter. Repeat this until all the food is finished ending with a layer of potatoes. Pour two-thirds of the stock over and cover first with a piece of buttered paper, then the lid. Either simmer very gently or cook in a slow oven at 275°F. (140°C.) or gas mark 1 for about 2–2½ hours, adding the rest of the stock at half cooking time. Sprinkle with the chopped parsley before serving.

Serves 4–6.

VARIATION: add about ½ lb. (225 g.) sliced ham or lean bacon with the chicken. Mix the shallots with 4 oz. (125 g.) sliced mushrooms.

WET DEVIL

From a recipe of Lady Clark, Tillypronie, 1880s.

4 raw or cooked joints poultry or game	1 tablespoon curry powder
2 oz. (50 g.) melted butter	1 teaspoon dry mustard
	salt

For the Devil sauce
½ pint (300 ml.) cream

If raw, dip the joints of the birds in the melted butter and grill or fry until golden brown all over and cooked, about 7 minutes on each side.

Then mix all the sauce ingredients together, put the chicken in and bring it to just under boiling point. Serve with boiled rice.

Enough for 2.

ROAST DUCK WITH GOOSEBERRY SAUCE

Recipe from Lady Clark of Tillypronie, c. 1880s.

1 duck, about 4 lb. (2 kg.)	*For the sauce*
salt	½ pint (300 ml.) sorrel or spinach juice
juice of 1 lemon	
2 tablespoons bacon dripping or 3 of oil	¼ pint (150 ml.) dry white wine
oatmeal stuffing, see *Skirlie*, page 88 optional	½ lb. (225 g.) green gooseberries
	2 oz. (50 g.) sugar
	1 oz. (25 g.) butter

First wipe the duck inside and out, then sprinkle all over with the lemon juice, salt and pepper. Stuff with the skirlie if using and secure well. Put on to a rack in the baking tin and spread the dripping or oil over, then roast in a hot oven, 400°F. (200°C.) or gas mark 6, for about 20–25 minutes to the pound, basting from time to time, and half way through cooking prick the breast skin lightly with a fork.

To make the sorrel or spinach juice boil up about 1 lb. (450 g.) sorrel or spinach in ¼ pint (150 ml.) water for 15 minutes, then strain pressing the vegetable very well to extract all liquid.

Mix this sorrel or spinach juice with the wine, gooseberries, sugar and butter, bring to the boil and simmer until it is a purée; or liquidize. Beat it well, taste that it is sweet enough, then serve with the duck.

This sauce is extremely good with a rich duck, goose and with roast pork.

Goose

Goose is not eaten a great deal in Scotland, but when it is it is often a green goose at Michaelmas, that is a young goose, also known as 'stubble goose'. This goose is not always stuffed, but simply roast and sometimes served with the above sauce. Older geese usually have a sage and onion stuffing and are roasted, or braised.

ROAST GOOSE WITH
SAGE AND ONION STUFFING

1 goose about 10 lb. (4·5 kg.)	*For the stuffing*
	4–6 medium onions
salt, pepper	salt, pepper
2 tablespoons oil	pinch nutmeg

95

½ teaspoon sugar
3 chopped sage leaves or
 ½ teaspoon dried
2 cooked mashed medium
 potatoes

2 tablespoons coarse
 oatmeal
the chopped goose liver

Cook the chopped onions in boiling salted water until they are soft, about 10 minutes, then drain, leaving just a very little liquid. Add all the other ingredients in the order given and mix well. It should be dry enough not to stick to the fingers. Put into the bird and secure. This stuffing can go into the body or the crop, but if preferred the crop end can be stuffed with sausage-meat mixed with a few whole, cooked chestnuts. Allow half a pound (225 g.) sausage-meat to 8–10 chestnuts.

Stand the goose on a rack and rub with salt and pepper, then pour over the oil, prick the breast skin slightly, then roast for 20 minutes to the pound and 20 minutes over in a moderate oven, 350°F. (170°C.) or gas mark 4 with a piece of foil over the breast and legs. Baste from time to time, and to serve pour off any excess fat after having removed the bird to a hot serving dish, and add a glass of red or white wine to the pan juices, then boil up to reduce and taste for seasoning.

Serves 10.

ACCOMPANIMENTS to roast goose are Apple Sauce and *Bread Sauce*, page 190; the gooseberry sauce given above is also good as is the following one given by Lady Clark.

SAUCE FOR GOOSE OR DUCK

Mix together 2 tablespoons dry mustard powder, the juice of 1 lemon, a sprinkle of cayenne pepper and ¼ pint (150 ml.) port wine. Heat to boiling point and serve hot, separately.

CASSEROLED GOOSE

1 goose, approx. 8 lb.
  (3·6 kg.)
1 large onion stuck with
  cloves
3 medium carrots
2 large leeks
1 bay leaf, sprig thyme
  and sage
salt and pepper
1½ pints (1 litre) chicken
  stock

For the stuffing
1 lb. (450 g.) chopped
  cooked potato
2 oz. sautéed salt pork,
  chopped
1 medium chopped onion
1 tablespoon chopped
  parsley
juice and peel of 1 lemon

Wipe out the goose and rub it with pepper and salt. Then prepare the stuffing and put into the bird and secure well. Peel and chop the vegetables and put into the bottom of a large casserole or oven-proof dish with the bay leaf and season them. Lay the goose over the top and prick the skin lightly. Then barely cover with the stock, bring to the boil, simmer gently either on top of the stove or in a slow oven, 325°F. (150°C.) or gas mark 2, for 25 minutes to the pound.

Serves 8.

Serve with freshly cooked root vegetables or *Red Cabbage*, page 100.

POTTED GOOSE

Recipe of Lady Forbes, *c.* 1900.

This is excellent for leftovers: chicken and ham, rabbit, tongue, turkey or game can also be used.

Remove the skin, bone, fat or gristle from the leftover poultry or game. Then mince it or chop finely (a food processor does it in seconds). Weigh the meat and beat it up with half a pound (225 g.) of butter to every pound (450 g.) of poultry, and season it with a little mace or nutmeg, salt and pepper. Mix very thoroughly and add 2 tablespoons stock or gravy to every 1½ lb. (700 g.) of the mixture and beat well.

Put into a large deep dish, or smaller ones, and press down, cover with foil, then set in a slow oven in a pan of hot water to half way up the sides, 325°F. (150°C.) or gas mark 3 for 40–60 minutes. Take from the oven, press down again and when slightly cooled cover the top with melted butter. Chill and serve with slices of dry toast.

It will keep for some time in a cold place if the butter seal is not broken.

Turkey

Mrs Major Farquharson's method for a hen turkey, 1876.

'This recipe does for a hen, or a hen turkey. Blanch a hen turkey half an hour in water or mutton barley broth, but a hen only 15 minutes. The bird being wet out of the pot, rub it well over with fresh butter. Then breadcrumb all over. Roast or cook in a pan in the oven. Baste it now and again. Very tender and juicy.'

Cooking time is 20 minutes to the pound (450 g.) and it can be basted with a little of the hot stock.

ROASTIT BUBBLY-JOCK

Mrs Buchanan's recipe, 1891.

This is a traditional Scottish method of cooking turkey, and probably gets its curious name from the gobbling voice of the live bird.

1 hen turkey about 10 lb. (4·6 kg.)	*For the stuffing* 1 lb. (450 g.) sausage- meat

4 oz. (125 g.) breadcrumbs
¼ pint (150 ml.) milk
6 oysters, fresh or canned, optional
8 large, peeled cooked chestnuts
2 stalks chopped celery
chopped turkey liver
2 teaspoons chopped parsley

pinch of dried sage
2 oz. (50 g.) melted butter
1 pint (600 ml.) giblet stock, hot
1 heaped tablespoon redcurrant jelly
salt and pepper

Wipe the turkey inside and out and prick the breast lightly. Then soak the breadcrumbs in the milk and squeeze dry before adding all the other stuffing ingredients, then put this into the body and crop of the bird.

Put the bird in the roasting tin and brush with the melted butter, then add half the stock, cover with foil and roast at 350°F. (170°C.) or gas mark 4 for 20–25 minutes to the pound. Baste half way through cooking time, season and add the rest of the giblet stock, warmed. Boil up before putting back in the oven, and continue cooking.

Take off the foil 15 minutes before it is ready to let it brown, and add the redcurrant jelly to the pan juices, stir well, boil up rapidly to reduce slightly and serve separately.

Enough for 10.

Game

BLACKCOCK (*Lyrurus tetrix*)

This bird, which is also known by the names of Black Game, Heathcock and Black Grouse, is of the *Tetraonidae* family and thus related to the Capercaillie and the Red Grouse. The female is sometimes known as the Grey Hen. It is in season from August to December, but is at its best from October. It should preferably be roasted, made into pies or casseroled, treated, in fact, as grouse, which it somewhat resembles in taste, though it is not so highly thought of. Feeding on shoots, berries and seeds, it can weigh up to 4 pounds for the cocks and about half this for the hens. Both must be hung for at least a week and preferably longer in cold weather or they will be without flavour and require too much cooking which will make them dry. Pluck and draw them but do not wash the body cavity, rub them inside with a little salt, squeeze a little lemon juice into them and truss like a chicken.

SEE ALSO: *Grouse*, page 103, *Partridge*, page 111 and *Pheasant*, page 113.

BLACKCOCK WITH RED CABBAGE

1 blackcock or 2 greyhens	1 medium red cabbage
2 heads celery	2 apples
1 bay leaf	1 tablespoon brown sugar
2 pints (1·1 litre) chicken stock	1 glass red wine (150 ml.)
2 tablespoons wine vinegar	3 tablespoons wine vinegar
	$\frac{1}{2}$ pint ($\frac{1}{4}$ litre) water
juice of a lemon	cloves and allspice
salt and pepper	$\frac{1}{2}$ oz. (15 g.) butter or margarine

Put the cleaned and plucked birds on to stew on a low heat, with the stock, vinegar, lemon juice and prepared and sliced celery, seasoning to taste. Simmer them gently for about 1$\frac{1}{2}$ hours, then remove the birds and the celery.

Put the sliced red cabbage into a large saucepan with the peeled, cored and sliced apples, onion, sugar, spices, wine and water. Season, and let them come gently to the boil, then lower the heat and add the 3 tablespoons of wine vinegar. Let it cook gently for around 3 hours, turning from time to time. When it is cooked, put the birds on the top without the lid and allow them to warm up thoroughly, meanwhile heat up the celery in a little butter and serve with the blackcock and the red cabbage.

CAPERCAILLIE, also spelled CAPERCAILZIE, ROASTED

This excellent game bird (Wood Grouse – *Tetrao urogallus*), which likes to feed on the young shoots of conifers, needs to be drawn as soon as it has been shot, hung for at least a week, or even longer in cold weather, and stuffed with raw potatoes before it is cooked, the latter being removed before the bird is served. This procedure eliminates the otherwise excessively turpentine-like flavour given by the pine shoots.

1 capercaillie	8 slices of fat ham or
sliced raw potatoes to fill	bacon
bird	salt and pepper
1 tablespoon redcurrant	½ pint (¼ litre) chicken
jelly	stock
3 tablespoons dry sherry	

Wipe the bird inside and out and season, inside and out, with salt and pepper, then stuff it with the raw potato slices. Cover it well with the ham or bacon slices and bake at 400°F. (200°C.) or gas mark 6 for 15 minutes, then reduce the heat to 375°F. (190°C.) or gas mark 5 and continue cooking for a further 35 minutes. Remove from oven, reserving the bird on a hot dish and keeping warm. Pour off any fat from the baking-tin juices, then put them into a saucepan with the chicken stock, the red-currant jelly and the sherry. Boil up the sauce until it is reduced by half. Taste and season if necessary. Remove and discard the potato from the inside of the bird and serve the capercaillie with *Bread Sauce*, page 190, and the sauce made from the juices in separate sauce boats.

CAPERCAILLIE, BRAISED

If the bird is a cock, it should be prepared for this recipe by steeping it in milk, for an hour or two, immediately after it has been plucked, which will also reduce the turpentine flavour.

1 capercaillie
6 oz. (175 g.) breadcrumbs
4 chopped shallots
2 tablespoons cranberry jam or jelly
1 tablespoon chopped parsley
4 medium onions, sliced
4 carrots, sliced
half red wine and half boiling water to cover

For the sauce
2 oz. (50 g.) butter or margarine
3 tablespoons cranberry jam
1 oz. (25 g.) flour
salt and freshly ground black pepper

Mix together the breadcrumbs, shallots, parsley and the 2 table-spoons of cranberry jam or jelly and stuff the bird with the mixture. Make a bed of the sliced onions and carrots in the bottom of a deep oven-proof dish, put the bird on top of them and pour on half red wine and half boiling water to cover it. Put a well fitting cover on the dish and simmer it very slowly for two hours. Meanwhile, combine the flour and the butter and to them add the 3 tablespoons of cranberry jam. When the bird is cooked, remove it from the oven-proof dish and reserve it on a hot dish in a warm oven. Strain the liquor in which the bird was cooked into a saucepan and boil it up until it is reduced by half, then, on a very low heat, add this, little by little and blending continuously, to the butter, flour and jam mixture, then allow it to come just to a simmer for 3 or 4 minutes, stirring all the while to ensure that no lumps form. Pour the sauce around the bird and serve immediately.

Grouse

The red grouse (*Lagopus scoticus*) of Scotland is generally considered one of the great gastronomical delights. For roasting, mid-September to mid-October is the best time to eat the birds of that year, after they have been hung for a week to ten days, depending upon the weather temperature. The older birds of the previous year are better kept for use in pies and terrines.

The young bird is easy to recognize by its having clean claws and no moulting ridge as well as the fact that the tip of its breast-bone bends readily. For *Wood Grouse*, see *Capercaillie*, for *Black Grouse*, *Blackcock* and for *White Grouse*, *Ptarmigan*.

ROAST GROUSE

As these birds have a delicate skin, they need to be carefully plucked, so as not to injure it. After drawing, wipe well, both inside and out. If you are lucky enough to have some cranberries or whortleberries, these make the best stuffing of all and keep the bird deliciously moist, which it is important with grouse, as they can easily be made dry and spoiled.

2 grouse
6 slices of fat bacon
2 grouse livers
2 slices of toast large enough to go under the birds
2 teaspoons rowanberry jelly
4 oz. (125 g.) butter
2 teaspoons lemon juice
salt and freshly ground black pepper
$\frac{1}{4}$ pint (150 ml.) red wine, warmed
2 small bunches of watercress
game chips

Work the lemon juice, a little salt and black pepper into 3 oz. (75 g.) of the butter, divide it, and put half into the body cavity of each bird (but not the crop). Wrap the birds well with the fat bacon and, in addition, cover the bacon in the breast region with kitchen foil.

Bake at 425°F. (220°C.) or gas mark 7 for 20 minutes. Meanwhile, heat the remaining butter and lightly fry the livers, season them, mash them well and spread them on the toast, reserving on a hot serving dish and keeping warm. After 20 minutes, remove the kitchen foil from the breasts of the birds and take off the bacon slices. Pour the warmed wine over the birds and continue baking for a further 10–15 minutes, basting frequently.

Smear the bacon slices generously with the rowanberry jelly, roll them and arrange around the toast and keep warm. When the birds are *à point*, remove them and mount them on the toast slices, in a warm but not hot oven. Pour off any fat from the juices in the baking tin and boil up until reduced by half, then serve in a sauce boat with the birds, which have been additionally garnished with the watercress and game chips. *Bread Sauce*, page 190, is sometimes served with roast grouse. Peeled and stoned white grapes make a very good alternative accompaniment.

Serves 4.

SEE ALSO: *Grouse Sauce*, page 192.

GROUSE PIE

This traditional nineteenth-century recipe from the Forbes's family does not make use of a pastry case. It is what we should today call a *terrine* and is particularly suitable for using birds of the previous year.

3 grouse, young or old
¼ lb. (125 g.) minced lean pork, with just a little fat
salt and freshly ground black pepper

½ lb. (225 g.) streaky bacon slices
1 medium onion
grouse stock, made from the carcases and strained

Take the breasts from old or young grouse, removing any skin, gristle or tough fibres. Cut them into thin layers and beat to further flatten. Pound in a mortar or work in a food processor the lean pork together with the onion, until you have a smooth paste, then season evenly with the salt and black pepper. Line a terrine or other suitable oven-proof dish with the slices of streaky bacon, then, spreading each flattened breast fillet with a layer of the paste, lay them one on top of the other layer by layer until the terrine is full. Fill the dish half full with a good grouse stock made from the carcases and cover the top with the remainder of the streaky bacon. Put on the cover of the terrine (or cover your dish with cooking foil), stand it in a meat tin containing water coming half way up the side of the terrine and bake in the oven at 300°F. (150°C.) or gas mark 2 for 2 hours, taking care that the water in the tin does not dry up, but replenishing with boiling water if needed.

Meanwhile, boil up the remainder of the stock* until it is reduced by half. When done, remove the terrine from the oven, take off the lid and pour the reduced stock over it until it comes to two-thirds of the way to the top. Let it cool until it is just warm, then cover the top with kitchen foil and put a weight about 4 lb. (2 kg.), conforming in shape to that of the terrine, on top of the foil. If a good weight is not available, use approximate tins of food. Allow to grow cold overnight, remove the weight, metal and foil and place in the refrigerator to chill. When chilled, remove any fat or grease from the top. Be sure to remove from the refrigerator at least an hour before serving, so that it is not too cold. This is also a good recipe for partridge, pheasant or pigeon.

* If the stock is made from old birds it might not jell. In which case add 1 level tablespoon per ½ pint (300 ml.) gelatine or aspic, dissolving it thoroughly.

It can be covered with *Short Crust Pastry*, page 218, instead of weighting and served hot or cold.

Serves 6–8.

POTTED GROUSE

Lady Forbes's recipe, *c.* 1900.

4 old grouse and their
  giblets
1 lb. (450 g.) butter
½ teaspoon cayenne pepper

¼ teaspoon freshly ground
  black pepper
salt

Prepare the birds as for roasting. Keep the necks, livers and gizzards. Split the birds lengthwise by cutting down the backs and break the bones by beating them with a rolling-pin. Take the butter and work it with the cayenne pepper, black pepper and salt to taste. Rub the birds all over with this and place the rest of the seasoned butter inside them, then close them up. Place all the giblets in an oven-proof casserole and put the birds on top. Cover with a tight-fitting lid and bake for two hours at 300°F. (150°C.) or gas mark 2. The birds should be so well done that the bones will pull out. Lift out of the casserole to remove the bones. After removing the bones, the birds must be pressed down in a deep dish and some of the gravy and butter in which they have been cooked poured over and among them. Let them get cold naturally, and then cover them with melted butter. Do not stint on either butter or pepper in this recipe. The potted birds will keep a week or so done in this way (in a reasonably cool place).

Serves 6–8.

SALMI OF GROUSE

For older game birds of all kinds.

2 grouse, liberally rubbed
  with butter, approx.
  2 oz. (50 g.)
1 pint (½ litre) stock or
  consommé, hot
3 fl. oz. (90 ml.) claret or
  port

1 oz. (25 g.) butter or
  margarine
1 oz. (25 g.) flour
salt and freshly ground
  black pepper

Roast the birds at 400°F. (200°C.) or gas mark 6 for 15 minutes, then joint them and put them into a saucepan with the stock and seasoning, to cover and simmer gently for 15 minutes or until tender. Remove the grouse joints and keep warm on a hot dish in a warm oven. Add the claret or port to the stock in which the birds have been cooked, boil up and reduce by half, meanwhile working the butter and flour together. When the sauce is reduced take off the heat and blend in the flour and butter in small pieces, stirring all the time, then reheat until simmering, stirring continuously until the flour cooks and the sauce thickens. Taste for seasoning and pour the sauce over the grouse and serve at once. All game birds can be made into a salmi, or a mixture is good.

Serves 4.

SEE ALSO: *Quenelles*, page 81.

Hare

Two species of hare are met with in Scotland, the blue or mountain hare (*Lepus timidus*), which is quite common in the highlands, changing its coat to white in the winter, and the larger English brown hare (*Lepus europaeus*) which is better for the table. Hares should be hung head downwards for a week or even ten days and should not be drawn until just before they are to be cooked. After skinning, the blood, which collects under a membrane inside the ribs, should be carefully reserved, as it is needed to thicken and enrich the gravies or sauces.

Young hares are best for roasting and it is easy to tell them by the readiness with which the edge of the ear may be torn. If to do this is difficult, then the hare will be an old one, as may be confirmed by its having blunt claws as well as a larger cleft in the lip; such hares are better jugged or made into pâté.

JUGGED HARE

1 hare approx. 3–4 lbs. (1·4–1·8 kilos)

4 oz. (125 g.) butter or 4 tablespoons cooking oil

6 oz. (175 g.) chopped bacon or chopped raw ham

1 celery heart sliced

4 medium onions, sliced, or 12 button onions left whole

4 medium carrots, sliced

1 tablespoon chopped parsley

2 teaspoons chopped thyme

2 bay leaves

3 tablespoons redcurrant jelly

1 heaped tablespoon flour

1½ pints (850 ml.) approx. water to cover

blood of the hare

salt and freshly ground black pepper

For the marinade

3 tablespoons olive oil

¼ pint (150 ml.) red wine

2 tablespoons red wine vinegar

2 shallots, sliced

6 juniper berries, crushed

4 allspice berries, whole

a sprig of rosemary

2 bay leaves

salt and freshly ground black pepper

Joint the hare (dividing the back into three or four pieces) and put it into the marinade overnight. Melt the butter in a large pan, shake off excess marinade from the hare pieces and fry them on all sides until they are brown. Transfer the hare pieces and the pan juices to an oven-proof metal casserole with a tight-fitting lid and add the chopped bacon or ham, the onions, the carrots and the herbs. Sift the flour over all, while stirring to ensure that everything gets a flour coating. Season to taste and then pour the stock over barely to cover and top up with a little of the marinade.

Cover and cook in the oven at 325°–350°F. (170°–180°C.) or gas mark 3–4 for about 3 hours, or until it is tender. Add the redcurrant jelly and the port half an hour before cooking is complete. If you are not using the blood, mix 1 tablespoon of cornflour in a little of the marinade and add it at this stage. I instead of thickening the gravy with cornflour you wish to use the blood, then remove the lid and allow it to cool until it is no longer boiling, then take a few spoonfuls of the hot stock and blend this into the blood before adding the blood to the gravy in the casserole, stirring well all the while to avoid lumps forming. Put the hare joints back and reheat but do not allow it to come to the boil and it is ready to serve.

Serves 6–8.

HARE FORCEMEAT BALLS

In Scotland, forcemeat balls are frequently served to accompany many game dishes.

1 onion, finely chopped
1 slice streaky bacon, chopped
liver of the hare, finely chopped
3 tablespoons cooking oil
1 tablespoon chopped suet or margarine
2 teaspoons chopped parsley
1 tablespoon chopped marjoram or thyme
6 tablespoons fresh brown breadcrumbs
2 eggs, beaten
salt and freshly ground black pepper
cooking oil for deep-frying

Heat the oil and fry the chopped onion, bacon and liver together until they are soft, then add 4 tablespoons of the breadcrumbs together with the remaining ingredients and bind them with half the beaten eggs. Shape into balls. Dip the balls in the remaining egg and breadcrumbs before frying in the deep fat until golden brown

ROAST SADDLE OF HARE

1 saddle of hare
3 oz. (75 g.) sugar, moistened
salt and freshly ground black pepper
a handful of parsley, chopped

4 tablespoons cooking oil
2½ fl. oz. (75 ml.) port, warmed
½ pint (¼ litre) stock
2 oz. (50 g.) redcurrant jelly

Rub the joint well with the moistened sugar, salt and freshly ground black pepper. Arrange the chopped onion and parsley in a layer on the bottom of a roasting tin, lay the joint on top and paint it over with the oil. Put a sheet of oven foil over the joint and roast at 375°F. (190°C.) or gas mark 5 for 1½ hours, then remove the foil, baste with the warmed port and return to the oven for a further 15 minutes, basting frequently. At the end of that time, test for tenderness, remove the hare and reserve on a hot dish in a warm oven. Put the roasting tin on the top of the stove, add the stock and boil up until it is a little reduced, then stir in the redcurrant jelly, heat until it is melted and serve in a heated sauce boat or *écrèmeuse.** *Hare Forcemeat Balls* (see page 109) make a very good accompaniment to this dish, as also is *Red Cabbage* (see page 100). The legs can be used for *Jugging*, page 108, *Pâté*, see below, or *Bawd Bree*, page 4.

* An *écrèmeuse* is a French gravy boat which pours fat at one end and without fat at the other. They are available at good kitchen stores, called variously gravy separator or 'creamer'.

HARE PÂTÉ

This recipe can also be effectively used for grouse, partridge, pheasant or venison.

½ lb. (225 g.) leftover
    pieces from the hare
    saddle or legs
½ lb. (225 g.) belly of
    pickled pork
3 cloves garlic

1 bay leaf
salt and freshly ground
    black pepper
2 tablespoons medium
    sherry or brandy
1 egg, lightly beaten

Chop finely or mince all the leftover meat, the pork and the garlic, mix together with all the other ingredients but the bay leaf and put into a greased pâté dish or terrine. Lay the bay leaf on top and cover with foil or the terrine cover and bake at 350°F. (180°C.) or gas mark 4 in a tin half way up with hot water for 1½ hours. When almost cold, it should be weighted on top and left overnight. Serve with toast.

Serves 4–6.

SEE ALSO: *Bawd Bree*, page 4.

PARTRIDGE, ROAST

See *Grouse*, page 103.

PARTRIDGE, WITH CABBAGE

Extract from a letter from Mary Parke, September 1841, to Lady Clark before her marriage. Mr Justice Coltman is Lady Clark's father.

'Go out shooting in the morning and bring home a good many birds; have 2 brace trussed as for boiling. Take a cabbage or two, first scalded in salt and water, then take off the leaves and wrap each bird in them, tying them up close.

'Season with pepper, salt and a very little mace and some ground peppercorns. Have ready a little good stock and put with the birds into a small, deep, stewpan. Cover very close and let the birds stew till sufficiently done. [40–60 minutes is long enough. T.FG.] Then cut the string around each bird, and leave them covered by the cabbage. Have also some more cabbage in the gravy. Take out the birds but keep them warm. Also the cabbage. Reduce the gravy on a hot fire, and add half wine glass of sherry to it. Then put the partridges and cabbage into a dish; have them served up very hot with the cabbage and sauce – and let yourself and Mr Justice Coltman eat them. I hope they will be good!

'N.B. Should the partridges be old they must be stewed some time *alone* before you add the scalded cabbage, otherwise the vegetables get overcooked and give too strong a flavour to the birds.'

[I always cut the extra cabbage in quarters, and I can assure Mary Parke they *are* good. T.FG.]

PARTRIDGE CASSEROLE

6 oz. (175 g.) diced bacon
2 partridges
4 oz. (125 g.) button onions
2 oz. (50 g.) mushrooms, chopped
1 oz. (25 g.) flour
2½ fl. oz. (75 ml.) Madeira wine
¼ pint (150 ml.) stock
salt and freshly ground black pepper
juice of ½ lemon
½ oz. (15 ml.) water

Line the bottom of a casserole with the diced bacon, place the partridges on top and all in with the onions and mushrooms. Pour on the Madeira and stock, sprinkle with the salt and pepper and cover tightly, sealing with a paste made from the flour and water. Cook in the oven at 400°F. (200°C.) or gas mark 6 for 40–45 minutes (depending on how young the birds are). Remove the lid of the casserole, and squeeze the lemon juice over the birds and serve immediately.

Serves 4–6.

This is also an excellent recipe for grouse or pheasant.

Pheasant

Though not, of course, indigenous, the pheasant (*Phasianus colchicus*) is the most decorative of the game birds and though the cock is the more attractive in appearance, the hen is best to eat, being more tender and plump.

The young hen can be recognized by its soft feet and light plumage, young cocks by their rounded spurs, which become more sharply pointed as the birds get older.

It is important to be able to assess the age of the birds, since the young ones make very much better eating, particularly if they are to be roasted; and while the shooting season is from October to .February, the best period is from November to January. In very warm weather, young hens may need only four or five days hanging, while the older birds, especially the cocks, may require up to 10–12 days when the weather is very cold and some gourmets prefer them even a little longer. A rough guide as to whether the bird is ready to cook is if the main tail feather can be easily plucked out. All pheasants should be hung by the neck.

PHEASANT WITH CREAM SAUCE

4 oz. (125 g.) butter or
  margarine
1 well hung pheasant
salt and freshly ground
  black pepper
4 oz. (125 g.) smoked ham,
  diced

½ pint (¼ litre) veal or
  chicken stock
3 fl. oz. (90 ml.) white
  wine
¼ pint (150 ml.) cream

Melt the butter in a casserole and when it is foaming add the pheasant and brown it well, turning about so that this is done all over. Season with the salt and pepper, add the diced ham, then the veal stock to cover with the white wine, bring gently to the boil and allow to simmer for around 2 hours with the casserole lid on. Just before serving, remove the lid, take off the heat until it stops simmering, stir in the cream and serve immediately in the casserole in which it was cooked.

Serves 3–4.

STUFFED ROAST PHEASANT

For the stuffing
½ lb. (225 g.) pork sausage-meat
1 apple, cored, peeled and chopped
1 tablespoon chopped parsley
1 egg, lightly beaten
salt and freshly ground black pepper
1 well hung pheasant
2 thin but large slices of bacon to wrap the bird in

3 oz. (75 g.) butter or margarine
2½ fl. oz. (75 ml.) sherry
1 tablespoon redcurrant jelly
juice of ½ lemon
pheasant liver
1 egg yolk, hard-boiled
1 slice of toast large enough to support the bird

Mix together all the stuffing ingredients and stuff the bird. Wrap the bacon about it, being careful to cover the breast, and smear 2 oz. (50 g.) of the butter liberally all over. Roast at 350°F. (180°C.) or gas mark 4 for about 1 hour. Meanwhile, melt the remaining butter in a pan and lightly fry the pheasant liver and pound it to a paste with the yolk of a hard-boiled egg (or process in a food processor). Spread this paste on to the toast and reserve on a hot dish in a warm oven. 15 minutes before the pheasant is roast, drain off any surplus fat from the roasting tin juices and pour the sherry over the bird and into the juices, then add the redcurrant jelly, lemon juice, salt and pepper and baste, several times at least, with this gravy. When it is *à point*, mount the pheasant on the pâté-covered toast and serve at once, with the gravy served separately in a sauce boat or *écrèmeuse*.

Serves 4.

PTARMIGAN

Three species of ptarmigan occur in Scotland; the common ptarmigan (*Lagopus mutus*), the rock ptarmigan (*L. rupestris*) and the willow ptarmigan (*L. lagopus*), like the red grouse, to which genus they belong, they have feathered legs, but they are slightly inferior in flavour to the red grouse. In winter, they change their feathers to white.

September and October are the months when they are at their best for the table and, allowing one bird for two people, all recipes for *Grouse*, pages 103–7 and *Partridge*, pages 111–12 can be used.

QUAIL

This small migratory game bird (*Coturnix coturnix*) from tropical Africa and India once nested in these islands, but is now imported alive from Egypt and fattened here before being put on the market. Quail should be eaten the day after they have been killed or as soon as possible after that. They should be plucked and singed, the head and neck removed and the drawing should be carried out from the head end. Lady Playfair gives a very good and simple recipe for the preparation of these excellent and delicately flavoured little birds which dates from 1887: 'A quail should have a small piece of capsicum (red or green pepper) put inside it, and then be boiled (in stock) for 8 minutes. No more cooking is required. Serve with a sauce of skinned and stoned white grapes, seasoned with their own juice and pepper and salt.'

BRAISED GAME BIRDS

Where a number of game birds, perhaps of different ages and hung for varying lengths of time, require to be used, there is always the problem that some will cook more quickly than others, so that some will be overcooked and falling to pieces when others are only just *à point*. The best way of dealing with this problem is as follows: make a bed of roughly cut root vegetables, such as carrots, turnips, parsnips together with some leeks and the broken carcases of any game birds or chicken, so that the whole is about 5 to 6 inches in depth at the bottom of a deep, cast-iron stew-pan with a well fitting lid. Pour over game stock or chicken stock or water in which several stock cubes have been dissolved, until the liquid comes within about a half an inch of the top of the bed, then add a bouquet garni.

Melt butter in a frying-pan and brown the birds on all sides, then set them on the top of the vegetable bed and, covering closely, simmer very gently for several hours until the birds are tender. Remove the birds and serve on a hot dish accompanied by a sauce appropriate to the game in question. See *Sauces*, pages 190–7.

GAME PÂTÉ OR CHICKEN, RABBIT etc.

See *Hare Pâté*, page 110.

RABBIT, KINGDOM OF FIFE PIE

This magnificent traditional recipe dates from the eighteenth century at least.

1 large or 2 small rabbits, jointed
1 lb. (450 g.) lean pickled pork, sliced and soaked in cold water
salt and freshly ground black pepper
nutmeg, grated
1 egg, hard-boiled
forcemeat balls
½ pint (¼ litre) rabbit stock
1 lb. (450 g.) rough puff or short crust pastry
1 tablespoon milk

For the forcemeat balls
1 rabbit liver, finely chopped
1 slice of fat bacon, finely chopped
4 oz. (125 g.) breadcrumbs
1 tablespoon finely chopped parsley
1 teaspoon chopped thyme
zest of half a lemon
nutmeg, grated
salt and freshly ground black pepper
1 egg, lightly beaten

Soak the rabbit joints in salted cold water for at least 1 hour, then drain them and simmer them in fresh water to cover for ½ hour. Cool and take the meat from the bones, returning the latter to the stock, and leave to simmer until it is reduced by half. Drain and chop the pork and combine it with the rabbit fillets. Make the forcemeat balls by combining all the ingredients in the order given and shape into balls about half an inch across. Slice the hard-boiled egg and, in a deep pie-dish, make a layer of the mixture of rabbit fillets, forcemeat balls and pickled pork, season each layer with salt, pepper and nutmeg and the chopped marjoram, spread some egg slices on the top and repeat the process until the pie-dish is full. Strain the rabbit stock, taste and season if needed, then pour the required amount over the contents of the pie-dish. Damp the edges of the dish and cover with the pastry, pressing the edges well down, make 3 small slits on the top for the steam to escape and brush the pastry with the milk to glaze it. Bake at 400°F. (200°C.) or gas mark 6 for 15 minutes, then lower the heat to 325°F. (170°C.) or gas mark 3 for a further 1½ hours, covering the top with grease-proof paper if the pastry is getting too brown. Serve either hot or cold; if the latter, allow to grow cold slowly and then chill in the refrigerator, when the contents will jelly.

Serves 8–10.

CIVET DE LAPIN

Recipe adapted from Lady Clark, *c.* 1880.

1 young rabbit, skinned, jointed and soaked in water for 1 hour

salt and freshly ground black pepper

¼ lb. (125 g.) bacon, diced

3 oz. (75 g.) butter or 4 tablespoons oil

For the sauce

3 tablespoons oil

3 medium onions, sliced

3 medium carrots, sliced finely

1 small celery heart, sliced

bouquet garni of herbs

1 lb. (450 g.) peeled tomatoes or 1 × 16 oz. (450 g.) can

Wipe the rabbit joints dry and season with the salt and pepper. Heat the butter or oil in a frying-pan and quickly brown the joints all over and then put them into a fireproof dish with the diced bacon. Add the 3 tablespoons of oil to the pan juices and just soften the sliced onion, carrots and celery in it, then add the bouquet garni and the peeled tomatoes, coarsely chopped. Simmer gently for ½ hour until the contents of the pan are reduced and thickened slightly. Then season to taste. Liquidize (or put through a food mill) this sauce and pour it over the rabbit and bacon, cover closely and cook in a moderate oven at 350°F. (180°C.) or gas mark 4 for about 1½ hours, checking for tenderness after an hour.

NOTE: if no liquidizer or food mill is available, sauté the vegetables, add them to the casserole, then simmer the tomatoes until they are a purée and add them also before cooking as above.

Serves 4.

This recipe is also excellent for chicken or turkey joints.

SEE ALSO: *Hare Pâté*, page 110, *Potted Grouse*, page 106 and *Quenelles*, page 81.

SNIPE

This is the name given to a considerable number of small game birds of which the most widely distributed is the Common Snipe (*Capella gallinago*). Though small it makes excellent eating, as also do the jack-snipe, red-breasted snipe and the great snipe, though the latter can attain a weight of up to 10 oz. (275 g.). All snipe, of whatever species, should be skinned and *not* plucked.

The easiest way to do this is as follows: cut off the head and wings and gently ease the skin at the neck apart and draw it away from the breast. If care is exercised the whole of the skin and feathers will come away like a jacket, but gentleness is required as the skin tears easily. No form of snipe is drawn before cooking; the entrails or *trail* are left inside or else partly protruding and resting on a piece of paper (by those who prefer them a little more done) and they are considered an essential delicacy. The crop of the bird should, however, be removed before cooking. If snipe are to be roasted they should first be liberally rubbed with butter after being skinned and then cooked for 15 minutes in a hot oven at 425°F. (220°C.) or gas mark 7. They are also good grilled as woodcock, and particularly delicious well buttered and grilled over a peat fire. The slight tang of the peat smoke lends an especial piquancy to their flavour. Recipes for *Woodcock*, page 126, can be used for snipe.

TEAL

See *Wild Duck*, page 125.

Venison

Venison is the name nowadays applied to the flesh of any kind of deer, especially red deer, fallow deer and roebuck. Scotland is indeed fortunate in still having supplies of good venison, which form one of the crowning glories of her gastronomy. The meat of the buck (male) has more flavour than that of the doe (female), though it may require to be hung a little longer. The animal should be cleaned and hung, unskinned, for 3 days in summer or 5 in winter, and then be skinned, dismembered and hung for a further 3 days in summer or in winter, in very cold weather for as long as 3 weeks.

Venison is at its best when from an animal between 18 months and 2 years old, for if over 3 years in age it may be somewhat dry, though this may to some extent be tempered by the use of a good marinade. Indeed all venison benefits from being kept in a marinade for 2 or 3 days. It should then be taken out, patted dry and roasted with good dripping, butter or oil in a moderate to hot oven, 375°F. (190°C.) or gas mark 5–400°F. (200°C.) or gas mark 6, for 25–30 minutes to the pound. Some of the marinade can be used for the gravy.

VENISON MARINADE

For a 4–5 lb. (2–2½ kg.) joint.

1 pint (½ litre) red wine	1 medium onion, thickly
½ pint (¼ litre) red wine	sliced
vinegar	1 clove of garlic

¼ pint (150 ml.) olive oil
1 pint (½ litre) water
2 carrots, thickly sliced
bouquet garni of herbs

salt and whole black
    peppercorns
4 juniper berries

Mix all the ingredients and soak the joint in the marinade for at least 2 days in summer and 3 in winter, turning the joint at least 3 times a day.

ROAST VENISON À LA MORRISON

1 large haunch of venison,
    well hung but not 'high',
    approx. 4 lb. (2 kg.)
2 bottles of dry white
    wine
2 peeled shallots, thinly
    sliced

4 small branches of
    lavender leaves
    (rosemary can be
    substituted)
1 bay leaf
4 oz. (125 g.) beef
    dripping or butter

Choose a deep dish and put all the ingredients into it, crushing the bay leaf, and allow to marinate for at least 48 hours, turning the joint at least 3 times a day. Take a deep roasting dish, smear the venison liberally all over with the beef dripping, put it into the roasting dish, pour ½ pint (¼ litre) of the marinade over it and roast at 375°F. (190°C.) or gas mark 5 for 3–4 hours or 25 minutes to the pound, basting frequently with some of the remainder of the warmed marinade and also with the roasting pan juices. When cooked, place on a hot dish in a warm oven, pour away any surplus fat from the pan juices and transfer them to a saucepan, boil up and reduce to half the quantity and serve with the venison in a sauce boat or *écrèmeuse*. Redcurrant jelly is the usual accompaniment.

Serves 8–10.

MARTINMAS STEAKS

½ lb. (225 g.) boned
  shoulder meat of venison
¼ lb. (125 g.) belly of pork
1 tablespoon finely
  chopped onion
salt and freshly ground
  black pepper
1 tablespoon breadcrumbs
1 lightly beaten egg
2 tablespoons cooking oil
pinch of powdered mace

For the garnish
2 oz. (50 g.) butter
1 teaspoon finely chopped
  chives
1 teaspoon finely chopped
  parsley
redcurrant jelly
4 lemon wedges

Mince the meats very finely, then add the onion, salt, pepper, breadcrumbs and finally, when all the ingredients are evenly mixed, the egg. Shape into 4 cakes about 1½ inches thick and fry on both sides in the hot but not smoking oil. Meanwhile work the butter with the parsley and chives and divide into 4 portions. Serve the Martinmas steaks with a pat of the herb butter and a lemon wedge with each and redcurrant jelly in a sauce boat.

Serves 3–4.

VENISON CUTLETS WITH ORANGES AND REDCURRANT JELLY

4 neck of venison cutlets
1 fl. oz. (25 ml.) olive oil
salt and freshly ground
  black pepper

2 oranges
2 tablespoons redcurrant
  jelly, melted

First pound the cutlets well to tenderize them, then brush them with the olive oil and grill under a moderate grill for 10 minutes each side.

Meanwhile, cut the oranges in half (or slice thickly if large), take out all the pips and bake them at 400°F. (200°C.) or gas mark 6 for 15 minutes, then arrange them on a hot dish and put the grilled cutlets on top. Brush the cutlets with the melted redcurrant jelly and serve with *Port Wine Sauce*, page 194.

Serves 4.

VENISON PIE

1 2-lb. (900 g.) shoulder venison
salt and freshly ground black pepper
pinch of powdered mace
pinch of powdered allspice
2 tablespoons flour
¼ pint (150 ml.) red wine
¼ pint red wine vinegar

½ pint (¼ litre) approx. stock made from venison bones
2 medium onions, sliced
1 tablespoon redcurrant jelly
½ tablespoon chopped parsley
10 oz. (275 g.) puff pastry, see page 218

Tenderize the meat by beating it, then remove any fat, gristle or bone. Put the salt, pepper, mace, allspice and flour into a polythene bag and shake them together until thoroughly mixed, then dust the meat all over with this mixture and put it into a saucepan with the wine, the vinegar and the stock, putting in sufficient to cover the meat.

Simmer gently for an hour, put in the onions and parsley, cover and simmer very gently for a further ½ hour or so until the meat is tender, then take off the heat, allow it to get quite cold and remove any fat from the top. Put the meat into a pie dish with the redcurrant jelly and pour stock over until it is within ½ an inch of the top. Cover with a good puff pastry (see page 218) moistening the edges and pressing them well down so that they adhere to the pie dish. Make 3 slits in the top to allow the steam to escape, and bake at 450°F. (230°C.) or gas

mark 8 for 25–30 minutes, keeping a close watch towards the
end to see that the pastry does not become too brown.

Serves 4.

VENISON SAUSAGES

This is a delicious way of serving the cheaper cuts of venison.

2 lb. (900 g.) venison
shoulder or neck,
minced
½ lb. (225 g.) veal, minced
½ lb. (225 g.) pork, minced
3 oz. (75 g.) flour or
breadcrumbs
½ teaspoon powdered
nutmeg
½ teaspoon powdered
allspice
¼ teaspoon powdered
marjoram

1 bay leaf, crushed
pinch of thyme
salt
½ teaspoon black pepper,
freshly ground
1 large onion, finely
chopped
2 cloves garlic, crushed
4 tablespoons cooking oil
redcurrant jelly

In a deep bowl, mix together the minced venison, veal and pork,
together with the flour, herbs, spices, salt and pepper. When all
the ingredients are evenly mixed put through a mincer or food
processor and add the onion and garlic. With floured hands,
form into sausage shapes, roll lightly in flour and fry in the hot
but not smoking oil for about 10 minutes for each side, until
they are golden brown. Serve very hot with redcurrant jelly.

Serves 10–12.

DEER LIVER, IN HAGGIS

See *Haggis*, page 140, *Game Pâté*, page 116 and
Game Soup, page 13.

WILD DUCK

Also for *Widgeon* or *Teal*.

2 wild duck
4 slices streaky bacon
4 tablespoons cooking oil
salt and freshly ground
 black pepper
juice of 1 lemon
¼ teaspoon cayenne
 pepper

8 tablespoons port wine
½ teaspoon mushroom
 ketchup
1 tablespoon brandy,
 warmed

Wild duck require to be hung for a week before cooking unless
cooked within hours of shooting. Cover the breasts with the
bacon slices, put them into a roasting tin and pour the oil over
them. Roast at 400°F. (200°C.) or gas mark 6 for about 40
minutes, basting once after about the first 20 minutes. When the
birds are done, remove the bacon slices, roll them and arrange
them as garnish on a hot serving dish. Score the breasts of the
birds lengthwise two or three times and transfer them to the
serving dish, keeping hot in a warm oven. Pour away all surplus
fat from the roasting tin juices, transfer them to a saucepan,
boil up and add the port wine and the mushroom ketchup.
Sprinkle the salt, black pepper, cayenne pepper and the lemon
juice over the breasts of the birds. Put the sauce into a hot
sauce boat and serve with the birds. At the moment of service,
pour the warmed brandy over the breasts of the birds and ignite.

Serves 4.

Widgeon or teal can also be treated in this way, but, being much
smaller birds, the number will have to be doubled and the
cooking time reduced to approximately 30 minutes.

WOODCOCK, IN A CHAFING DISH

Like snipe, the woodcock should be cooked undrawn, the 'trail' being a particular delicacy.

4 woodcock	2 tablespoons port wine
4 oz. (125 g.) butter	½ teaspoon freshly ground
¼ pint brandy, warmed	black pepper
juice of 1 lemon	

Roast the woodcock, in the butter, at 425°F. (220°C.) or gas mark 7 for around 15 minutes. Take them out and joint them, splitting the bodies lengthwise and removing the legs, reserve them in a hot dish over a lamp after having removed the trail. Transfer the juices in the roasting tin to a frying-pan and keep warm. Chop the intestines finely, squeeze out and remove any blood and mix them well with the juices in the frying-pan, seasoning to taste. Pour the warmed brandy into the pan and ignite. Let the contents of the pan reduce on a hot flame while stirring, add the lemon juice, port and black pepper. Let it boil up again and reduce a little more, then pour over the hot joints of woodcock and serve at once.

Serves 4–6.

WOODCOCK, SPLIT AND GRILLED OVER A PEAT FIRE

See *Snipe*, page 119 and *Salmi*, page 106.

MEAT

Despite the well-known hardiness of the Scots, they were not in the past a great meat-eating race, always preferring fish, game and oatmeal dishes. The famous names in beef, such as Aberdeen Angus, Galloway and Shorthorns, are all Scottish breeds but most of the finer cuts found their way to Smithfield market and the cheaper cuts were used in soups, braises and minced dishes. There were of course the roasts in richer homes, but generally speaking traditional recipes for meat are sparse compared to those for fish or game.

The mountain lamb and mutton is delicious, equal to the French *pré-salé*, and this is eaten in many ways, again with the cheaper cuts being used in the good Scotch Broth and other soups.

For a reason which I cannot quite understand pork was almost taboo until the nineteenth century, owing to a superstition that it was inhabited by the devil – a view to which James VI of Scotland vehemently subscribed. Even as late as 1835 Mrs McEwen in *Elements of Cookery* wrote: 'In Scotland we do not manage pork well. In England they kill it at the proper age and size ... Servants in Scotland will seldom touch it ...' However all these meats were used in pickled form and beef and mutton hams were made as well as ham. In Aberdeen, no doubt again due to Norse influence, pork was pickled in the mid-eighteenth century, and of course it is used in the old *Kingdom of Fife Pie* (page 117). Ayrshire bacon is very delicious, the pigs formerly being fed on potatoes and milk. The whole side is rolled, and sliced across both fat and lean in Ayrshire bacon.

Bull calves were often killed off so veal dishes were popular and fairly plentiful; this could also be part of the heritage left by the Auld Alliance. Generally speaking traditional meat dishes in Scotland show the ingenuity and economy of the Scottish *cuisine*. All over the world today, many of these traditions are being passed over in favour of foreign food, but in the remoter parts of Scotland many still exist for the pleasure of both native and tourist alike.

SCOTCH BRAISED BEEF

Recipe from Lady Forbes, *c.* 1910.

2 lb. (900 g.) stewing beef
   in one piece, preferably
   rib or shoulder
2 medium onions, sliced
3 medium carrots, sliced
1 clove garlic
1 tablespoon parsley,
   coarsely chopped
½ teaspoon mixed spice
1 pint (600 ml.) beef
   stock, approx.

salt and pepper
2–3 tablespoons sherry or
   or red wine
1 lb. (450 g.) each:
   carrots and small
   turnips and ½ lb. (225 g.)
   mushrooms to garnish
1 oz. (25 g.) butter

Trim the beef of any fat, gristle or bone and leave whole. Put into a casserole with the sliced onions, carrots, chopped garlic, parsley, mixed spice, salt and pepper, then just cover with the stock. Bring to the boil, then cover and cook in a low oven 325°F. (170°C.) or gas mark 3 for about 2 hours, checking towards the end of that time that it is not drying up. Test also for tenderness before taking from the oven.

In a separate saucepan cook the extra carrots and turnips, adding the mushrooms 10–15 minutes before they are ready. Strain, toss in butter and keep hot. Meanwhile, when the beef is ready, put it on to a warmed serving dish and sieve (or liquidize) the vegetables, add the sherry or red wine to them and

pour over the beef, garnishing with the freshly cooked vegetables.

Serves 4.

COLLARED BEEF

Recipe of Dr Hervey, Aberdeen, 1867.

2 lb. (900 g.) beef flank,
  trimmed
salt
2 tablespoons parsley
2 sage leaves or a pinch
  ground sage

pinch of marjoram and
  allspice
1 chopped garlic clove
pepper

Rub about 1 tablespoon salt over the trimmed beef on both
sides, then leave overnight. The next day, wipe it dry and cover
one side with the chopped herbs and spices. Then roll the meat
up as tightly as possible and secure with small skewers or
kitchen string like a parcel. Wrap it in a cloth or foil (2 thick-
nesses) and put it into boiling water, bring the water back to the
boil, then simmer gently for about 3 hours. Take out when the
water has cooled, and still in the cloth or foil, put into a dish
and weight the top of it overnight if possible. When quite cold
take off the wrappings, and serve cold in slices.

It can be glazed with a little browning or meat extract if liked.

Serves about 4.

VARIATION: mix the herbs and spices into 1 lb. (450 g.)
sausage-meat (either beef or pork) and hard-boil 1 egg. Put
the egg inside the sausage-meat and spread this on to the flank,
then roll up and secure as above. This makes a very pretty dish
for a cold buffet or for a picnic.

BEEF COLLOPS, MINCED

The word 'collop' comes from the French *escalope* and means any small piece of meat. It can refer to both beef and veal, and sometimes to hare and venison. Minced collops and mash is as common to the Scotsman (especially the Glaswegian) as sausages and mash are to the English. It is also a popular breakfast dish.

1 lb. (450 g.) minced lean steak
1 tablespoon butter or oil
2 small finely chopped onions
salt and pepper
1 tablespoon oatmeal, optional
½ pint (300 ml.) beef stock
1 tablespoon Worcestershire sauce or mushroom ketchup
toast or mashed potatoes

Break up the mince so that there are no lumps. Heat the butter or oil and soften the onions in it but do not colour. Push aside, then add the steak, in batches if the pan is small, and fry it quickly until it is brown all over. Mix well with the onions, season to taste and stir in the oatmeal, mix well, then finally add the stock. Cover and simmer gently for about half an hour, add the sauce to taste, mix well and taste for seasonings.

Serve either with triangles of dry toast or mashed potatoes. It can also be served with sliced hard-boiled or poached eggs.

Serves 2–4.

NOTE: if game is used it is often seasoned with a pinch of ground allspice and half port wine and half stock is used.

SCOTCH COLLOPS

See page 156.

BEEF OLIVES

Recipe from Lady Forbes, *c.* 1910.

These little rolls are very like the French *paupiettes*, and combine economy with imagination, which is so often found in Scottish cooking.

12 thin slices of raw, lean beef (topside is good) 6 × 4″ (15 × 10 cm)	2 egg yolks
4 oz. (125 g.) breadcrumbs	salt and pepper
1 medium onion, grated	2 tablespoons oil
grated rind of 1 lemon	a little flour
1 tablespoon mixed chopped parsley and marjoram	1 pint (600 ml.) beef stock

Trim the beef slices of any fat or gristle, then beat them until they are flatter and thinner. Mix the breadcrumbs with the onion, lemon rind, herbs, egg yolks and seasoning and mix well. Put a small spoonful on each piece of meat, roll up and skewer with kitchen string or a cocktail stick. Rub all over in seasoned flour and brown them in the heated oil. Put side by side in an oven-proof dish, add the stock, bring to the boil, then cover and cook in a moderate oven, 350°F. (180°C.) or gas mark 4, for about 1½ hours. Serve with freshly cooked root or green vegetables.

Serves 4–6.

VARIATION: thin gammon rashers, pork or veal can also be used for 'olives', and a teaspoon of tomato purée can be added to the stock if liked, also a tablespoon of red wine or sherry.

PICKLED BEEF

Recipe from Lady Clark, *c.* 1880s.

This is what we would call nowadays a marinated steak. Beef was however pickled in brine, see page 160.

1 steak, either rump or
  sirloin about 2¼ lb.
  (1 kg.) in one piece
1 medium onion, sliced
6 whole peppercorns
salt
1 bay leaf, sprig or thyme,
  marjoram and rosemary

3 tablespoons oil (olive is
  best)
3 tablespoons red wine
  vinegar
2 oz. (50 g.) butter
2 tablespoons stock or
  consommé

Trim the steak so that no fat or gristle remains, then score it lightly across in diamond fashion with the tip of a sharp knife. Put it into a dish with the onion, peppercorns, salt, bay leaf and other herbs, then add the oil and vinegar. Cover and leave overnight, turning occasionally.

Take it out, pat dry, then heat up the oil and quickly fry it in a hot pan so that it is brown on both sides and cooked as you like it. Take out of the pan and keep hot, then add the stock and a little of the marinade (about 3–4 tablespoons) according to taste, boil up to reduce a little, taste for seasoning and serve over the beef. Slice thickly.

Serves 4.

VARIATION: this can also be cooked longer if well-cooked meat is liked. After browning the steak add the stock and the marinade, bring to the boil, cover and simmer gently for half an hour.

FORFAR BRIDIES

These pasties are traditional to Scotland and are mentioned by Sir James Barrie in *Sentimental Tommie*. He was born at Kirriemuir (Thrums), a village in Forfarshire. Although originally made with suet this is not everyone's taste today and butter or margarine can be used instead.

1½ lb. (700 g.) rump steak, well hung
2 oz. (50 g.) suet, butter or margarine
3 small onions, finely chopped
salt and pepper
1½ lb. (700 g.) short crust pastry, see page 218

See that the meat is well-hung or else it will be tough to eat. Cut into thin strips and beat them well, then cut again until they are no longer than 1 inch. Season with salt and pepper and reserve.

Make the pastry and leave to rest for half an hour, then roll into 4 equal portions and see that it is quite thin but unbroken. Divide the meat between the pastry, putting it on one half only. Add a little onion and some suet, butter or margarine. Dampen the edges, then fold over, pressing the edges well, and notch with a fork or the fingers. Make a small slit in the top of each, then bake in a hot oven, 450°F. (230°C.) or gas mark 8, for 15 minutes, then lower to 350°F. (180°C.) or gas mark 4 for about 45 minutes or until the meat is tender when tested. If they are getting too brown during cooking cover loosely with a piece of greaseproof paper.

Serve 1 per person.

NOTE: if a cheaper Bridie is required, then use a cheaper cut of meat and cook it first until it is tender as for a pie. Drain off the liquid and use with freshly sliced onion. Or use lean minced beef seasoned well, and with a little chopped onion. Leftover or raw venison can also be used.

POTTED HOUGH

This is a traditional Scottish dish, very simple but pure in flavour and excellent for sandwiches, for supper with toast, or for picnics. Hough is the Scottish name for shin of beef.

2¼ lb. (1 kg.) shin beef (hough)
piece of shin bone, cracked

salt, pepper and a pinch of cayenne pepper
pinch ground allspice

Put the meat in one piece with the bone and seasonings into a large saucepan, then just cover it with cold water. Bring to boiling point, skim and at once turn to a low simmer, almost a shudder, and let it cook like this for about 6 hours or over-night. (The electric crockery pot slow cookers are ideal for this, and the time can be up to 12–14 hours at LOW. Pour boiling water over to begin with and cook on HIGH for half an hour.) Then strain all the liquid off, let it get cold and take off any fat. Mince the meat finely and put back in the defatted stock, taste for seasoning, then cook again for not longer than 15 minutes.

Wet some small moulds or dishes and divide the mixture between them, then chill until cold and set. Unmould to serve. It will keep well if the top is covered by melted butter.

MUSSELBURGH PIE

This is traditional to the great oyster and mussel-eating district of the past, but alas oysters have risen steeply in price since this recipe was first made. However it is a delicious dish for special occasions.

2 lb. (900 g.) rump or sirloin steak, cut very thinly

1 dozen oysters, fresh or canned
6 thin streaky bacon rashers

salt, pepper and cayenne
pepper
2–3 shallots or button
onions, sliced
2 oz. (50 g.) flour

½ pint (300 ml.) beef stock
½ lb. (225 g.) rough puff
or shortcrust pastry,
pages 218

First make the pastry and let it rest in a cold place. Then trim
the steak and cut into strips, then beat them well to flatten and
tenderize. Beard the oysters, then cut in half and roll each one
in a small piece of thin bacon, then in the meat and press down
well to prevent them opening. Chop the shallots finely and
scatter in a deep pie-dish, then roll the meat in seasoned flour
and pack tightly (seam side downwards) around the pastry
funnel until the dish is full. Pour the stock over, then dampen
the edges and put the pastry lid over the top, pressing down the
edges well. Brush with a little milk or beaten egg and bake at
450°F. (230°C.) or gas mark 8 for 15 minutes, then at 350°F.
(180°C.) or gas mark 4 for a further 1¼ hours. Cover the top with
greaseproof paper if it is getting too brown.

Serves 4.

OX KIDNEY CASSEROLE

2 lb. (900 g.) ox kidney
flour
salt and pepper
1 large sliced onion
pinch ground cloves
1 tablespoon mixed:
chopped parsley and
marjoram

1 pint (600 ml.) beef
stock, approx.
salt and pepper
crisply fried onions for
garnish

Slice the kidney and take out the fatty core, also take off any
skin, then cut into convenient serving pieces. Season the flour,
then roll the kidney in it. Put into a casserole with the finely
sliced onions, herbs and seasonings.

Barely cover with the stock, bring to the boil, then cover and cook in a moderate oven, 350°F. (180°C.) or gas mark 4, for ½ hour, then lower to 300°F. (150°C.) or gas mark 2 for a further 1¼ hours. Check that it does not dry up, if so add a little more stock, and stir while so doing.

While it is cooking, fry some more onions until they are crisp but not too brown and serve these over the top as a garnish.

Serves 4–6.

VARIATION: pig's kidneys or veal kidneys can also be used.

SEE ALSO: *Pickles for Meats*, pages 159–61 and *Meg Dods's Brown Soup*, page 6.

Lamb and Mutton

BRAISED BREAST OF LAMB OR MUTTON WITH SAUCE PIQUANTE

2 lean breasts mutton or
    lamb, about 2 lb.
    (900 g.) each
3 medium carrots, sliced
3 medium onions
1 bay leaf
sprig of thyme
salt and pepper
2 oz. (50 g.) melted butter
2 oz. (50 g.) breadcrumbs

For the sauce
3 shallots or 1 medium
    onion
2 tablespoons white wine
    vinegar or vinegar from
    the capers
¾ pint (450 ml.) lamb
    stock or consommé
salt and pepper
2 tablespoons capers
1 tablespoon chopped
    parsley

Trim the meat of any excess fat, roll it and tie up with kitchen string. Put into a saucepan with the sliced vegetables, bay leaf, thyme and seasonings. Cover with water, bring to the boil and take off any scum, then cover and simmer gently for about 1–1½ hours.

Remove from the stock, untie, and if cooked sufficiently the bones will pull out. If they don't, put back for further cooking. Put the bones back into the stock, boil up and let it reduce at a steadily rolling boil. Put the boned meat on a flat dish and cover either with foil or another dish, weight it and leave to get cold. When it is cold, trim off any fat or gristle and cut into oblong pieces from where the bones have been. Season well, dip into the melted butter and then into the breadcrumbs.

Meanwhile make the sauce by chopping the shallots finely and cooking them with the vinegar until it reduces by half. Then add the defatted stock or consommé and season to taste, boil up and simmer for about 15 minutes, then add the capers and finally the parsley and heat up again and keep hot.

Grill the egg and breadcrumbed slices of mutton on both sides until crisp or brown and serve with the Sauce Piquante separately.

VARIATION: sliced mushrooms can be used instead of capers; sliced cocktail gherkins also give a pleasantly sharp flavour, or even a tablespoon of sultanas.

BOILED GIGOT OF LAMB OR MUTTON WITH CAPER SAUCE

As in France, 'gigot' is the word for a leg of lamb or mutton in Scotland.

1 leg lamb or mutton about 4 lb. (1·8 kg.)
2½ pints (1·4 litres) half milk and half water
4–6 medium onions, sliced

4 medium carrots, sliced
1 small sprig rosemary
1 bay leaf
6 whole black peppercorns
salt

For the sauce
2 tablespoons butter
2 tablespoons flour
1–1½ pints (600–900 ml.)
   lamb stock

3 tablespoons capers
salt and pepper
2 tablespoons cream,
   optional

Remove any surplus fat from the meat, put into a large, deep saucepan and add the milk and water. It should come about three-quarters of the way up; if not, add a little more. Add the sliced vegetables, herbs and peppercorns, then season to taste. Cover and bring gently to the boil, removing any scum, then simmer for at least 30 minutes to the pound or until the meat is tender. Skim the fat from the top and take out 1½ pints (900 ml.) for the sauce. Keep the meat hot but do not let it boil furiously.

To make the sauce melt the butter, stir in the flour and let it cook for about 1 minute, then add the warm milky stock, stirring all the time to prevent lumps, season to taste and keep it hot at a simmer. Add the capers, let them heat up and finally the cream, if using, but do not reboil. Carve the lamb in fairly thick slices and arrange on a hot ashet (Scottish word for a dish) and mask with some of the sauce, keeping the rest for serving separately.

It should be served with small to medium boiled potatoes garnished with chopped parsley, carrots and turnips, boiled, drained and served with a little butter, sugar and chopped mint.

Serves at least 8.

VARIATION: serve with a creamy onion sauce instead of the caper, see *Club Cutlets* below, or page 196 in the chapter on sauces.

CLUB CUTLETS

Recipe from Dr MacGregor, Edinburgh, *c.* 1912.

1 lb. (450 g.) onions, sliced

2 oz. (50 g.) butter

1 rounded teaspoon sugar

1 rounded tablespoon flour

½ pint (300 ml.) onion stock

¼ pint (150 ml.) warm milk

2 tablespoons cream

salt and black pepper

4 thick chump lamb cutlets or chops

1 oz. (25 g.) butter

4 tablespoons breadcrumbs

Slice the onions and cover with water, then bring to the boil and cook for about 10 minutes. Strain, but reserve the liquor. Heat the butter in a saucepan and sauté the onions in it, adding the sugar and a little salt. They should be cooked until they are quite soft and puréed. Stir in the flour, cook for about 1 minute, then add the warm onion stock, mix well, then add the milk and finally the cream. Heat but do not reboil.

Trim and sprinkle the cutlets with black pepper and grill them well on *one side only*, then put them cooked side down in a baking tin. Cover the tops with the sauce, then sprinkle the breadcrumbs over and add a small nut of butter to each chop. Cook in a hot oven, 425°F. (220°C.) or gas mark 7, for between 15–20 minutes depending on how well cooked you like your meat.

Serves 4.

NOTE: if preferred the cutlets can be cooked in the usual way, or roasted in one piece for 20 minutes to the pound at 400°F. (200°C.) or gas mark 6, and the onion sauce served with them. However the crisp topping to creamy sauce is very good. Pork chops can also be served this way.

HAGGIS

Recipe from Lady Login, 1856.

Haggis is perhaps the best known and most traditional of all Scottish foods. It is eaten at Hogmanay (New Year's Eve) and is often served at banquets and dinners especially on St Andrew's Day (30 November) and Robert Burns anniversary (25 January) dinners. Burns described it as the 'great chieftain of the puddin' race', and it is in fact a large sausage-like pudding cooked in a sheep's paunch originally, but often nowadays made in a cloth or basin. It has been known since Roman times, the earliest reference to the dish (but not the name) being in *De Arte Coquinaria* of Caelius Apicius who lived in the reigns of the Emperors Augustus and Tiberius. The name haggis is thought to derive from the French *hachis* – to chop.

At these banquets it is served to bagpipe music played by a kilted Highlander and it is traditional to drink a glass of neat whisky with it, and also to serve it with *Clapshot*, page 170.

1 cleaned sheep or lamb's paunch	1 lamb's lights boiled and minced
2 lb. (900 g.) dry oatmeal	1 large finely chopped onion
1 lb. (450 g.) chopped mutton suet	$\frac{1}{2}$ teaspoon each: cayenne pepper, ground allspice, salt and pepper
1 lb. (450 g.) lamb's liver, boiled and minced	
1 lamb's heart, boiled and minced	1 pint (600 ml.) stock

See that the paunch is well cleaned, then soak it in salt and water for about 2 hours, take out and let it dry. Put the oatmeal on a baking tray in a low oven and let it dry out and crisp up a little. Then cook the liver, heart (trimmed) and lights in salted water to cover and cook for about $\frac{1}{2}$ hour. Strain, but reserve the stock, and chop the meats up finely, or mince. Mix all ingredients (except the paunch) together and season well. Then add the stock. Put into the cleaned paunch (fill to about half) and sew up loosely, but securely.

Have ready a large pot of boiling water mixed with the rest of the liver stock, prick the haggis all over with a small knitting needle to prevent bursting, then cook in the water and stock, at a slow simmer uncovered, but keep up water level, for about 3 hours.

Serves about 16.

VARIATION: the finest haggis is said to be made with the liver and heart of a deer. Meg Dods's recipe adds about 6 onions. For Haggis Royal a small leg of mutton is used; the meat removed from the bones and minced, instead of the heart, liver etc. and it is flavoured with 3 anchovies, grated lemon rind, parsley, 4 egg yolks and half a pint (300 ml.) of red wine. This can be cooked in a small calves' paunch or in a basin.

It can be covered with suet dough as for a beefsteak pudding and cooked the same way if desired. The variety cooked in a basin with or without the suet crust is known as Pot Haggis. Half quantities can of course be made.

HARICOT OF LAMB OR MUTTON

This is also a well-known French dish, *haricot de mouton*. It is named after the small, white, dried haricot bean.

½ lb. (225 g.) haricot beans
soaked overnight
1 lb. (450 g.) lean lamb
1 medium onion, sliced
1 medium sliced carrot
and 1 small sliced
turnip
2 tablespoons dripping or
oil

1 tablespoon flour
1 pint (600 ml.) stock,
bean stock will do
salt and pepper
1 tablespoon chopped
parsley

Soak the beans in cold water to cover overnight, then drain, put into a saucepan, cover with water and cook for about 2 hours (or pressure cook for ½ hour). Trim the meat and cut into cubes and prepare the vegetables. Heat up the oil and lightly fry all these ingredients, sprinkle the flour over, cook for 1 minute until golden brown, then add the stock, mix well and season to taste.

Add to the beans, seeing that it is not too liquid, bring to the boil, cover, then simmer or cook in a slow oven at 325°F. (170°C.) or gas mark 3 for about 1 hour. Garnish thickly with parsley before serving.

Serves 4.

VARIATION: cold, cooked lamb can also be used: shin of beef (called hough in Scotland) can be used instead of the lamb, but you may need to increase cooking time slightly, so check for tenderness after 1 hour.

HOT POT

This delicious hot pot of lamb and lamb's kidneys comes from the manuscript book of Lady Forbes, *c.* 1900.

6 lamb chops, lean	pepper and salt
6 lamb's kidneys	approx. 1 pint (600 ml.)
1 lb. (450 g.) potatoes, sliced	consommé or rich lamb stock, defatted
1 medium onion, sliced	

Trim the chops so that no fat or bone remains, then put a layer on the bottom of a deep casserole and season well. Add a layer of skinned, defatted, sliced kidneys, a little finely sliced onion and a layer of peeled, raw sliced potatoes, seasoning each layer as it is put in. Continue this until the ingredients are used up, ending with a layer of potatoes.

Heat up the consommé or stock and pour over gently. It should barely cover the ingredients. Put the lid on and cook in a moderate oven, 350°F. (180°C.) or gas mark 4, for about 1½–2 hours, removing the lid for the last half an hour to let the top brown slightly. It should be quite free of fat, relying for its excellence on the purity of taste.

Serves 6.

ROAST LAMB WITH PORT AND ANCHOVY SAUCE

A Scottish recipe from the 1850s with an unusual tang.

1 shoulder or leg lamb, about 4 lb. (1·8 kg.)
2 medium garlic cloves, sliced
black pepper
3 tablespoons oil
½ teaspoon chopped rosemary
4 anchovy fillets, drained

½ pint (300 ml.) brown stock or consommé
¼ pint (150 ml.) port wine
1 teaspoon butter rolled in the same of flour
1 teaspoon mushroom ketchup or soy sauce
salt and pepper

Score the meat over the top in diamond fashion, then sliver the garlic and insert the slivers both under the skin and in the flesh, then dust well with black pepper. Heat up the oil and brown the meat all over quickly, then put into a baking tin and trickle what oil remains over the top, then sprinkle the rosemary over.

Roast at 400°F. (200°C.) or gas mark 6 for 20 minutes to the pound plus 20 minutes over, if liked pink in the middle, or 25–30 minutes for well-cooked meat. Meanwhile mash up the anchovies and add the stock or consommé, port and seasoning. Bring to the boil, stirring well, and cook for about 10 minutes. After the meat has been cooking for 40 minutes, baste with the hot anchovy and wine mixture. Do this again before cooking time is completed.

When cooked put the joint on to a warmed serving dish and keep warm. Boil up the pan juices after removing any excess fat, and add small pieces of the butter rolled in flour stirring all the time until the sauce thickens slightly. Add the mushroom

ketchup or soy, taste for seasoning, and either serve over the
joint or separately.

Serves about 8.

MUTTON HAMS

See page 161.

MUTTON PIES

These pies are traditional to all parts of Scotland, and have been
praised by many eminent people, including Dr Johnson, who
was not known for his kindly remarks. They are usually made
with hot-water pastry crust but shortcrust can also be used.

For the pastry
¼ lb. (125 g.) lard,
   dripping or margarine
½ pint (300 ml.) hot water
1 lb. (450 g.) plain flour
salt
a little milk to glaze

For the filling
1 lb. (450 g.) lean lamb,
   free from fat, bone or
   gristle, minced

salt and pepper
1 small minced onion
pinch ground mace or
   nutmeg
4 tablespoons stock or
   gravy
dash of Worcestershire
   sauce

Prepare the meat and the onion, then add the spice, season it
well and reserve. To make the hot-water pastry all ingredients
and the room should be warm.

Put the fat and water into a saucepan and bring to the boil.
Sift the flour and salt into a basin, make a well in the centre and
pour the hot liquid into this and mix quickly with a spatula

until cool enough to handle, then form into a ball. This must be done quickly before the fat hardens. Put on to a floured surface, and pat flat. Divide it in four and keep the rest warm, then roll out to a circle, putting a small jar about 3 inches across in the middle. Mould the pastry around the jar and when it stands well remove the jar and do three others the same way. Roll out remaining pastry and cut out the lids.

These circles can be put into small Yorkshire pudding tins if desired or the pastry can be shaped into one large pie in a spring-sided tin. Fill up the pastry cases and add a little gravy or stock to each pie, then dampen the edges and put the lids on, making a small slit in the centre and brushing the top and sides with a little milk. Bake on a baking sheet in a low oven, 250°F. (130°C.) or gas mark $\frac{1}{2}$, for about 45 minutes.

NOTE: if using shortcrust pastry use $\frac{1}{2}$ lb. (225 g.) fat to 1 pound (450 g.) flour and see that the oven is at least 400°F. (200°C.) or gas mark 4 for 15 minutes when the pies are put in. Pork can also be used.

LAMB'S KIDNEYS, DEVILLED

Recipe from Mrs Goodwin, Aberdeen, *c.* 1872.

Lamb chops or cutlets can also be served in this way.

12 lamb's kidneys or 4 lamb chops	pinch of cayenne
3 tablespoons oil	6 oz. (175 g.) butter
1 tablespoon Worcestershire sauce	2 teaspoons each: dry mustard powder and French mustard
1 tablespoon mushroom ketchup	salt

Trim and skin the kidneys (or cutlets) and slice in half, heat up the oil and cook them quickly on both sides, but do not over-cook as they should be a little pink in the middle. Mix together all the other ingredients in a basin, then pour off any fat left in the pan and spread the devil mixture over the kidneys or chops. There is no need to melt it as the heat from the meat will do so.

Serves 4.

VARIATION: add 1 tablespoon chutney to the devil mix, home-made is best, but if using a mango chutney then see that the mango slices are well chopped up.

SEE ALSO: *Barley Broth*, page 3, *Hairst Bree*, page 14 and *Pickles for Meats*, pages 159–62.

Pork and Pork Products

Owing to the curious pork taboo mentioned on page 127, there are virtually no traditional recipes for pork, although bacon is mentioned and used in many recipes. Ayrshire bacon has a sweet and pleasant flavour and is very highly thought of. See *Kingdom of Fife Pie*, page 117.

AYRSHIRE GALANTINE

6 oz. (175 g.) fresh
  breadcrumbs
¼ teaspoon ground nutmeg
¼ teaspoon fresh ground
  black pepper
½ teaspoon salt
1 lb. (450 g.) minced lean
  beef
1 lb. (450 g.) minced
  Ayrshire bacon

2 beaten eggs
¼ pint (150 ml.) beef
  stock
2 hard-boiled eggs
parsley for garnish
2 pints (1·2 litres) stock or
  half stock and water
2 medium carrots
1 halved onion

Mix the breadcrumbs with the nutmeg, salt and pepper. Then trim the beef and bacon of all skin, bone, fat or gristle and mince it up. Mix with the breadcrumbs very thoroughly, add the beaten eggs and enough stock to moisten it a little.

With floured hands and on a floured surface shape into flat oblong. Shell the eggs, cut them in half and arrange on the meat mixture, then shape into a roll. Formerly this was then put into a buttered and floured cloth, but today it can be either securely wrapped in buttered foil or put into a greased loaf tin. If in the cloth or foil, secure well, bring the stock to boiling point with the vegetables, and add the galantine. Let it come back to the boil, then simmer gently for about 2 hours. Take out, leave it in the cloth or foil, put on to a large dish and weight it overnight.

If using a loaf tin, it should be covered with foil, then baked in a moderate oven, 350°F. (180°C.) or gas mark 4, in a pan of hot water to come half way up the sides of the tin, for the same time. Let it cool, then weight it as above. Serve cold, cut into slices with a parsley garnish.

Serves about 8–10.

VARIATION: for economy reasons, sausage-meat can be used instead of the bacon. It will not have quite the fine flavour but will make an agreeable meat loaf.

Oatmeal and breadcrumbs can be used, half and half, but if using oatmeal add about 2–3 tablespoons more stock. Some chopped fresh herbs such as parsley, chives and marjoram can also be added, about 2 teaspoons.

STUFFED CABBAGE

Recipe from Lady Forbes, *c.* 1910.

1 medium to large firm white cabbage
1 lb. (450 g.) minced pork, not too fat
salt and pepper
1 oz. (25 g.) butter
1 oz. (25 g.) flour

1 pint (600 ml.) stock
3–4 tablespoons sherry, optional
2 medium onions, sliced
4 medium carrots, sliced
pinch caraway seeds, optional

Remove the tough outer leaves of the cabbage, but see that the heart does not fall to pieces. Pour boiling water over the heart in between the leaves to blanch them, and to let you separate them easily.

Get a pan very hot and quickly fry the minced pork, so that it browns, and season it. Put the pork between each leaf and when it is all used up tie round the cabbage with kitchen string.

Heat up the butter until foaming, then add the flour and cook for a minute, then add the stock, bringing to the boil and stirring until it is thick and smooth. Add the sherry, the caraway seeds if using, and season to taste. Prepare the vegetables and slice them finely and add to the stock, then pour this around the cabbage in a saucepan, bring to the boil, cover and simmer for about $1\frac{1}{2}$–2 hours. Check that it is not drying up, if so add a little more stock.

To serve, take off the string, and serve the cabbage in its sauce with the vegetables.

Serves about 4.

VARIATION: sausage-meat can be used instead of pork, or a mixture of pork and bacon. Minced beef or leftover minced meats can be used as well.

Another method is to remove the leaves separately and to fill each one with the meat, then to wrap each one up like a parcel, putting them seam side down in a casserole. The stock and root vegetables are added as above. If liked 2 teaspoons of tomato purée can be added to the stock.

CLUB CUTLETS

See page 139, and use pork chops instead of lamb.

PORK PIE

For the pastry
10 oz. (275 g.) flour
1 level teaspoon salt
5 oz. (150 g.) butter or margarine
4 tablespoons water, approx.
a little milk to glaze

For the filling
1 lb. (450 g.) lean pork, chopped

4 oz. (125 g.) bacon, Ayrshire if possible, chopped
pinch dried sage or thyme
2 hard-boiled eggs, sliced
½ pint (300 ml.) approx. chicken or pork stock
salt and pepper

First make the pastry by mixing the salt with the flour and then sifting it. Add the fat in small pieces and rub it in until it resembles coarse breadcrumbs. Add the water gradually until you have a firm but pliable dough. Then roll into a ball, and chill while preparing the meat.

Trim the pork well, so that no fat, gristle, bone etc. remains, then chop into half-inch pieces. De-rind the bacon and chop finely, and slice the eggs fairly thickly. Line a deep pie-dish with layers of the pork, bacon and egg, seasoning well and adding the herbs to each layer. Pour over the stock to come to about two-thirds of the way up the dish. Then moisten the edges with water, roll out the pastry and cover the dish pressing the edges down firmly and notching with the fingers or a fork. Roll out any leftover pastry and cut out some leaves for decoration, and dampen them so they stick to the pastry. Then brush over with a little warmed milk, and bake at 400°F. (200°C.) or gas mark 6 for 15 minutes, then lower to 350°F. (180°C.) or gas mark 4 for a further 1½ hours. If it is getting too brown, then cover loosely with a piece of buttered greaseproof paper or foil. Serve hot, or cold when it will be softly jellied.

Serves about 4–6.

VARIATION: if liked the pork and bacon can be simmered for

about 45 minutes in water to barely cover, then strained and the stock used for the pie. In this case the pie will only take about 30–35 minutes to cook.

Veal and ham in equal quantities can be used instead of pork and bacon, or cooked game can be used for a very good game pie.

HAM WITH CHESTNUT SAUCE

Recipe from Lady Forbes, *c.* 1910.

1 joint ham about 4–5 lb. (1·8–2·3 kg.)
½ lemon
5 oz. (150 g.) brown sugar mixed with 1 tablespoon made mustard, French or English
1 lb. (450 g.) chestnuts or equivalent can of unsweetened chestnuts

2 oz. (50 g.) butter, melted
¼ pint (150 ml.) consommé or stock
salt and pepper

Soak the ham overnight, then take out and scrape the skin before putting into cold water to cover with the half a lemon. Bring to the boil, then simmer very gently for 25 minutes to the pound and 25 minutes over. When cool, take from the stock, peel off the skin and trim the fat evenly to your taste. Make a diamond pattern over the top with a sharp knife. Then mix up the sugar with the mustard and spread this over evenly. Put into an oven-proof dish adding about 1 pint (600 ml.) of the ham stock around it, and bake in a hot oven, 425°F. (220°C.) or gas mark 7, for about 35 minutes or until the top is set and slightly crisp. Do not worry if a little of the sugar rolls off into the stock, for it will give it a pleasantly sweet flavour.

Meanwhile, cook the chestnuts, by first making a slit down one side, then covering them with water and boiling for about half an hour or until they are soft when pricked with a fork.

Leave in the warm water and lift each one out separately and remove both shell and skin. The warm water makes this much easier to do. Mash them up, or put into a liquidizer with the consommé, adding a little more if it seems too thick. Season to taste and finally mix in the melted butter. Stir well and serve hot with the hot ham. If using canned chestnuts, drain before using, but the juice can be poured around the ham when baking. This sauce is also very good with venison or turkey.

Serves about 8–10.

VARIATION: the bone can be removed from the ham and about 4 oz. (125 g.) of coarsely chopped chestnuts mixed with 1 oz. (25 g.) butter can be inserted in place of the bone, keeping the remainder for making into the sauce given above, but cutting down slightly on the other ingredients.

HAM TERRINE OR BRAWN

Recipe from Lady Clark, *c.* 1880s.

3 lb. (1·4 kg.) ham
½ calf's foot or 2 pig's
    trotters
2 medium carrots, sliced
1 large onion, sliced
sprig of thyme, parsley,
    tarragon and bay leaf
½ pint (300 ml.) dry white
    wine

water
1 large garlic clove, sliced
1 teaspoon tarragon
    vinegar
2 tablespoons chopped
    parsley
¼ pint (150 ml.) red wine
salt and pepper

Soak the ham overnight, then take out and scrape the skin, before putting it into a saucepan with the calf's foot or pig's trotters, the herbs and vegetables with the white wine and enough water to cover. Bring to the boil and remove any scum, then season and simmer for 25 minutes per pound and 25 minutes over. When cool, take out and put on to a large dish. Take out the bones, skin and any gristle, and remove excess fat. Then chop the ham coarsely adding a little of the calf's foot or pig's trotter cut very small, and put into a deep dish or basin.

Reduce the stock to about two-thirds, then strain it. Put into a clean saucepan with the chopped garlic, parsley, vinegar and wine, and bring to the boil and simmer for about 10 minutes. Taste for seasoning, then when cool pour over the chopped ham so that it is covered all over. Chill until set in a cold place, removing any fat from the top, and serve cut into thick slices before serving.

Enough for about 6–8.

VARIATION: use a mixture of half veal and half ham. Sliced hard-boiled eggs can be added to the mixture if liked just before adding the final stock. This can also be made with a pig's head or calf's head, and its tongue, but be quite certain to remove the fatty parts as well as the bones before putting in the dish. The tongue should be skinned, then cut in half lengthways and set in the centre of the dish. Using a pig's head is, of course, a much more economical dish.

Another alternative is to use rabbit and either boiling bacon such as collar, or pickled belly of pork.

BLACK PUDDINGS

Also called Blood Puddings.

These blood puddings are traditional to all Celtic countries, and are one of the earliest prepared foods known to man. Pig's, lamb's and goose blood can also be used.

> 'It fell about the Martinmas time
> And a gay time it was then, O;
> That our gudewife had puddins to mak'
> And she boiled them in the pan, O.'
> from 'The Barrin' of the Door'.

2 pints (1·1 litre) blood	2 oz. (50 g.) oatmeal
1 tablespoon salt	pinch grated nutmeg
½ pint (300 ml.) milk	½ teaspoon mixed herbs
3 medium onions, chopped	½ teaspoon cayenne pepper
12 oz. (350 g.) shredded suet	

Let the blood run into a deep pan, then when cold add the salt. The butcher will often do this for you. Add all the other ingredients, seasoning very well, and either put into prepared skins or into a large ovenproof dish, or basin. This can then be either baked, the tin standing in another tin half filled with water, covered and baked at 300°F. (150°C.) or gas mark 2 for about 1½ hours, or covered and steamed for the same length of time. It is left to get cold, then sliced and fried up with eggs, bacon, or sausages.

VARIATION: cooked rice or breadcrumbs can be used in place of oatmeal if liked.

PIG'S LIVER CASSEROLE

This liver makes a delicious casserole, but do not cook longer than the stated time for full flavour.

1 lb. (450 g.) pig's liver	½ pint (300 ml.) stock, approx.
a little flour, seasoned	
6 rashers streaky bacon	1 tablespoon chopped parsley
1 large onion, sliced	
pinch of dried sage	salt and pepper

Trim the liver of any pipe or gristle, then take the rind from the bacon. Roll the liver in the seasoned flour, and prepare the onion. Put a layer of liver in a fireproof casserole, then a little sage, bacon and onion, seasoning as you go. When the ingredients are used up, pour the stock over the top, bring to boiling point, then cover and bake in a moderate oven, 350°F.

(180°C.) or gas mark 4, for not longer than 1¼ hours. Just before serving sprinkle the parsley over the top.

Serves 4.

VARIATION: leave the liver in one piece and wrap it up in the bacon rashers, then flour it and rub the sage over. Add the onion and stock, but increase cooking time to 2 hours.

SEE ALSO: *Pickles for Meats*, pages 159–62.

Veal

Veal was eaten a lot in Scotland formerly, no doubt partly due to the French influence and also to the vast cattle breeding when bull calves would be culled. Certainly some of the recipes are early ones which I have adapted for modern use. Unfortunately the price of veal has risen very steeply so nowadays it is a luxury.

VEAL FLORY

This dish, a Florentine pie, is mentioned by Sir Walter Scott in *The Bride of Lammermoor*, and 'flory' possibly comes from Florence. The Medici family came from Florence and both Catherine and Mary de Medici influenced French food greatly; through Mary, Queen of Scots, this would have been brought to Scotland early on.

4 veal chops or cutlets, about 1½ lb. (700 g.)	pinch of ground mace
4 lean bacon rashers or ham	3 hard-boiled egg
salt and pepper	½ lb. (225 g.) mushrooms, sliced
1 teaspoon chopped tarragon	2–3 boiled sweetbreads, if available OR 6–8 forcemeat balls*

| 1 pint (600 ml.) approx. stock | 10 oz. (275 g.) puff or shortcrust pastry, page 218 |

* Forcemeat balls
These are made from 4 oz. (125 g.) breadcrumbs, mixed with 1 teaspoon mixed herbs, 2 oz. (50 g.) suet or butter and bound with 1 small egg, then shaped into walnut-sized balls. Or use a stuffing mix of your choice, but not a strong tasting one. Trim and bone the chops, then put the bones on to cook covered with water to make stock. Season the meat with salt, pepper, tarragon and mace. Shell the eggs, cut in half and take the yolks, whole, from them but coarsely chop the whites. Take any rind from the bacon and cut into strips, then roll up. Slice the mushrooms, and also the sweetbreads if using, otherwise make up the force-meat balls.

Take a deep pie-dish and layer all the ingredients, seasoning well, tucking in the egg yolks and the forcemeat balls into corners and between the meats. Cover to within 1 inch (2·5 cm) of the top of the dish with the veal stock, dampen the edges of the dish, roll out the pastry to the required size and press over. Make a slit on the top.

Bake at 400°F. (200°C.) or gas mark 6 for 15 minutes, then reduce to 350°F. (180°C.) or gas mark 4 for a further 45 minutes testing through the slit at the top that the meat is tender.

Serves 4–6.

This pie can be served hot or cold but if the latter then make certain you use veal stock or consommé that will jelly when cold. If neither are available then use 2 teaspoons gelatine with your stock.

VARIATION: this can also be made with sliced veal kidney, in which case use consommé for the stock.

FRICANDEAU

Recipe from Lady Forbes, *c.* 1900.

Fricandeau was a popular dish in the nineteenth and early twentieth centuries and it was made with what was called a 'cushion' of veal which is boneless and comes from just by the fillet.

2 lb. (900 g.) veal fillet	3 cloves
4 rashers bacon	¾ pint (450 ml.) white
4 carrots, sliced	stock, warmed
4 small onions, sliced	1 tablespoon potato flour
2 teaspoons each chopped	or arrowroot
thyme and parsley	salt and pepper

Wrap the trimmed meat in the bacon rashers, then put the vegetables, herbs, cloves all seasoned in the bottom of a fireproof dish. Put the veal on top of this and then pour the stock around, adding a little more if the vegetables are not quite covered. Do not put a lid on, but bake in a moderate oven, 350°F. (180°C.) or gas mark 6, for about 1½ hours or until the meat is tender. Baste from time to time until it browns. Put the veal on to a warmed serving dish and keep hot. Then mix the potato flour or arrowroot with a little water and paint this over the fricandeau and let it glaze in a low oven for 15 minutes. Serve with some of the stock and vegetables.

Serves 4–6.

SCOTCH COLLOPS

This is a traditional Scottish dish and the word collop comes from the French *escalope*. Recipe is adapted from *Cookery and Pastry as Taught and Practised by Mrs Maciver, Teacher of those Arts in Edinburgh,* 1783–97.

4 slices of veal escalope	3 tablespoons chicken or
a little seasoned flour	veal stock
3 oz. (75 g.) butter	1 egg yolk
½ lemon peel finely grated	2 tablespoons cream
pinch of ground mace	salt and pepper
3 tablespoons white wine	

Trim and beat the escalopes, then roll them in seasoned flour.
Heat the butter and when it is foaming brown them well on
both sides. Add the lemon rind and the mace, then pour over
the wine and stock and simmer gently for about 20 minutes or
until the meat is tender. Taste for seasoning, put the veal on to a
warmed dish, then beat the egg yolk with the cream, stir into
the pan juices, reheat, stirring well, but do not reboil. Pour over
the veal and serve.

Serves 4.

VARIATION: about 6 oz. (175 g.) sliced mushrooms can also be
added if liked.

BRAISED VEAL TONGUE

This recipe comes from Lady Caledon, *c.* 1900.

Ox tongue can also be used, and sheep or pig's tongues, but the
latter will only need cooking for about 1½ hours.

1 large calf's tongue or	3 cloves and 8 white
medium ox tongue	peppercorns
1 onion, sliced	a sprig of parsley
1 carrot, sliced	

Soak the tongue overnight, then put on to boil with the vegetables and cover with fresh, cold water. Add the herbs and
seasonings when it has come to the boil and any scum is
removed. Simmer gently for about 3 hours or until it is tender.
(It can be done in a slow-cooker crockery pot overnight or

pressure cooked in 1 hour.) When it is cooked put it straight away in cold water and take off the skin and any horny or gristly parts. It is very good served hot cut into thick slices, in which case put it back in the stock, heat it up, then serve with *Sauce Piquante*, page 136.

Serves about 4–6.

TO SERVE COLD: roll it and put into a basin, then cover with made-up aspic. The directions are to be found on the packet. When cold, press lightly and serve sliced.

BALMORAL TRIPE

Veal tripe is thought to be the most delicate, but other tripe can be used for this dish if that is not available. This is a delectable recipe showing the French influence on Scottish cooking.

$1\frac{1}{2}$ lb. (700 g.) veal tripe
6 thin slices lean bacon or
  ham
2 bay leaves
salt and black pepper
3 medium onions, sliced
2 tablespoons chopped
  parsley

1 pint (600 ml.) chicken
  or veal stock
4 oz. (125 g.) mushrooms,
  sliced
2 tablespoons cream

Wash the tripe and cut it into rectangles about 3 inches (8 cm.) long and cut the bacon or ham the same shape but slightly smaller. Put a slice of the ham on top of the tripe, season with pepper, then roll up and secure with a stick or skewer. Put the bay leaves at the bottom of a saucepan or casserole, then lay the rolls on top, seam side downwards, pushing them against one another so that they are packed tightly. Sprinkle with salt, then add the chopped onions and half the parsley. Cover with the stock, bring to the boil and simmer (or put into a moderate oven, 350°F. (180°C.) or gas mark 4) for $1\frac{1}{2}$–2 hours checking at the first time as to tenderness.

Meanwhile wipe the mushrooms and slice them thinly, then blanch them in hot salted water to cover. Strain and add them to the tripe, mixing as well as possible without disturbing the rolls. Cook for about 10 minutes, then taste for seasoning. Finally mix in the cream, reheat but do not reboil and serve garnished with the rest of the parsley.

Serves 4.

GLASGOW TRIPE

This is adapted from an old recipe of Meg Dods's, *c.* 1826.

1½ lb. (700 g.) tripe	salt and pepper
knuckle bone of veal or a	water
marrow bone	

Wash the tripe well and cut into thin strips and season it, then roll up each piece and put side by side in an earthenware jar with the knuckle bone and cover with water. Cover and put the jar in a saucepan of water, then simmer gently for 8–10 hours replenishing with water when necessary. This pure and beautiful tripe can be kept in its own jelly and is excellent for soups, or it can be fried in batter and served with lemon wedges, or heated up in a fresh *Onion Sauce, Mushroom Sauce,* or *Parsley Sauce,* page 196.

Serves about 4.

Pickles for Meats

The pickling of meats is very traditional in Scotland, and their mutton hams have been famous for centuries. In the eighteenth century the Scottish border was the centre for these 'hams' and many were exported from Glasgow to the West Indies and America.

PICKLE FOR BEEF

The pickle should cover the meat entirely and a lid should be kept on. Beef requires at least a week in pickle if it is about 8 lb. (3·6 kg.) in weight. Leave in pickle for an extra day for each pound. The beef should be well washed before cooking, and put into cold, not hot water, with the root vegetables of your choice. This pickled beef is known as 'corned' beef in Ireland and parts of England. This is a traditional recipe.

For an 8 lb. (3·6 kg.) beef you will need the following:

3 bay leaves
½ lb. (225 g.) brown sugar
1 teaspoon cloves
1 teaspoon allspice
1 teaspoon black
   peppercorns

2 heaped teaspoons
   saltpetre
2 lb. (900 g.) coarse salt

Trim the meat and tie into shape loosely. Then mix all the ingredients excepting 1 lb. (450 g.) of salt and rub it well all over the joint, stuffing as much as possible into the bone and seams of meat. Stand in a large earthenware or glass container, cover and leave for at least a week, turning it every day and taking the pickle from the bottom of the dish. After three days add the extra pound (450 g.) of salt rubbing it well all over the meat.

For use, drain from the pickle and hang it up to dry slightly. If you want to smoke it, then hang it over a barrel in which peat is burning slowly, and see that the smoke reaches all parts, for 3 or 4 days.

PICKLE FOR HAM OR PORK JOINTS

1 ham, about 8–10 lb. (3·6–4·5 kg.)	2 cloves garlic
3 lb. (1·4 kg.) coarse salt	1 few sprigs of thyme and marjoram
2 oz. (50 g.) saltpetre	1 bay leaf
1 lb. (450 g.) brown sugar	½ lb. (225 g.) black treacle
1 oz. (25 g.) each: bruised cloves and mace	1 pint (600 ml.) dark ale
1 teaspoon allspice	

Mix all ingredients except the treacle and ale together and rub thoroughly all over the meat, turning every day. After three days add ½ lb. (225 g.) black treacle and 1 pint (600 ml.) dark brown ale. Leave for at least 14 days, then take out and hang up to dry.

It is not necessary to smoke them, but if desired then follow instructions for beef above.

MUTTON HAMS

These were often served for breakfast in the Highlands of Scotland, after boiling like a pork ham. It is served cold, cut into thin slices.

'The Scottish border is famous for the excellence of its mutton-hams. They are carefully pickled with salt, a little coarse sugar, and very little saltpetre, kept in the pickle for three weeks, and hung for months in the shepherd's chimneys, where peat and wood are the only fuel. Without previous steeping, they are boiled quickly for an hour, or a little more, if large, and allowed to soak in the pot-liquor for twenty-four hours.' Meg Dods, c. 1826.

1 leg or shoulder mutton, about 4–5 lb. (1·8–2·3 kg.)	1 oz. (25 g.) saltpetre
1 lb. (450 g.) coarse salt	4 oz. (125 g.) moist brown sugar

1 oz. (25 g.) allspice	1 tablespoon crushed
1 oz. black peppercorns	coriander seeds
1 teaspoon crushed juniper	
berries	

Mix all ingredients together very well, then rub all over the joint. Put into an earthenware or glass container, cover and leave for 12–14 days, turning and rubbing it every day. Drain and smoke as above if desired.

NOTE: I strongly advise steeping the joint for at least 1 hour and preferably 3–4 before cooking, despite Meg Dods's advice.

Geese can be pickled the same way and Caithness was the centre for this. Ducks are very good pickled but both geese and ducks should not lie in the pickle for longer than 2 days for a duck and 4 days for a goose.

VEGETABLES
AND OTHER
ACCOMPANIMENTS

Vegetables

The harsh climate of large parts of Scotland was not favourable to the growing of the more delicate vegetables in former years and the main staples of diet, apart from oatmeal and barley, were the root vegetables and kail, that hardy colewort which can withstand frost and indeed is said to taste better for it. It is claimed that if you want to taste vegetables at their best in Scotland then you should eat one of the fine soups such as Hairst Bree or Scots Broth where many kinds are cooked to perfection in a good broth.

Potatoes were introduced into Scotland in the eighteenth century and were first cultivated on a large scale in 1739 by Robert Graham of Tamrawer, who planted a half-acre field of potatoes which caused many people, including the Earl of Perth, to come from far afield to witness such a thing and also to enquire into the growing of them. It is interesting to note that many of our best varieties of potatoes carry the names of Scottish cultivators. Turnips were introduced from Holland at about the same time, Mr Cockburn of Ormiston being the first to grow turnips in drill in 1725. It was during the eighteenth century that Scottish gardens and gardeners were attracting attention in England and Europe: it became the thing to have a Scottish gardener and among others, Thomas Blaikie was gardener to the Duc de Chartres, later Duc d'Orléans. Bishop Pococke wrote in 1760: 'The most beautiful kitchen-garden, I

believe, in the world, was at Blair Castle' (home of the Duke of
Atholl).

However, at this time these vegetables were a prerogative of
the rich; the poor and those living on the islands made great use
of wild vegetables such as nettles (used like spinach), a kind of
wild lovage (*Ligusticum scoticum*) called *shemis* in Scotland, wild
garlic and particularly the wild carrot of which the following is
written:

> '*Is e mil fo'n talamh*
> *A th'anna a' churran gheamhraidh,*
> *E'adar Latha an Naoimh Aindreadh agus An Nollaig.*'

> 'Honey underground
> is the winter carrot,
> Between St Andrew's Day and Christmas.'

The 'kail-wives' of Edinburgh carried creels of varying kinds of
greenstuffs to the High Street for general use but there were
great improvements seen in the late eighteenth century to better
the quality and variety. Meg Dods (Mrs Isobel Christian Johnstone) wrote in 1826: '. . . much has been done of late years to
improve the quality, to hasten the season and to spread the
cultivation of vegetables. Whereas a turnip, or a cabbage, or a
leek was fifty years ago the only vegetable luxury found on a
country gentleman's table, we now see a regular succession of
. . . the more recondite asparagus, seakale, endive and artichoke . . . The vegetable markets of most towns have within the
same period undergone a wonderful improvement . . . so that a
healthful luxury is now within the reach of all classes.'

ARTICHOKES, JERUSALEM, SCALLOPED

Recipe from Lady Forbes (1867–1953).

1½ lb. (700 g.) Jerusalem
  artichokes
1 teaspoon vinegar
salt and freshly ground
  black pepper

½ pint (¼ litre) beef stock
3–4 tablespoons cream
2 oz. (50 g.) breadcrumbs
1 oz. (25 g.) butter (or
  margarine)

Wash and peel the artichokes, putting them into water with a little vinegar in it to stop them going brown. Parboil them in boiling salted water and when cold cut them into thin slices. Put them in an oven-proof dish with the beef stock, season to taste and add a little cream.

Sprinkle the breadcrumbs on the top, dot with the butter and bake at 350°F. (180°C.) or gas mark 4 until it is a pale brown on top.

Serves 4

VARIATION: use 1 pint (½ litre) of white sauce, see page 195, mixed with 2 teaspoons of anchovy essence instead of the stock and cream.

This recipe is also excellent for *salsify*. See also *Artichoke Soup*, page 2.

FRENCH BEANS

Recipe from Lady Clark, *c.* 1880.

1½ lb. (700 g.) French
  beans
salt and pepper
1 large onion, sliced
2 oz. (50 g.) butter
2 teaspoons each: chopped
  thyme and parsley

1 oz. (25 g.) flour
1 tablespoon tarragon
  vinegar
1 tablespoon white wine
¼ pint (150 ml.) Jersey
  milk or cream
1 oz. (25 g.) butter

String the beans and boil them in boiling salted water for 15 minutes, then drain them. Peel and slice the onion and sauté it in 2 oz. of butter with the chopped thyme and parsley, frying it until it is soft and golden brown. Shake over 1 oz. flour and let it cook for a minute, then add the tarragon vinegar and the white wine, the Jersey milk or cream and the ounce of butter cut in small pieces. Season to taste and stir all together until it becomes creamy, then add the cooked beans.

Serves 6.

BEETROOT WITH POTATO, AS AT CAIRNTON

Recipe from Mrs Burnett, *c.* 1880s.

3 young cooked beetroot, sliced
2 small onions, sliced
1½ oz. (40 g.) butter
1 oz. (25 g.) flour
½ pint (¼ litre) milk
2 tablespoons cream

salt and freshly ground black pepper
1 teaspoon castor sugar
1 tablespoon tarragon vinegar
1 lb. (450 g.) hot mashed potato

Fry the onions with ½ oz. butter, but do not let them brown. Melt the remaining butter in a saucepan, stir in the flour and add the milk and cream stirring all the time until the flour cooks. Season to taste and add the sugar and the tarragon vinegar. Cook the sauce for a few minutes more and then warm up the beetroot in it. Surround the inside of a deep serving dish with a thick layer of hot mashed potato, put the beetroot and sauce in the centre and serve very hot. It is excellent with any cold meat.

Serves 4.

BEETROOT SALAD

Recipe from Lord Elphinstone, 1880.

2 egg yolks
½ teaspoon made English
   mustard
¼ pint (150 ml.) olive oil
2 teaspoons chili vinegar
2 teaspoons tarragon
   vinegar

¼ pint (150 ml.) cream,
   stiffly whipped
salt and freshly ground
   white pepper
2 large beetroot, cooked
   and peeled

Put the egg yolks into a basin and beat with a whisk, or into a food processor set for making mayonnaise, add the mustard, salt and pepper, then, drop by drop at first, the olive oil. When the mayonnaise begins to make, cautiously add the two vinegars, and lastly the whipped cream. The sauce should be made half an hour before it is wanted and kept cold. Just before serving, slice the beetroot into a dish and pour the sauce over them.

Serves 4.

CABBAGE AND BACON

Recipe from Aboyne Castle, 1883.

2 Savoy cabbage, halved
boiling salted water to
   cover
12 thin but large slices of
   bacon

salt and freshly ground
   black pepper
10 cloves
10 whole allspice
1 pint (½ litre) ham stock

Cook the halved cabbages in the boiling salted water for ¼ hour, then remove and drain them. Line the bottom of a large flat pan with half the bacon and distribute the cabbage evenly on top. Season to taste and scatter the cloves and allspice over, then cover with the stock and put the remaining bacon on top. Cover the pan closely and simmer very gently for 1½ hours; at the end of this time the cabbage will have absorbed most of the stock. Remove the cloves and allspice corns and serve the cabbage with the bacon.

Serves 4.

CABBAGE, RED

See page 100; see also *Colcannon*, page 170,

CARROTS

'Honey underground': see page 164.

CARROTS WITH LEMON JUICE

This recipe is especially good when made with the very young carrot 'thinnings'.

1 lb. (450 g.) young carrots, scraped	1 oz. (25 g.) butter
1 level teaspoon salt	1 tablespoon finely chopped parsley to which
1 heaped teaspoon sugar	has been added the salt
juice of ½ lemon, about 1 tablespoon	and the sugar

Boil the young carrots whole in the salted boiling water until they are tender when tested with a fork. Drain them, return them to the saucepan and toss them in the butter, lemon and parsley. Serve at once.

Serves 4.

SCOTS CARROTS

1 lb. (450 g.) young carrots,
  boiled
1 lb. (450 g.) sausage-
  meat
½ lb. (225 g.) cooked
  mashed potato

salt and freshly ground
  black pepper
1 egg, lightly beaten
2 oz. (50 g.) breadcrumbs
cooking oil for deep
  frying

Drain the carrots and pat dry. Mix the sausage-meat and the
potato thoroughly together and season to taste, then wrap the
mixture around each carrot, retaining the carrot shape, drip in
the egg, coat with breadcrumbs and fry in the deep oil until
golden brown. Serve very hot.

Serves 4.

CAULIFLOWER, SCALLOPED

1 cauliflower, lightly
  boiled
1 oz. (25 g.) butter or
  margarine
1 oz. (25 g.) flour
½ pint (¼ litre) milk
2 tablespoons cream

salt and freshly ground
  black pepper
3 tablespoons grated
  cheese
4 tablespoons browned
  breadcrumbs

Divide the boiled cauliflower into sprigs. Make a white sauce
with the butter flour and milk (see page 195). Remove the sauce
from the heat and stir in the cream, season to taste and stir in
one tablespoon of the grated cheese. Put a layer of the cauliflower in an oven-proof dish, pour a little of the sauce over it and
scatter a little of the cheese on the top. Repeat this layer by layer
until the cauliflower is used up, remembering to retain enough
cheese to scatter liberally on the top of all, together with the

breadcrumbs. Bake at 400°F. (200°C.) or gas mark 6 for about
½ hour until the top is nicely browned.

Serves 2 as a main course, 4 as a vegetable accompaniment.

CLAPSHOT

1 lb. (450 g.) potato, boiled	salt and freshly ground black pepper
1 lb. (450 g.) turnips, boiled	2 oz. (50 g.) butter or margarine
2 tablespoons finely chopped chives	

Boil the potatoes and turnips separately and let them dry in a
colander over the stove. Then mash them together with the
butter or margarine ensuring an even mix, stir in the chopped
chives, season to taste, put into a hot dish and serve very hot.
This is traditionally served with *Haggis*, page 140.

Serves 4

COLCANNON

1 lb. (450 g.) potatoes, boiled and drained	1 oz. (25 g.) butter or margarine
1 lb. (450 g.) cabbage, boiled and drained	salt and freshly ground black pepper

Mash the potatoes thoroughly and chop the cabbage fairly
finely, then mix the two in a large saucepan in which the butter
has been melted, working over the heat so that all is kept piping
hot. Season to taste and serve in a piping hot dish. It can also
be put into a greased oven-proof dish and baked at 400°F.

(200°C.) or gas mark 6, until the top is browned. Variations: a variety of this dish popular in the Highlands also includes a couple of medium-sized boiled and mashed carrots and a couple of boiled and mashed turnips are added as well as the other ingredients. In the Border country, *Colcannon* is known as *Rumbledethumps*. In the North East, particularly Aberdeenshire, another variation is found known as *Kailkenny*, which consists of the first form of the recipe but using 4 tablespoons of cream in place of the butter.

Serves 4–6.

CUCUMBERS, SAUTÉED

Recipe from Lady Clark, *c.* 1880s.

Lady Clark writes that these cucumbers are very good served in the centre of the dish with grilled veal cutlets.

2 medium cucumbers	2 oz. (50 g.) butter
1 tablespoon white wine vinegar	1 tablespoon white sugar salt and white pepper

Peel and cut the cucumbers into fairly thick rounds, then put into a saucepan, barely cover with boiling water and add a little salt. Bring back to the boil and simmer gently for about 5 minutes, then strain thoroughly.

Heat up the butter until foaming, then add the sugar and vinegar and mix well. Add the cucumber and gently sauté them in this, turning the slices gently so that they do not break up. They should be tender, unbroken and covered with a glaze.

Serves 4–6.

DULSE

Dulse is an edible seaweed (*Rhodymenia palmata*), reddish-brown in colour and eaten in Scotland, particularly on the islands. Other seaweeds eaten there are Carrageen (*Chondrus crispus*) which is made into blancmange-like puddings, see page 203, and Redware or sea-tangle (*Porphyra lacinata*) which is similar to Sloke (*P. vulgaris*). Some of these can be found already prepared in health shops. All seaweeds are rich in minerals and form a basis for sauces (with roast lamb), soups, or served as a vegetable with mashed potatoes.

When the seaweed is gathered it must be very well washed in running cold water to remove the sand and grit. Soak it after that in cold water for at least 2 hours, then strain.

Put into a saucepan, cover with water and bring to the boil, then simmer for at least 3-4 hours or until it shows signs of getting tender. Strain and if possible liquidize, then beat with pepper and salt to taste, a large nut of butter and a squeeze of lemon and orange juice. It should resemble a soft jelly, and the taste resembles a mild-tasting anchovy.

This jelly can also be mixed with half of its quantity of medium oatmeal, shaped into small, flat cakes and fried up for breakfast.

ENDIVES MEUNIÈRE

Recipe from Lady Clark, *c.* 1880s.

1 lb. (450 g.) endives	juice of 1 lemon
2 oz. (50 g.) butter	water or chicken stock

Scoop a small hole in the bottom of the endives to prevent them tasting bitter, then heat the butter until foaming and put them into it, turning over frequently so that they get soft but do not colour. Add the lemon juice, water or stock to barely cover, salt and pepper. Cover with a little greaseproof paper pressed down to meet them, then a lid and simmer gently for about half an hour until they are soft when pricked.

VARIATION: add small pieces of pickled pork or ham when simmering the endives or cook as above, then drain and serve in a cheese sauce (page 196) made with half milk and half endive stock.

Serves 4

Kail

Kail is the most traditional of Scottish vegetables, for it withstands frost and snow and is said to be more delicate in taste after it. To 'come to kail' can also mean an invitation to a meal, and not one at which kail is served. Soup is made from it, see *Kail Brose*, page 15, and it is also served in several ways as a vegetable. *Kailkenny* is another name for *Colcannon*, page 170, in Aberdeenshire and the North East of Scotland.

TO COOK KAIL
Kail – also called Lang Kail – should be taken off the hard stalks and then the leaves stripped of any tough fibres before washing it thoroughly. Put into plenty of boiling salted water and cook quickly until tender, about 20–30 minutes. Formerly it was then sieved, but today it could be liquidized with far less trouble. It is then heated up with a knob of butter, salt and pepper to taste. It is good served with boiled beef, or boiled bacon, or fresh pork.

SIR JOHN CLARK'S RECIPE

Sir John – husband of Lady Clark – reheats it with a good tablespoon of double cream and 2 tablespoons of meat gravy or stock, all reduced by rapid boiling.

In some parts of Scotland it is served with a sprinkling of oatmeal and served with *Oatcakes*, page 187.

KAIL AND KNOCKIT CORN

This is the way they serve it on the Shetland Isles; from an old
Shetland song:

'Kail an' k-nock, kail an' k-nock,
Kail an' knockit coen,
Tak' dee fill wi' heart will
O' kail an' knockit corn'

Knocked corn is groats made from bere, a native type of barley,
which was dried, put into the knocking-stone with a little warm
water, then bruised with a mallet in order to break the husks.
These husks were removed by floating the meal in water, thus
leaving the grain whole. It was used in place of pearl barley. In
this recipe cooked groats were mixed with kail or cabbage that
has been cooked with a little smoked mutton (known as *reisted*)
or boiled pork or bacon, all well seasoned.

LEEKS

See *Cock-a-Leekie*, page 7.

Leeks are also lightly boiled then put into a shortcrust pastry
case (see page 218) with 2 beaten eggs mixed with $\frac{1}{2}$ pint
(300 ml.) milk and baked in a moderate oven, 350°F. (180°C.) or
gas mark 4, for about half an hour. Depending on their size
about 4–6 leeks would be needed for a 9-inch (23-cm.) dish.

STUFFED MARROW

This unusual and delicious method of stuffing marrow comes
from Lady Forbes, *c.* 1900, and can also be used for large onions.

1 medium to large marrow	1 large beaten egg
2 oz. (50 g.) butter or	salt and pepper
margarine	2 oz. (50 g.) grated hard
1 medium onion, sliced	cheese

Cut the marrow in two, lengthways, remove the seeds and also the flesh, but leave the skin on. Heat up the butter and quickly soften the onion in it. Then chop the marrow small and add it to the onion and butter and about 2–3 tablespoons of water. Simmer gently until it is all tender – but not mushy – and let it cool.

When cold, add the beaten egg, salt and pepper and half the cheese. Mix well and put it into the half shells sprinkling the tops with the remaining cheese. Bake high up in a hot oven, 400°F. (200°C.) or gas mark 6, for about 20 minutes or until the top is delicately browned.

The onions are peeled, and the centres scooped out without breaking the outer layers. It is not necessary to have another onion for this dish, but if liked a little chopped cooked meat or poultry can be added if making a light meal of them.

MUSHROOM KETCHUP

As will be noticed this is a popular flavouring in Scotland, taking the place of the widely used Worcestershire sauce in England. This recipe is from the Scottish Women's Rural Institutes, c. 1947.

'Gather nice fresh mushrooms (the morning preferred), go over them all and put in a large earthenware dish. Sprinkle with common salt. Go on adding more mushrooms for three or four days, always adding a sprinkling of salt, and stirring with a wooden spoon. After adding the last lot, let them remain overnight, then put the contents into a pan, bring to the boil and let it simmer for 30–35 minutes, then strain through muslin. Put this liquid on again and boil for the same time, but seasoning this time with black peppercorns, cayenne pepper, cloves and a blade or two of mace. Strain all and bottle when cold; this ketchup will keep for two years if well-made.'

POTTED MUSHROOMS

Recipe from Lady Clark, *c.* 1880s.

Take 2 lb. (900 g.) of button mushrooms and peel and clean them well. Heat up 2 oz. (50 g.) butter and sweat them in it, but do not let them get crisp, and add 3 oz. (75 g.) more butter when they have absorbed the first lot, salt, pepper and a pinch of ground mace to flavour. When they have nearly absorbed all the butter add a tablespoon of anchovy essence, mix well and simmer for 10 minutes.

If not wanted for immediate use put into pots and cover with melted butter. They will keep for some time in a cold place. If anchovy is not liked, then omit it. These mushrooms are most useful for adding to grills or roasts, sauces etc.

NEEP PURRY

'Neep' is the Scottish word for turnip, and purry means purée. This recipe of Meg Dods's boils the turnips in plenty of boiling salted water, then drains them and mashes them into a purée. They are put back in the saucepan with some butter, white pepper, salt and a good pinch of ginger, put into a dish and marked diamond fashion on top when being served.

'The Cleikum Club put a little powdered ginger to their mashed turnips, which were studiously chosen of the yellow, sweet, juicy sort, for which Scotland is celebrated . . . Mashed turnips may be eaten with boiled fowl or veal, or the more insipid meats are considerably improved by the Cleikum seasoning of ginger,

which besides, corrects the flatulent properties of this esculent.'
Meg Dods, c. 1826.

NETTLES

Nettles, when young, are eaten quite a lot in rural parts of Scotland where they are also known as 'Ivar's Daughter'. They are well washed and cooked like spinach with very little water, and they can be left as they are after draining, or puréed with a little butter and seasonings. They make a good soup with stock and this can be thickened with a handful of oatmeal. See also *Hairst Bree*, page 14.

PEAS, THE TILLYPRONIE WAY

Tillypronie was where Lady Clark lived.
The recipe dates from 1892.

'Take 1 quart (approx. 1 lb. (450 g.)) shelled new, fresh-shelled peas. Put them into a little boiling water with a pinch of salt, 2 lumps of sugar and a walnut of butter. Boil, *uncovered* until just tender, about 5–7 minutes. Then strain them and put on again with 2 oz. (50 g.) butter, a tablespoon stock, the same of castor sugar and simmer uncovered until they are pretty dry. Then dish and sprinkle with chopped mint.'

Serves 4.

VARIATION: if the peas are very young they can be cooked in butter without the water, and with the other ingredients for about 10 minutes.

PEA SOUFFLÉ

Recipe from Rei-na-charn, Aberdeenshire, 1890.

This is a very good way of using up older peas which have become large and tough. Served with grilled gammon it makes a very good light meal.

2 oz. (50 g.) butter or margarine	3 eggs, separated
1½ oz. (40 g.) flour	2 oz. (50 g.) grated Parmesan or hard cheese
½ pint (300 ml.) milk	
salt, pepper and cayenne pepper	½ lb. (225 g.) sieved, cooked peas

First lightly grease a 1½–2 pint (850 ml.–1·1 litres) soufflé dish, then heat up the rest of the butter until it is foaming but not coloured. Stir in the flour and cook for 1 minute, then add the milk, stirring all the time until the mixture thickens and is smooth. Season to taste, then beat the egg yolks and when the paste cools, add them gradually mixing them well through the mixture. Add the cheese and the peas which have been liquidized or put through a vegetable mill. Then whip the egg whites until stiff and fold them into the soufflé, seeing that they get right down to the bottom of the mixture. Pour into the dish and bake in the centre of a preheated oven at 350°F. (180°C.) or gas mark 4 for approximately 30 minutes if you like the centre liquid, or 40 minutes if preferred set.

Serves 2–4.

VARIATION: this basic soufflé recipe can be used for many vegetable or cheese soufflés, but if you are using a heavy, damp-ish vegetable such as spinach, then it is advisable to increase the egg whites to 3 instead of 2. Shellfish or leftover fish such as Finnan Haddie make a very good soufflé but would need the extra egg white.

Potatoes

Potatoes are eaten a lot in Scotland and served in imaginative ways. They are also mixed with other vegetables, see *Colcannon*, page 170. This recipe of Lady Harriet St Clair is delicious, eaten either on its own or served with steak, chops or bacon.

SCOTS POTATO FRITTERS

6 large kidney potatoes
2 eggs
salt

1 heaped tablespoon breadcrumbs mixed with the same of minced lean ham or bacon
oil for frying

Peel the potatoes, half-cook them in boiling salted water, drain, and cut them into thickish slices. Beat up the eggs well and add the breadcrumbs and ham, then dip the potato slices in this on both sides. Heat the oil and quickly fry the egg and bread-crumbed potato slices in it until they are golden brown all over. Drain on absorbent paper and serve hot.

Serves 4–6.

POTATO SCONES

½ lb. (225 g.) boiled mashed potatoes
2¼ oz. (65 g.) flour

3 tablespoons melted butter or bacon dripping
½ teaspoon salt

Mash the potatoes well, add the melted fat and salt, then as much flour as the potatoes will absorb without becoming too dry. This depends on the type of potato used. Turn out on to a floured surface and roll until they are ¼ inch (0·5 cm.) thick, then cut into circles, then into quarters. Prick all over with a fork and cook either on a hot griddle or in a heavy pan, which has been lightly greased. Turn over to cook the other side. Makes approximately 3 large scones or 12 quarters or farls.

VARIATION: to the above mixture add 4 oz. (125 g.) grated cheese and 2 well-beaten eggs. Shape into small round cakes, dip in breadcrumbs or flour and fry on both sides until golden. Makes about 12 cakes. These are called Cheese Potato Cakes and make a good supper or picnic dish.

STOVIES

Or stoved potatoes, from the French *étouffée*,
to stew in a closed vessel. Lady Clark's recipe, *c.* 1890.

Take 8 potatoes of good quality and the same size (preferably the the floury kind) and peel them. Then put into a heavy saucepan with not more than ½ inch (1·5 cm.) water. Sprinkle with salt and dot lavishly with butter. Cover closely and simmer over a very low heat until they are cooked. Shake from time to time to prevent sticking.

Serves 4.

VARIATION: in country districts bacon or good meat dripping is heated and 2 medium onions are quickly softened (but not browned) in it, then the potatoes cut into thick slices are added with salt and pepper and about ½ pint (300 ml.) water. They are covered and cooked as above, the butter being omitted. Quantities would be about 2 tablespoons dripping, 2 onions, 6 medium potatoes.

They are served on their own or with cold meats.

STUFFED BAKED POTATOES

Also called 'potato pies'. In Angus large potatoes (4) are baked in their jackets until soft, then the tops are cut off, (or they are cut in half lengthways) and the potato removed and mashed. This is mixed with ½ lb. (225 g.) cooked, boned, skinned and flaked Finnan Haddie which has been mixed with 2 tablespoons butter and the top of the milk, then seasoned. When well amalgamated it is piled high into the potato skins, then heated up in a moderate oven for about 20 minutes.

VARIATION: 4 oz. (125 g.) grated cheese and 1 tablespoon chopped parsley can be used instead of the fish. Or use the same amount of minced ham, but in these cases use only half the butter.

SCOTS POTATO PIES

This method is quite peculiar to Scotland and very good it is too. Large potatoes of equal size are peeled and the tops cut off. The centre is hollowed out leaving a rim of about half an inch (1·5 cm.) and the centres are filled with minced cooked meat which has been mixed with chopped part-cooked onion, salt, pepper and a drop or two of ketchup and a little stock. This is put into the centre of the potatoes and the tops are put back.

They are then put into a heavily greased baking tin and rolled in the fat and baked in a hot oven at 400°F. (200°C.) or gas mark 6 for at least 1 hour, basting from time to time with the dripping or oil. Test for tenderness as the variety of potato makes a difference to the cooking time.

These delicious little 'pies' are served with a good meat gravy or fresh, hot tomato sauce. Allow at least 1 large potato per person. In Banffshire, the potato is mixed with an egg yolk, butter, breadcrumbs, herbs and milk.

SEE ALSO: *Colcannon*, page 170, and *Arran Potato Salad*, below.

SALSIFY

See *Artichokes*, page 165.

Accompaniments

ARRAN POTATO SALAD

6 Arran Chief potatoes, cooked
2 oz. (50 g.) fresh peas
4 oz. (125 g.) cooked beetroot
salt and pepper
1 teaspoon each: fresh chopped tarragon, chervil, parsley
1 medium finely chopped shallot
3 tablespoons olive oil and 1 tablespoon wine vinegar

Cook the vegetables and drain them well, then cube the potatoes and beetroot. While they are warm put them into the salad bowl, season and mix in the herbs. Mix the oil and vinegar well, then pour over and mix thoroughly, but gently so that the potatoes are unbroken. Arrange the peas around the edges and serve cold.

Serves 4–6.

BUTTERED BARLEY

This is often served with *Mince Collops*, page 130, stews or boiled chicken.

- 4 oz. (125 g.) pearl barley approx. 1 large teacupful
- 3 teacups of water
- 1 tablespoon butter
- salt

Boil the barley in the water with a little salt and cook until the water has been absorbed, stirring from time to time. Then add the butter and simmer gently until it is quite soft.

Serves 4.

DUTCH SALAD

This recipe was brought over by the Dutch fishermen, see page 23.

- 2 salt herrings
- 8 small to medium cold boiled potatoes
- 1 small cooked beetroot
- 1 apple, peeled, sliced and cored
- 2 hard-boiled eggs, sliced
- 1 small lettuce
- 2 tablespoons oil and 1 wine vinegar
- 2–3 tablespoons mayonnaise, page 193
- 4 cocktail gherkins
- pepper

Clean the herrings which have been soaked in cold water or buttermilk for 2–3 hours. Take out the bones and chop into small pieces. Clean and dry the lettuce, and chop all the other ingredients. Mix together most of the herring with the lettuce and pour the mixed oil and vinegar over the top and toss them in it. Pile up like a cushion and put the beetroot, apple and eggs on top and season with the pepper. Cover with the mayonnaise and decorate the top with the remaining herring and sliced gherkins.

Serves 4–6.

GREEN DUMPLINGS

These traditional dumplings are only made in the spring when the greenstuff is young and fresh. They are delicious in soups, stews or with boiled meats or chicken.

8 oz. (225 g.) flour	cold water, about 3
4 oz. (125 g.) shredded	tablespoons
suet	young green shoots about
1 teaspoon baking powder	1 cupful
salt, pepper	

The green shoots can consist of hawthorn buds, tips of young nettles, young dandelion leaves, turnip tops, shoots of young corn etc. Sift the flour and baking powder into a bowl, then add the suet and mix well. Pour in enough water to make a stiff but elastic dough, then add the shoots, washed and chopped very fine, and mix until the dough is quite green all over.

Shape with floured hands into small balls about the size of a large walnut, then drop into boiling liquid and cook for about 15 minutes, turning them once. Makes about 20–25 dumplings.

VARIATION: for serving with boiled salted beef add 1 tablespoon creamed horseradish.

WINTER SALAD

Recipe from Lady Clark, *c.* 1880s.

2 large Spanish onions
½ pint (300 ml.) milk and water mixed
3 raw celery hearts
1 medium cooked beetroot

For the sauce
2 hard-boiled egg yolks

1 teaspoon each: dry mustard powder and anchovy essence
4 tablespoons olive oil
1 tablespoon wine vinegar
2 tablespoons cream
pinch castor sugar
salt and cayenne pepper

Cook the peeled onions, until tender, whole, in the milk and water for some time before you want the salad. Then drain well. Rub the eggyolks until smooth with the mustard, anchovy, salt and pepper, then drop by drop add the olive oil, then the vinegar mixing it all very well. Finally add the cream and sugar.

Slice all ingredients finely into a bowl, pour the sauce over and let it marinate for at least 1 hour before serving, then mix it all thoroughly.

Serves 4–6.

Oatmeal Accompaniments

CARCAKES

This variety of oatcake is served with breakfast bacon rashers.

5 oz. (150 g.) oatmeal
pinch of soda bicarbonate
pinch of cream of tartar

salt and pepper
a little milk to mix
hot bacon fat

Mix the dry ingredients together, then add enough milk to make a thickish pouring batter. Heat up the fat and when hot put spoonfuls of the batter into it (it should sizzle as it goes in) and

fry for a few minutes until brown underneath, then turn and fry
the other side. Makes 12–15.

OATMEAL 'CUTLETS'

Recipe from the Scottish Women's Rural Institute,
c. 1940s.

4 oz. (125 g.) oatmeal	¼ pint (150 ml.) milk
1 oz. (25 g.) flour	1 egg
2 tablespoons finely	3–4 tablespoons
chopped leek, or spring	breadcrumbs
onions	fat or oil for frying
salt and pepper	

Mix the oatmeal, flour, leek and pepper, then add the milk and
stir to make a soft dough, adding a very little more if needed.
Leave to swell and get firm. Then with floured hands shape into
cutlets, brush with beaten egg and roll in breadcrumbs, then fry
on both sides in the hot fat or oil. Garnish with mixed vegetables.

Serves 2–4.

FITLESS COCK

This was eaten formerly at Fastern's Eve (Shrove Tuesday) and
in the eighteenth century cock fights were often held to celebrate
the festival. Fitless is thought to come from 'festy' – 'fastyn'. In
the south of Scotland it was called 'Dry Goose'. Recipe from the
Scottish Women's Rural Institute, *c.* 1940s.

4 oz. (125 g.) oatmeal	salt and pepper
2 oz. (50 g.) shredded	1 large egg
suet	a little milk if needed
1 small finely chopped	
onion	

Mix all dry ingredients and bind with the beaten egg adding a little milk if it seems too dry. Scald a pudding cloth, shape mixture like a chicken, then tie in the floured cloth, secure it well and cook in boiling water for 2 hours. Serve alone or with meat or fowl.

OATMEAL DUMPLINGS

8 oz. (225 g.) oatmeal   1 medium onion, chopped
4 oz. (125 g.) shredded   1 egg
  suet   salt and pepper

Toast the oatmeal lightly in the oven or under a slow grill, then add the suet and onion, mix well and season. Add the beaten egg, then put into a floured cloth and tie loosely. Put into boiling water and simmer uncovered for $1\frac{1}{2}$ hours seeing that the dumpling is under water all the time.

It is usually served with boiled chicken and it is almost a meal in itself.

Serves 4.

OATCAKES

Oatcakes or bannocks are traditional Scottish fare and are eaten for breakfast, with fish (particularly herrings) or plain with butter and heather honey. They are also served with soups, buttermilk, jam or marmalade. Traditionally they are cooked over a girdle or griddle, one of the oldest cooking utensils, but a heavy frying pan can be used.

It is easier to make 1 large oatcake at a time, then to cut it into farls or quarters, as the mixture stiffens if left too long. They can be stored in a tin and heated in the oven or under a low grill.

4 oz. (125 g.) medium
  oatmeal
2 teaspoons melted fat
  (bacon if possible)
a pinch of bicarbonate of
  soda

pinch of salt
about 3–4 tablespoons
  hot water
additional oatmeal for
  kneading

Mix the oatmeal with the salt and bicarbonate of soda in a bowl, then pour the melted fat into a well in the centre. Stir well and add enough water to make a stiff paste. Scatter a surface thickly with oatmeal, turn out the mixture and roll into a ball. Knead well with the hands covered in oatmeal to prevent sticking. Then roll out to $\frac{1}{4}$ inch (0·5 cm.) thickness and shape by putting a plate the size of your pan over the top and cutting round it. Cut into farls, lightly grease the pan or griddle, heat it up and when hot put them in and cook until the edges curl slightly.

Turn and do the other side or put under a medium hot grill. Formerly they were finished on a toasting stone. Mix another oatcake while this one is 'finishing'. The above amounts make 2 bannocks about the size of a dessert plate, that is 8 farls.

HODGILS

These dumplings for soup come from the Border counties.

4 oz. (125 g.) oatmeal
salt and pepper
1 tablespoon chopped
  chives

2–3 tablespoons fatty
  beef broth

Put the oatmeal and seasonings into a bowl, adding the chopped chives, then moisten with the fatty broth, mix well and put small spoonfuls into the boiling soup and boil for about 20 minutes.

MEALIE PUDDING

MEALIE PUDDING: put all the ingredients into a greased basin, raw, cover and steam or boil for about 1 hour.

These mealie puddings can be bought in Scotland stuffed into skins like a sausage. They are then heated in water and browned in a frying pan, not unlike a white pudding.

SKIRLIE AND MEALIE PUDDING

This boiled oatmeal pudding is often served with *Boiled Cod and Mustard Sauce*, page 28, and also with meats and game. Uncooked it is used as a stuffing for chicken, see page 88, and if it is fried in bacon fat for 7–10 minutes it is called Skirlie, or Skirl-in-the-pan.

2 oz. (50 g.) shredded
 suet, dripping or oil
2 medium onions, finely
 chopped

4 oz. (125 g.) medium
 oatmeal
salt and pepper

Heat the suet or fat and when very hot add the onions, soften and let them become golden brown. Then add the oatmeal, keeping the mixture thick. Season and cook, stirring well till it is well cooked.

Serves 4.

SAUCES

There are not many truly Scottish sauces, most are variants on the Béchamel or white sauce theme. However Scotland has contributed at least two original sauces to the world, one being bread sauce and the other egg sauce. There are also some sauces for game which are included below.

Savoury Sauces

BREAD SAUCE

An early form of this is given in Mrs Cleland's *A New and Easy Method of Cookery* (1759) for serving with chickens, ducks, partridges, moor-fowl and grouse. Nowadays it is also served with turkey. Before the eighteenth century many gravies and sauces were thickened with breadcrumbs but it took the Scots to make it into a creamy and delectable sauce.

1 medium onion, peeled
4 whole cloves
small blade mace
¾ pint (450 ml.) milk
8 rounded tablespoons
    fresh white
    breadcrumbs

½ oz. (15 g.) butter
2 tablespoons thick cream,
    optional
salt and white pepper

Stick the cloves into the onion and put into a saucepan with the mace, peppercorns and the milk, bring to the boil, then take

from the heat at once and leave, covered, to infuse for about
half an hour.

Strain the milk into another saucepan and stir in the breadcrumbs. Put back on the heat and, stirring all the time, cook
until the mixture boils and it becomes thick. Season to taste,
then add the butter in small pieces and finally the cream. Serve
warm, but do not reboil.
Serves 4.

CHESTNUT SAUCE

See page 150.

DUCK OR GOOSE SAUCE

2 tablespoons mild French mustard	juice of 1 lemon
dash of cayenne pepper	$\frac{1}{4}$ pint (150 ml.) port wine
3 tablespoons redcurrant jelly	

Mix all ingredients together in a saucepan and simmer gently
for 5–10 minutes. Serve hot. Enough for 1 small duck.

DEVIL SAUCE

See page 94.

GROUSE SAUCE

Recipe from Mrs Macleod.

pan juices of the roast
3 tablespoons brandy or
  single malt whisky

½ pint (300 ml.) pouring
  cream
salt and pepper

Pour off any excess fat but leave the sediment in the pan juices. Pour the warmed brandy or whisky into the hot pan and set light to it. When the flames have died down pour in the cream, slowly, stirring well, heat but do not reboil. Taste for seasoning before use. Enough for a brace of grouse, it can also be served with other feathered game.

HOLLANDAISE

8 oz. (225 g.) butter
2 tablespoons white wine
  vinegar or lemon
1 tablespoon cold water
salt and white pepper

2 tablespoons water
3 egg yolks
lemon juice
cayenne pepper

All ingredients should be at room temperature. Divide the butter into small pieces and in a heavy saucepan put the vinegar and 2 tablespoons water with a little pepper and cook over a high flame until it is reduced by half. Take from the heat and add the cold water. Add the egg yolks and whisk briskly until it is thick and creamy, then lower the heat (or put over hot, not boiling water) and whisk until it is thick, adding the butter pieces one at a time, and make certain each piece is melted before adding the next. Lift the pan to cool from time to time. Continue to do this until all the butter is used up and the mixture is thick, then add the lemon juice and season to taste.

Keep in a shallow pan of warm, not hot water until it is needed and beat well before using. Makes about ½ pint (300 ml.).

BLENDER HOLLANDAISE

Heat 4 oz. (125 g.) butter in a saucepan until foaming, then put the egg yolks into the blender container with the lemon juice, salt and pepper. Cover and blend for 1 second, then turn off. Turn on to high, take off the lid and slowly pour the hot butter into the eggs. Then switch off. If the sauce is not needed at once pour into a thick saucepan or bowl and stand over tepid water. Heat up the water before serving and whisk until the sauce is fluffy and warm.

This is served with poached salmon, vegetables and eggs.

VARIATION: if 2–3 tablespoons thick cream are added it becomes sauce Mousseline and it is served with fresh asparagus, poached eggs or fish.

MAYONNAISE

Although not a truly Scottish sauce it is generally used all over. It is essential to have all ingredients at room temperature before starting.

2 egg yolks
2 teaspoons tarragon
    vinegar or lemon juice
½ pint (300 ml.) olive oil

salt and pepper
1 tablespoon boiling
    water

Break the egg yolks into a bowl and add half the vinegar. Add the olive oil, drop by drop, beating all the time until it becomes thick, then let it flow in a gentle stream beating well. When the oil is used up, season and add the rest of the vinegar, mixing well. Finally add the boiling water which improves its keeping properties.

If it should curdle (separate) then break another egg yolk and drop by drop add the curdled mixture beating all the time. Makes about ½ pint (300 ml.).

BLENDER MAYONNAISE

This can be done very easily in a Kenwood Chef or a Magimix machine in a matter of minutes with no fear of curdling, using the above method.

VARIATION: green mayonnaise is made by adding chopped parsley, chives and tarragon. Red mayonnaise has the pounded coral of lobster added, see page 54, and a little grated horse-radish can be added for serving with cold beef.

PIQUANTE SAUCE

See page 136.

PORT WINE SAUCE

Madeira or Marsala wine can be used instead of the port.

- 1 oz. (25 g.) butter
- 1 tablespoon finely chopped shallot
- 4 tablespoons port, madeira or marsala
- ½ pint (300 ml.) chicken stock
- 2 teaspoons chopped parsley
- salt and pepper
- 1 rounded teaspoon butter worked with the same of flour

Heat the butter and soften the shallot in it but do not colour. Add the port, boil and reduce to half. Add the stock, seasoning, lemon juice and parsley, bring to the boil, then lower to keep warm. Mix the flour and butter together thoroughly, break into

SAUCES

small pieces and add to the sauce, stirring until it is blended and the sauce thickened slightly.

Serves 4.

This sauce is excellent with wild duck, guinea fowl, duck, game, chops or steak.

Sauces made with a Béchamel or white sauce base

BÉCHAMEL SAUCE

1 small onion, finely chopped	pinch salt
1 oz. (25 g.) butter	4 white peppercorns
2 tablespoons flour	sprig of parsley with stalk
1¼ pints (750 ml.) scalded milk	½ bay leaf
	pinch nutmeg

Heat the butter until foaming, then sauté the onion in it until soft. Add the flour mix well and cook slowly until it starts to turn a golden brown colour, stirring all the time. Add the milk gradually and cook, stirring well with a whisk until it is thick and creamy. Then season with salt, peppercorns, nutmeg, bay leaf and parsley and simmer very slowly for about half an hour or until it is reduced to two-thirds. Strain through a conical strainer and it is ready for use. Makes approx. ¾ pint (450 ml.).

WHITE SAUCE

If being served with boiled fish, poultry or meats sometimes the appropriate stock is used instead of the milk. This is indicated in the recipe.

2 oz. (50 g.) butter   salt and pepper
1 oz. (25 g.) flour
¾–1 pint (450–600 ml.)
   scalded milk or thin
   cream

Heat the butter and stir in the flour and cook for about 1 minute, stirring well. Gradually add the milk, keep stirring and cook until it becomes smooth and creamy. Season and simmer slowly for about 5 minutes to ensure the flour is cooked. Makes about ¾ pint (450 ml.).

SWEET WHITE SAUCE

Omit the salt and pepper but add 1 oz. (25 g.) sugar or to taste.
BÉCHAMEL AND WHITE SAUCE form the basis for the following:

ANCHOVY: add 1 tablespoon anchovy essence to either of above, or 4 mashed anchovy fillets to the above quantities.

CAPER: add 2–3 tablespoons capers.

CHEESE: add 3–4 tablespoons grated cheese.

EGG: add 2 finely chopped hard-boiled eggs. See also page 87.

MUSHROOM: add 3 oz. (75 g.) sliced mushrooms.

MUSTARD: add 1–2 tablespoons made mustard. See also page 28.

ONION: see page 139, or add 3 medium, cooked onions, chopped or puréed.

PARSLEY: add 2–3 tablespoons chopped parsley.
For other herbs add 2 tablespoons if they are strong such as fennel, but if using dried herbs then half that quantity.

SHELLFISH SAUCE: to either sauces shelled prawns, scallops,

lobster or crab can be added. About 4 oz. (125 g.) is usually enough, but add more if liked.

TOMATO SAUCE: add 3 medium peeled and chopped tomatoes and 1 teaspoon tomato purée.

WATERCRESS SAUCE: add 1 bunch chopped watercress without the stalks. For *Watercress Butter*, see page 63.

Other sauces are given throughout the book with the appropriate dishes.

Sweet Sauces

ALMOND SAUCE

Recipe from Dr Williamson, Edinburgh, *c.* 1857.

2 eggs
2 oz. (50 g.) castor sugar
½ pint (300 ml.) milk
2 oz. (50 g.) ground
    almonds

2 tablespoons orange-
    flower water (obtainable
    at chemists)

In a saucepan beat the eggs and add sugar and all the other ingredients. Set on a low flame or in a double-boiler and beat with a wire whisk like a custard until it thickens, but do not let it boil. Serve hot with *Holyrood Pudding*, page 215, or with a lemon-flavoured steamed pudding.

CREAM SAUCE

Meg Dods, 1826, calls this 'Caudle Sauce', and omits the almonds but adds 1 teaspoon grated lemon rind and a pinch of cinnamon.

For Plum pudding or any steamed pudding, or mincepies.

½ lb. (225 g.) butter
1 teaspoon ground almonds
4 oz. (125 g.) castor sugar

2½ fl. oz. (75 ml.) brandy
or single malt whisky

Let the butter soften, but on no account let it oil. Gradually add the other ingredients, being careful to add the spirit slowly lest it should curdle the butter. When it is all well amalgamated, chill and serve chilled.

Enough for 4–6.

CUSTARD

See *Scots Trifle*, page 221.

This sauce can also be flavoured with brandy, rum, whisky or a liqueur of your choice, using about 2 tablespoons or to taste.

HONEY SAUCE

For serving with steamed puddings, milk puddings, pancakes and sweet omelettes.

½ lb. (225 g.) honey,
heather if possible
½ pint (300 ml.) water
finely grated rind and
juice of ½ large orange

finely grated rind and
juice of ½ lemon
1 rounded teaspoon butter
1 large beaten egg

Put the honey and water in a bowl or double saucepan and heat until it is well blended, then add the juice and rind of the fruits, the butter and finally the well-beaten egg. Heat over hot water, stirring constantly for about 10 minutes or until it has thickened slightly.

Serves 4.

MARMALADE SAUCE (1)

Apricot jam can also be used instead of marmalade. As marmalade is a Scottish creation this could be termed a traditional Scottish sauce.

For serving with steamed puddings, pancakes, sweet omelettes or sweet batter pudding.

¼ oz. (8 g.) cornflour   1 rounded tablespoon
2 teaspoons lemon juice   marmalade (if coarse
¼ pint (150 ml.) water   cut, sieve or chop peel)
a thin twist lemon peel   2 teaspoons castor sugar

Mix the cornflour and lemon juice. Then put the water into a saucepan with the peel and boil for about 3 minutes, then leave to infuse for 15 minutes and remove the peel. Stir in the cornflour, bring back to the boil and stir for about 1 minute until it thickens and is smooth and creamy. Mix the marmalade and sugar and add to the sauce, stirring until the sugar is quite dissolved.

Serves 2.

A tablespoon of whisky gives an excellent flavour.

MARMALADE SAUCE (2)

This is Lady Clark's recipe.

4 tablespoons sieved   4 oz. (125 g.) castor
    marmalade or apricot jam   sugar
¼ pint (150 ml.) medium
    white wine

Mix all ingredients together and heat for 5 minutes, stirring until the sugar is quite dissolved. Serve hot.

Enough for 4.

REDCURRANT SAUCE

Mrs Wellington, Aberdeen, 1878.

For serving with rice, steamed puddings or over ice-cream.

4 oz. (125 g.) castor sugar	grated rind of ½ lemon and
water	1 orange
2 tablespoons redcurrant	2 tablespoons Maraschino
jelly	liqueur

Boil the sugar with 2 tablespoons water for 10 minutes, but do not stir or let it colour. Add the redcurrant jelly, grated rinds and boil gently until the jelly has melted. Strain and add the Maraschino, just heat up if serving hot, or leave if serving cold.

Serves 4.

SWEET WHITE SAUCE

See page 196.

But it can also be made in the following way:

¼ oz. (8 g.) cornflour	1 tablespoon sugar, or to
½ pint (300 ml.) milk	taste
½ vanilla pod or piece of	
lemon peel	

Mix the cornflour with a little of the milk and boil up the remainder. Mix in the cornflour stirring well, and simmer gently for about 5 minutes with either the vanilla pod or lemon peel. Remove before serving by straining the sauce. Makes about ½ pint (300 ml.).

VARIATION: omit the vanilla or lemon and flavour with a spirit such as brandy, whisky, rum, or a liqueur; about 1 tablespoon should be enough. A pinch of ground cinnamon or nutmeg can also be added.

WHITE WINE SAUCE

Recipe from Lady Clark, *c.* 1880s.

Lady Clark suggests serving this with a steamed fig pudding, but it is also good with pancakes.

2 tablespoons flour or
    cornflour
½ pint (300 ml.) sweet
    white wine

1 oz. (25 g.) butter
2 tablespoons brown sugar
    grated peel of 1 lemon

Mix the flour with the wine very well, then heat to boiling point stirring well until it is thick and smooth. Simmer for 5 minutes, stirring from time to time. Then add the butter in small pieces, the sugar and finely grated lemon peel. Serve hot.

Enough for 4.

PUDDINGS
AND DESSERTS

Basically the Scots are a nation of soup-eaters rather than pudding-eaters, yet there are many puddings, and especially pastry covered ones in the Scottish cuisine. In Meg Dods's *The Cook and Housewife's Manual* published in 1826 (prior to Mrs Beeton) many traditional puddings are given most of which are served with sweet sauces such as custard or wine sauce, see page 201, or cream. It is interesting to note that Scottish pudding plates were like shallow soup dishes and Scottish brides who went to settle in Britain made a point of taking their pudding plates with them. These plates were useful to contain the sauce without any fear of it running over the edge.

BURNT CREAM OR CRÈME BRULÉE

Recipe adapted from Mrs Elizabeth Cleland's *A New and Easy Method of Cookery*, 1759. There is an amusing anecdote connected with this recipe. In the 1860s it was offered to the kitchens of Trinity College Cambridge by an undergraduate from Aberdeenshire (where the recipe originated at a country house) and it was rejected out of hand. Many years later when this undergraduate became a Fellow of the College he presented it again and it was accepted with pleasure. It became a speciality of Trinity College – sometimes it was called 'Cambridge Cream' – and was one of the favourite dishes served in May Week. This anecdote is given by Eleanor Jenkinson, the sister of a former Cambridge University Librarian, in *The Ocklye Cookery Book* (1909).

4 egg yolks	2 oz. (50 g.) approx.
1 tablespoon caster sugar	castor sugar
1 pint (600 ml.) cream	
a split vanilla pod or a few	
drops of essence	

Mix the egg yolks thoroughly with the sugar, then put the cream and the vanilla pod into a double saucepan. Bring to scalding point but do not boil, and add essence if the pod is not available. Pour on to the yolks, stirring well all the time until it thickens, but do not let it boil. Strain into a pie-dish and let it get cold, preferably overnight.

Get the grill very hot, then cover the surface of the cream evenly with the castor sugar, but do not make too thick a layer. Put at once under the grill and let the sugar melt and turn golden brown. Take from the heat and let it stand in a cold place for about 3 hours before serving.

Serves 4.

NOTE: originally this was browned with a salamander, a flat iron made hot and passed over the top of the pudding. It is very rich and is sometimes served with poached or stewed fruit.

This is the classical recipe still used today, but Mrs Cleland flavoured the cream with the finely grated rind of an orange and a stick of cinnamon. It is worth trying, but the pure flavour of the other takes a lot of beating.

CARRAGEEN BLANCMANGE

Carrageen (*Chondrus crispus*) is a branching mucilaginous sea-weed found on many coasts in Europe and North America. It is a speciality in both Ireland and Scotland where it is used for puddings and beverages. It contains iodine and sulphur and is recommended for chest and stomach troubles. It can be bought already prepared in health shops, but in the west of Ireland and on the Hebrides it is gathered from the rock pools, washed and dried, then put into muslin bags for future use. Contrary to what one would think, it doesn't taste mariney.

½ oz. (15 g.) dried carrageen   1 oz. (25 g.) sugar, or to
1 pint (600 ml.) milk   taste
peel of 1 lemon or a few
   drops of vanilla essence

Put the dried carrageen into a bowl and cover with hot water, then stir well and strain thoroughly.

Boil this carrageen in the milk with the lemon rind and simmer for about 15 minutes, or until it is soft and thick. Strain into a bowl and add the sugar stirring well to dissolve it. Pour into a wetted mould and leave to set.

Serves 4.

VARIATION: proceed as above and when it is cooked add the stiffly beaten white of 1 egg and 2 tablespoons cream. This is called *Carrageen Cream.*

CARRAGEEN JELLY

For coughs or colds, boil ¼ oz. (8 g.) carrageen with the juice and rind of 1 orange or lemon, sugar to taste and 1 pint (600 ml.) water. Simmer for 20 minutes, then strain and serve hot, or cold.

CHOCOLATE MARIE

Recipe from Lady Forbes, *c.* 1910.

½ lb. (225 g.) dark cooking
    chocolate such as
    Menier
4 large eggs, separated
2 tablespoons cold water

2 tablespoons sweetened
    black coffee, or coffee
    liqueur such as Tia
    Maria

Cut the chocolate into small pieces, then put into the water and melt it gently. Cool slightly, then add the egg yolks, one by one, mixing well. Then add the coffee or coffee liqueur and stir thoroughly. This can then be poured into small dessert cups when it will be found to be very good and rich when cold. Or whip up the egg whites until stiff and fold them in. This makes it more of a mousse. Make 12 hours before it is wanted.

Serves 4.

CALEDONIAN CREAM

Recipe adapted from Mrs Dalgairns, *c.* 1829.

1 lb. (450 g.) curds or
    cottage cheese
2 tablespoons minced
    Dundee marmalade

2 tablespoons castor sugar
1 tablespoon lemon juice
2 tablespoons approx.
    Highland malt whisky

Mix all ingredients together thoroughly, or liquidize, then put into a dish and freeze or chill very hard.

Serves 4–6.

NOTE: Mrs Dalgairns uses whipped cream but I have found this too rich. However, half cream and half curds is quite a good mixture.

CALEDONIAN ICE

Also called Iced Stapag, and Cranachan or Cream Crowdie*

1 pint (600 ml.) double
  cream
2 tablespoons castor sugar
a few drops vanilla
  essence or flavouring of
  your choice

2 rounded tablespoons
  coarse oatmeal, lightly
  toasted

Whip the cream stiffly, then add the sugar and the vanilla (or rum, orange liqueur etc.) and freeze until the edges are crystallized. Meanwhile lightly toast the oatmeal, either in a low oven or under a slow grill, so that it is dried but not browned. Then mix it into the cream thoroughly, put into a dish and freeze again until solid, but take out of the freezer about half an hour before serving.

Serves 4–6.

VARIATION: use vanilla ice-cream instead of cream. Add 1 cup fresh raspberries or other soft fruit at the same time as the oatmeal.

* This dish was traditionally served at Harvest time or on festive occasions in farmhouses, but it was not frozen, just set in a cold place.

CLOOTIE DUMPLING

Also spelt Cloutie, and so called from being boiled in a 'clout' or cloth. It is a traditional pudding especially in country districts.

4 oz. (125 g.) shredded suet, or margarine	1 teaspoon each: ground cinnamon and ginger
8 oz. (225 g.) flour	1 tablespoon golden syrup
4 oz. (125 g.) oatmeal	2 eggs
3 oz. (75 g.) sugar	3-4 tablespoons buttermilk or sour milk
1 rounded teaspoon baking powder	
8 oz. (225 g.) mixed sultanas and currants	

Rub the fat into the sifted flour, then add all the other dry ingredients. Make a hole in the centre and add the syrup and beaten eggs and mix well. Then add enough buttermilk or sour milk to make a soft but firm batter. If using a pudding cloth dip it first into boiling water and then flour it well before adding the pudding mixture. Tie up, but allow a good space for expansion.

Or the mixture can be put into a lightly greased basin allowing a one inch (2.5 cm.) space at the top. Tie down securely and boil with boiling water coming up to the rim for 2½-3 hours. If using the cloth, put a saucer or plate in the bottom of the saucepan and stand the pudding in the cloth on top, then cover with boiling water, and cook for 2½-3 hours. Turn out and serve with *Custard Sauce*, page 198.

DRAMBUIE CREAM

Recipe from Mrs Mackinnon, formerly Chairman of
the Drambuie Liqueur Company.

For the wine jelly
¼ pint (150 ml.) port or claret
¼ pint (150 ml.) water
1 oz. (25 g.) sugar or powdered glucose

squeeze of lemon juice
1 level tablespoon gelatine
1 teaspoon redcurrant jelly
20 sponge fingers (boudoir biscuits) approx.

¾ pint (450 ml.) milk,
scalded
3 oz. (75 g.) castor sugar
¾ oz. (20 g.) powdered
gelatine

2 beaten eggs
½ pint (300 ml.) double
cream
4 fl. oz. (100/125 ml.)
Drambuie

First make the wine jelly by putting all the ingredients except the port into a rinsed pan and stir over heat until the gelatine and jelly are dissolved. Draw pan aside and infuse for 15 minutes. Add the port, strain and it is ready for use. (If making wine jelly on its own for a dessert, then double the quantities and pour into 6 small individual dishes.)

Let the jelly cool until it is the consistency of raw egg white, then pour into the bottom of a mould and line the sides with the sponge fingers sticking them into the jelly to about 1 inch (2·5 cm.). Let it set in a cold place.

Meanwhile make the cream by scalding the milk. Then blend the sugar with the gelatine and the well-beaten eggs. Pour the milk over this mixture and put into a saucepan over heat and cook, stirring all the time, but do not let it boil. Let it cool, but not set. Then whip the cream, adding the Drambuie finally, and when the custard cream is cool fold in gently and pour into the sponge and jelly mould. Chill until set, and wrap a hot towel around it before turning out.

Serves about 6.

DUNFILLAN BLACKBERRY PUDDING

Blaeberries can be used instead of blackberries.

For the Dunfillan paste
2 oz. (50 g.) butter or
margarine
2 oz. (50 g.) castor sugar
1 large beaten egg

4 oz. (125 g.) sifted flour
pinch baking powder
2 tablespoons milk
2 teaspoons finely grated
lemon rind

For the filling   squeeze of lemon, optional
1 lb. (450 g.) blackberries   water
  or blaeberries   sprinkling of cornflour
3 oz. (75 g.) sugar

Put the berries into a saucepan and barely cover with water, then add the sugar and lemon juice and cook until soft. Put into a dish in layers and sprinkle each layer with cornflour.

To make the pastry, cream the butter and sugar, then add the well-beaten egg. Mix the baking powder and flour and add it alternately with the milk mixing well. Finally stir in the lemon rind. Spread evenly over the fruit and cook in a moderate oven at 350°F. (180°C.) or gas mark 4 for 20–30 minutes or until the top is golden-brown, but test with a skewer before taking from the oven. Serve hot or cold.

Enough for 4.

VARIATION: stewed apples can also be used, or a mixture of blackberry and apple. Rhubarb is good, too.

DUNESSLIN PUDDING

Recipe from the Scottish Women's Rural Institutes.

4 tablespoons jam or   ½ pint (300 ml.) milk
  stewed fruit   squeeze of lemon juice or
2 oz. (50 g.) flour   vanilla
1 oz. (25 g.) sugar   2 eggs, well beaten
1 oz. (25 g.) butter

Put the jam or fruit at the bottom of a 2-pint (1 litre) pudding dish which has been lightly buttered. Mix the flour and sugar in a thick saucepan over heat, and gradually add the milk, stirring well, then add the butter cut into small pieces. Stir until it boils and becomes thick. Cool slightly, add the lemon juice and the well-beaten eggs. Beat until smooth, then pour over the jam or fruit evenly and brown in a moderate oven, 350°F. (180°C.) or gas mark 4, for about 20 minutes.

Serves 4.

EDINBURGH FOG

½ pint (300 ml.) double
  cream
1 oz. (25 g.) castor sugar,
  or to taste
a few drops almond
  essence

2 oz. (50 g.) small ratafia
  biscuits (see page 237)
  or small macaroons
1 oz. (25 g.) blanched,
  split almonds

Whip the cream until stiff, then sweeten to taste. Mix well with the small ratafia biscuits or crushed small macaroons and finally add the slivered almonds. Chill well before serving.

Serves 4.

VARIATION: use ice-cream instead of the sweetened cream and refreeze. It can also be flavoured with a liqueur, rum, whisky or brandy.

EDINBURGH TART

8 oz. (225 g.) puff or
  shortcrust pastry
  page 218
2 rounded tablespoons
  butter
2 oz. (50 g.) castor sugar
1 teaspoon grated orange
  or lemon rind

2 oz. (50 g.) chopped
  candied peel
1 rounded tablespoon
  sultanas
2 eggs, beaten

First make the pastry and chill for at least 1 hour. Then roll out on a floured surface and line an 8–9 inch (20·3–22·8 cm.) flan dish. Prick the bottom lightly and brush over thinly with a little of the beaten egg.

Heat the butter and sugar in a saucepan and when melted add

the fruit, peel and lemon rind and mix well. Pour over the well-beaten eggs, and then pour into the flan case. Bake in a hot oven, 450°F. (230°C.) or gas mark 8, for about 30 minutes. Serve warm or cold.

Enough for 4–6.

FAIRY PUDDING

Recipe from the Scottish Women's Rural Institutes.

½ pint (300 ml.) water
2 level tablespoons
cornflour
1½ oz. (38 g.) sugar

For the sauce
2 eggyolks

¾ pint (450 ml.) milk
1 large lemon, rind and
juice
2 eggwhites, stiffly beaten
1 teaspoon cornflour
2 teaspoons sugar
¼ teaspoon vanilla essence

Put the water on to boil with the sugar, lemon rind and juice. When it comes to the boil remove the rind. Mix the cornflour with a little cold water, stir in, and bring to the boil, stirring all the time until it thickens. Let it boil for about 2 minutes, then turn into a basin. Add the stiffly beaten eggwhites and mix thoroughly. Put into a wetted mould and chill. When cold turn out and serve with the sauce. To make the sauce, bring the milk to just under boiling point. Mix the cornflour with a little cold milk and the egg yolks, beating well. Then stir into the milk and over heat, keep stirring until it boils. Cool, and then serve it poured around the pudding.

Serves 4.

FRAIR'S OMELETTE

Recipe from Lady Forbes, *c.* 1910.

6 medium cooking apples	2 eggs, well beaten
4 oz. (125 g.) butter	½ oz. (12 g.) butter
2 oz. (50 g.) sugar	4 oz. (125 g.) breadcrumbs
squeeze lemon juice	1 oz. (25 g.) sugar

Peel, core and slice the apples, then put into a saucepan with about ¼ pint (150 ml.) water and cook until soft, as for apple sauce. Take from the heat and add the 4 oz. (125 g.) butter, sugar and lemon juice and mix well. When cold add the well-beaten eggs.

Take a deep baking dish and butter it well, then strew it thickly with breadcrumbs so that they stick to the bottom and the sides, but reserve enough for the top. Put the apple and egg mixture into the dish and cover the top thickly. Bake in a moderate oven, 350°F. (180°C.) or gas mark 4, for about half an hour. Serve warm or cold, but turn out on to a flat dish, and cover with sugar before dishing up.

Serves 4.

VARIATION: this can be also made with rhubarb, plums (without the stones), blackberry and apple etc.

FRUIT FLAN
WITH OATMEAL PASTRY

Rhubarb, apple, blackberry and apple, blaeberries, plums, cherries, etc. can all be used for this flan. The nutty pastry goes well with a tart fruit.

For the pastry	3 oz. (75 g.) butter or
2 oz. (50 g.) fine oatmeal	margarine
3 oz. (75 g.) flour	a pinch sugar

2–3 tablespoons water,
approx.

For the filling
1 lb. (450 g.) plums,
stoned

3 oz. (75 g.) sugar
1 rounded teaspoon
cornflour
2–3 tablespoons water

Cook the stoned plums very gently with the sugar and the water so that they are soft but not mushy, and reserve.

Mix the oatmeal and flour together and rub in the fat, and add the sugar, then mix to a stiff dough with the water, adding a little more if necessary. Put on to a floured surface and roll out to about ¼ inch (0·6 cm.) thick, and line an 8-inch (20·3 cm.) flan tin with it, trimming the edges and notching them. Prick lightly over the bottom, then bake in a moderate oven, 375°F. (190°C.) or gas mark 5, for 30–35 minutes. Let it cool. Then drain the plums and arrange them over the flan case. Measure a ¼ pint (150 ml.) juice, adding a little water if necessary, cream the cornflour with a little of the juice, then bring the liquid to the boil, add the cornflour, and stir over heat until it is thickened and opaque. Cool slightly, then pour over the fruit and serve warm or cold.

Serves 4–6.

GLISTER PUDDING

The Scots are fond of steamed puddings and there are several variations on the same theme. They are usually served either with fresh *Custard*, page 221, with *Wine Sauce*, page 201, or *Honey Sauce*, page 198.

4 oz. (125 g.) sifted flour
2 eggs
4 oz. (125 g.) butter
4 oz. (125 g.) sugar
2 tablespoons marmalade

2 teaspoons lemon juice
pinch ground ginger
1 level teaspoon
bicarbonate soda

First sift the flour and then beat the eggs. Cream the butter and sugar and beat in the eggs alternately with a little flour which has been mixed with the ginger. Dissolve the bicarbonate soda in a very little water and add to the mixture with the marmalade and lemon juice. Turn into a lightly greased basin, to within 1 inch (2·5 cm.) of the top to allow for rising. Cover with grease-proof paper or foil, tie down and steam over boiling water for 2 hours.

Serves 4–6.

VARIATION: if strawberry jam is used instead of marmalade it is called Urney Pudding. Two oranges, grated rind and juice can be used instead of the jam and lemon.

GREENGAGE FRUSHIE

'Frushie' is an old Scottish word meaning brittle or crumbly and probably refers here to the texture of the pastry used in this Victorian tart. It is traditional to the West of Scotland, and many different fruits are used, apple being the most common. This tart is made with rich shortcrust pastry, see page 219, which lines an 8-inch (20·3 cm.) flan dish, the stoned fruit is arranged on top with sugar to taste, then strips of the pastry are put lattice fashion over the top. The pastry whole is brushed with milk or beaten egg and baked at 400°F. (200°C.) or gas mark 6 for 30–40 minutes. It is served warm or cold with cream. About 12 oz. (325–350 g.) fruit is required and about 2 oz. (50 g.) sugar depending on the tartness of the fruit. It is good made with gooseberries.

Serves 4–6.

HOLYROOD PUDDING

This recipe comes from D. Williamson who was caterer pastry-cook and teacher of cookery in Dundas Street, Edinburgh in the mid-nineteenth century.

1 pint (600 ml.) milk	1 oz. (25 g.) butter
2 oz. (50 g.) semolina	3 eggs, separated
3 oz. (75 g.) castor sugar	2 teaspoons marmalade
2 oz. (50 g.) ratafia biscuits, see page 237	a little butter

Bring the milk to the boil and then stir in the semolina, the ratafia biscuits and the butter. Simmer for about 5 minutes, stirring all the time, then pour into a basin and cool.

Meanwhile beat the egg whites until stiff, and lightly butter a pudding dish. Beat the egg yolks and fold in to the mixture, one at a time, then stir in the marmalade. Finally add the beaten egg whites and mix gently. Pour into the buttered basin, cover with foil or a lid, and steam for 1¼–1½ hours. Turn out on to a warm dish and serve with *Almond Sauce*, page 197.

Serves 4–6.

MARMALADE TART

Recipe from the Scottish Women's Rural Institutes.

8 oz. (225 g.) shortcrust pastry, page 218	1 tablespoon sugar
2 large eggs, beaten	1½ oz. (38 g.) butter, melted
3 tablespoons milk	2 tablespoons marmalade

First make the pastry and chill for at least half an hour before using. Then roll out on a floured surface and line an 8-inch (20·3 cm.) tart plate with it, trimming the edges and notching them. Prick the bottom lightly and brush over thinly with a little of the beaten egg.

Beat the eggs in a bowl and add all the other ingredients, mixing well. Pour into the pastry shell and bake in a hot oven, 425°F. (220°C.) or gas mark 7, for 10 minutes, then reduce the heat to 400°F. (200°C.) or gas mark 6 for a further 20 minutes or until the filling is set. Serve warm or cold.

Enough for 4–6.

VARIATION: this creamy tart is also good made with cooked blaeberries, gooseberries, etc.

MELROSE PUDDING

This is an almond-flavoured steamed pudding and is good served with *Wine Sauce*, page 201.

8 oz. (225 g.) self-raising flour	2 oz. (50 g.) ground almonds
2 eggs	¼ pint (150 ml.) milk
4 oz. (125 g.) butter or margarine	a little butter
3 oz. (75 g.) sugar	2 oz. (50 g.) halved glacé cherries

First sift the flour and then beat the eggs. Cream the butter and sugar and add the eggs alternately with a little of the flour. Then add the almonds and the milk seeing that the mixture is soft enough to drop from the spoon.

Grease a 2-lb. (900-g.) basin well, then press the cherries on to the sides and bottom firmly. Pour in the pudding mixture to within 1 inch (2·5 cm.) of the top, cover with foil or grease-proof paper and a lid, and steam for 1½–2 hours. Turn out after leaving for a minute or so when first taken from the saucepan. Serve hot.

Enough for 4–6.

ORANGE COMPOTE

Also for fresh peaches, apricots, tangerines etc. or a mixture
of fresh fruits.

6 large juicy oranges or   8 tablespoons water
  1 lb. (450 g.) fresh   6 tablespoons whisky,
  peaches, apricots, etc.   preferably malt
8 oz. (225 g.) sugar

First grate the rind of 3 oranges very finely and blanch it in
boiling water for 2 minutes, drain and reserve. (This is not done
if using stoned fruits; instead pour boiling water over the fruit
for a few minutes, then peel off the skins.) Put the sugar and
water into a heavy saucepan, bring to the boil and simmer for
about 15 minutes or until it is slightly reduced. Meanwhile
peel the oranges with a sharp knife making sure that no pith
remains, then slice thickly taking out any pips, catching the
juice in a bowl. Add the whisky to the syrup and juice, boil hard
for 5 minutes, then add the oranges (or whole, skinned fruit),
cook gently for 5 minutes (15 if the whole fruit), cool slightly
then pour into the bowl they will be served from. Garnish with
the orange peel. Leave to get quite cold and to marinate. Serve
at room temperature. Cream only spoils the good fresh flavour
of the whisky syrup and fruit.

Serves 6.

Pastry

Many different kinds of pastry are used throughout the book.
Hot Water Pastry is on page 144, *Oatmeal Pastry*, page 212.
Others mentioned throughout the book are given below.

PUFF PASTRY

6 oz. (175 g.) plain flour
pinch of salt
6 oz. (175 g.) butter, at
room temperature

1 tablespoon sugar, for
sweet dishes
3–4 tablespoons cold
water

Mix the flour in a basin with the salt, or sugar. Cut half the butter into small pieces and mix into the flour well, then add enough water to make a firm dough. Roll out on to a floured surface to about ½ inch (1·2 cm.). Add the remaining butter in little pieces on to half the dough, then fold over, pressing the edges well together. Let it stand for 10 minutes. With the sealed edges towards you, roll away from you, then fold the dough into three, and turn round again so that the open edges face you, then roll again. Repeat this twice more so that all the pastry has six turns of rolling and resting. Keep everything as cold as possible, and store in a cold place until wanted for use.

SHORTCRUST PASTRY

4 oz. (125 g.) margarine or
half margarine and lard
pinch of salt or sugar for
sweet dishes

8 oz. (225 g.) SR flour
2–3 tablespoons cold
water

Mix the fat and a pinch of salt (or sugar) into the flour and make into a stiff but elastic dough with the water. See that all ingredients are kept cold. Turn out on to a floured surface and roll into a ball if not using at once. Keep cold and let it rest in a cool place for at least half an hour before using.

RICH SHORTCRUST PASTRY

4 oz. (125 g.) butter
8 oz. (225 g.) plain flour
pinch of salt
2 teaspoons castor sugar
  (for sweet dishes)

3 tablespoons iced water
1 egg yolk

Mix the butter into the flour, salt and sugar if using. Add a
tablespoon of iced water to the egg yolk and beat lightly. Mix
this into the flour mixture and finally add the remaining iced
water, mixing it all to a stiff paste. Put on to a lightly floured
surface, roll out and rest if using at once for half an hour, or roll
into a ball and keep cold if using it at a later date.

PEACHES IN WHISKY SYRUP

See *Orange Compote*, page 217.

PRUNE FLORY

Also for plums, or a mixture of dried fruits.

1 lb. (450 g.) prunes,
  soaked for 2–3 hours
3 oz. (75 g.) sugar
2 tablespoons lemon juice
3 tablespoons port or red
  wine

8 oz. (225 g.) puff pastry,
  see page 218
1 teaspoon cornflour

Soak the prunes in cold water to cover, then cook them in the
same water until soft, about 20 minutes. Drain, but reserve
juice, cut in half and take out the stones, then crack some of the
stones and take out the kernels. Mix together the sugar, lemon

juice, port and about 4 tablespoons of the prune juice in a sauce pan, cream the cornflour with a tablespoon of the cold prune juice, add to the liquid, bring to the boil and stir until it thickens, then add the prunes. Leave to cool.

Cut the pastry in half, and line a tart plate with half of it, add the prune mixture, dampen the edges and lay the other half, rolled to fit on top, pressing down the edges well. Brush with a little milk, make a slit in the top, then bake in a hot oven, 450°F. (230°C.) or gas mark 8, for 15 minutes, then lower to 400°F. (200°C.) or gas mark 7 for a further 15 minutes. Serve warm or cold.

Enough for 4–6.

RHUBARB OATMEAL CRUMBLE

Other fruits such as apple, apple and blackberry, or goose-berries can also be used. The oatmeal crumble makes a nutty and crisp topping.

1 lb. (450 g.) rhubarb or other fruit

2 oz. (50 g.) sugar, or use 2 tablespoons redcurrant jelly

3–4 tablespoons water

a squeeze of lemon

For the crumble

2 oz. (50 g.) flour

1 oz. (25 g.) coarse oatmeal

2 oz. (50 g.) brown sugar

2 oz. (50 g.) butter or margarine

Cook the fruit with the sugar or jelly, water and lemon juice until soft, but not mushy, then put into a deep pie-dish. Mix up the crumble ingredients in the order given, seeing that the butter or margarine is soft but not oily. When well mixed sprinkle evenly over the fruit and bake at 400°F. (200°C.) or gas mark 6 high up in the oven for 20 minutes or until the top is crunchy and slightly brown.

Serves 4.

SAINT FILLAN'S PASTE

Recipe from the Scottish Women's Rural Institutes.

4 oz. (125 g.) flour
2 oz. (50 g.) castor sugar
½ teaspoon baking soda
    and ½ teaspoon cream of
    tartar
pinch of salt
1½ oz. (38 g.) butter or
    margarine

2 eggs
2 tablespoons milk,
    approx.
1 lb. (450 g.) stewed
    fruit, i.e. apples,
    rhubarb, gooseberries,
    prunes, figs, etc. with
    juice

Mix the dry ingredients together, then rub in the butter, make a well in the centre and add the eggs, unbeaten but mix well. Mix to a thick batter with the milk.

Put the stewed fruit and juice to cover in the bottom of an oven-proof dish, then drop the batter on top in spoonfuls. Bake at 375°F. (190°C.) or gas mark 5 for about half an hour, or until the paste is risen, golden and cooked through. Serve warm or cold.

Enough for 4–6.

SCOTS TRIFLE

For the custard
1 pint (600 ml.) milk
1 oz. (25 g.) castor sugar
4 egg yolks
2 egg whites
6 sponge cakes
2–3 tablespoons strawberry
    or raspberry jam
6 small macaroons and 6
    small ratafia biscuits,
    see page 237

¼ pint (150 ml.) sherry
2–3 tablespoons whisky or
    brandy
½ pint (300 ml.) double
    cream
ratafias, nuts and sliced
    angelica to garnish

First make the custard by putting the milk and sugar into a saucepan (or double boiler) and bringing to the boil. Beat the egg yolks and whites together and pour the hot milk over them, stirring very well. Return to the saucepan and stir with a wooden spoon over a gentle heat until it runs in ribbons down the back of the wooden spoon. Strain into a basin and cover the top with dampened greaseproof paper right down to the custard, to prevent a skin forming.

Take a large dessert bowl, then split the sponge cakes and spread them thickly with jam and cut into cubes. Put into the serving bowl, putting the crumbled macaroons and whole, small ratafias between each layer. Pour the sherry and whisky or brandy over, seeing that there is enough to make the sponge cakes moist. Leave to absorb the liquid. Pour the custard evenly over the top. Then whip the cream until stiff, sweeten a little if liked but do not make it too sweet, then spread over the trifle evenly. Garnish with slivered almonds, some more small ratafia biscuits and sliced angelica. Keep in a cold place until wanted.

Serves 6.

SYLLABUB

¼ pint (150 ml.) medium white wine	1 tablespoon lemon juice and grated rind of ½ lemon
¼ pint (150 ml.) red fruit juice or thin purée	2 level tablespoons castor sugar
sprig of rosemary	½ pint (300 ml.) double cream
pinch of nutmeg	

Mix together the wine, fruit juice, rosemary, nutmeg lemon juice and rind with the sugar. Cover and let it stand for some hours, if possible overnight. Then strain and half-fill 4 or 6 tall glasses with the liquid. Whip the cream until stiff and fill up each glass with it. Serve cold.

ATHOLL BROSE SYLLABUB

Put 4 tablespoons Atholl Brose liquid (see page 268) into 4 tall glasses and fill up with whipped, sweetened cream (about $\frac{3}{4}$ pint (450 ml.)). Sprinkle the tops with lightly toasted oatmeal mixed with a pinch of ground nutmeg. About 4 tablespoons oatmeal is enough. Serve cold.

Enough for 4.

WINE JELLY
See *Drambuie Cream* page 207.

BAKING

(Bannocks, Breads, Scones, Biscuits and Cakes)

Scotland has been renowned for its baking for many centuries: the two main meals, breakfast and tea, being remarkable for the amount and variety of homemade breads, scones of many kinds and rolls served, as well as porridge, trout, Finnan Haddie, Ayrshire bacon, eggs, venison and other pastries, smoked mutton ham, honey, marmalade, etc. The following description from Tobias Smollett's *Humphry Clinker* describes a breakfast graphically: 'One kit of boiled eggs; a second, full of butter; a third, full pot, full of honey; the best part of a ham; a cold venison pasty; a bushel of oatmeal, made into thin cakes and bannocks; with a wheaten loaf in the middle . . .'

Tea appears to have been introduced into Scotland by Mary of Modena, wife of James VII and II, and with the introduction of afternoon tea came the cakes, biscuits and tea-breads. Henry Mackenzie wrote in the early nineteenth century: '. . . tea was the meal of ceremony and we had fifty-odd kinds of teabread.'

F. Marian McNeill, the superb historian and writer about Scottish food (*A Scots Kitchen*, among other books), made the brilliant remark: 'If every Frenchwoman is born with a wooden spoon in her hand, every Scotwoman is born with a rolling-pin under her arm.'

T. F. Henderson in his book *Old World Scotland* (1893) wrote: 'To beat the Edinburgh baker, you must go – not to London but – to Paris or Vienna.'

The first tea-shop as we know it was opened in Glasgow by Miss Cranston (later Mrs Cochrane) in 1884 in rented rooms at Aitkin's Hotel, Argyle Street. Her tea-shop was so successful that she then acquired not only the whole building but also other premises in Buchanan Street, Ingram Street and Sauchiehall Street. The fame of some Scottish cakes such as Shortbread and Dundee Cake has spread all over the English-speaking world.

Bannocks

The word 'bannock' covers several different kinds of foods: generally it refers to griddle or girdle cakes made with oatmeal, barley meal, pease-meal or with flour, but there is the *Selkirk Bannock*, page 250, and the *Pitcaithly Bannock*, page 249, which are sweetened tea-breads or cakes. From the earliest years special kinds of bannocks were made for every Highland quarter day: on 1 February, the Bonnach Bride (St Bride's bannock) was cooked to celebrate the first day of Spring; the Bonnach Bealtain (Beltane bannock) for the first day of summer, Bonnach Lunastain (Lammas bannock) for the first day of autumn and the Bonnach Samhtain (Hallowmas bannock) for the first day of winter. Bannocks were baked for a child's birth (Cryin' Bannock) and there was a Teethin' Bannock baked with a ring in it which was later used as a teething ring, and when the bannock broke each person present got a small piece of it. There were special bannocks fired for St Columba's Eve, for marriage and for Christmas. Each one was a variety of oatcake (page 187) some made with eggs, butter, cream and sugar. Today many of these customs have died out but the bannock remains in several forms. If using a griddle then it must be warmed up before starting to cook.

FIFE BANNOCKS

Recipe from the Scottish Women's Rural Institutes.

6 oz. (175 g.) plain flour
4 oz. (125 g.) oatmeal
½ teaspoon bicarbonate
  soda
½ teaspoon cream of tartar

pinch of salt and sugar
1 rounded teaspoon lard,
  butter or margarine
¼ pint (150 ml.) approx.
  sour milk or buttermilk

Sieve the flour and mix all the dry ingredients together, then rub in the fat and add enough sour milk or buttermilk to make a soft dough. Turn out on to a lightly floured surface, knead lightly and roll out to a circle. Cut in four, then put on to a hot griddle which has been rubbed over lightly with a piece of fat, or use a thick-bottomed frying-pan and cook on both sides until golden brown. Or bake in a hot oven, 400°F. (200°C.) or gas mark 6, near the top, for about 15–20 minutes.

SEE ALSO: *Pitcaithly Bannock*, page 249, *Selkirk Bannock*, page 250, and *Scones*, page 231.

BARLEY BANNOCKS

Also called Bere bannocks – a traditional song has the lines

'Here's to the Hielandman's
Bannock o' barley!'

The former early method of making barley bannocks was with milk, barley-meal, salt and butter, or in Sutherland, whey was used without the butter. The modern method contains a little flour which makes them easier to handle.

½ lb. (225 g.) barley-meal
2 oz. (50 g.) plain flour
½ teaspoon salt
1 level teaspoon cream of
  tartar

1 level teaspoon
  bicarbonate soda
½ pint (300 ml.) buttermilk
  or sour milk

First heat up the griddle or heavy pan, so that it is hot when needed. Mix together in a basin the barley-meal, flour, salt and cream of tartar. Pour the buttermilk over the bicarbonate of soda and stir well. When it fizzes up pour into the centre of the barley mixture and work it into a soft dough, adding a little more buttermilk if needed. Dredge it with flour, then turn out on to a lightly floured surface, handling as little as possible, roll out to about half an inch (1·2 cm.) thickness and cut into circles the size of a dinner plate.

Lightly rub the griddle or pan over with a lump of fat, then put the bannock on and cook, not too quickly, until it is brown underneath. Then turn and brown the other side. Makes about 2 large bannocks.

BAPS

These are yeasted rolls eaten all over Scotland for breakfast. They are best hot from the oven.

1 lb. (450 g.) sifted flour	1 teaspoon sugar
1 teaspoon salt	$\frac{1}{2}$ pint (300 ml.) half milk
2 oz. (50 g.) lard	and half water, tepid
1 oz. (25 g.) fresh yeast or	a little milk for glazing
$\frac{1}{2}$ oz. (12 g.) dried	

Mix the flour and salt in a warm bowl, then rub in the lard. In another basin cream the yeast with the sugar by mixing well with a wooden spoon, then add the tepid milk and water mixed. Give it about 10 minutes to work well, then make a well in the centre of the flour mixture and pour it into it. Make it into a soft dough, cover and leave to rise in a warm place for about 1 hour.

Turn out on to a lightly floured surface, knead lightly, then shape into ovals about 3 inches (7·6 cm.) across and put on to a baking sheet which has been greased and floured. Brush with warm milk to give a glaze, or if floury-looking baps are liked, dust with a little flour just before they go in the oven. Leave to rise for about 15 minutes, then press a finger into the middle of each bap to prevent them blistering. Bake in a hot oven, 400°F. (200°C.) or gas mark 6, for 15–20 minutes. Makes about 10 baps.

BROWN BREAD

This is a very good recipe for wholemeal bread which has been tested and tried for many years. The quantities given below make 2 large loaves, approx. 2 lb. (1 kg.) each.

1 heaped tablespoon lard, butter or margarine

3 lb. (1·4 kg.) flour, warmed

1 oz. (25 g.) dried yeast

1 heaped teaspoon brown sugar

¼ pint (150 ml.) tepid water

1 tablespoon black treacle

a pinch salt

1 pint (600 ml.) warm water

Rub the fat into the warmed flour, then dissolve the yeast and sugar in the quarter pint (150 ml.) warm water, and stir until it begins to froth up. Dissolve the treacle and salt in the pint of warm water, then add the yeast mixture to the flour and then add the treacle and water, mixing well. Add a very little more water if the dough seems too stiff, but do not make it sloppy. Knead for about 5 minutes, then divide the dough in two and put into two greased and warmed pans (about 10″ × 4″, 25·4 cm. × 10 cm.). Cut a deep groove down the middle of the dough and put in a warm place covered with a cloth for about 1 hour or until the dough has almost doubled in size.

Pre-heat the oven to 425°F. (220°C.) or gas mark 7 and put the loaves in and 10 minutes later reduce the heat to 400°F. (200°C.) or gas mark 6 for a further 40 minutes. If a glaze is liked then brush over with warm milk at this stage and put back in the oven for another 10 minutes. Turn out on to a wire rack and cool. The loaves will sound hollow when tapped on the bottom, when they are cooked.

VARIATION: use 4 oz. (125 g.) oatmeal in place of the same amount of flour. All white flour can also be used, or a mixture of white flour and the oatmeal.

BUTTERMILK BREAD

8 oz. (225 g.) white flour	or use all white, strong, unbleached flour
8 oz. (225 g.) wholemeal flour	
1 teaspoon bicarbonate soda	1 pint (600 ml.) scant, buttermilk
3 teaspoons baking powder	1 egg, beaten with the
2 teaspoons salt	buttermilk

Sift all dry ingredients together, then beat in the buttermilk mixed with the beaten egg. Turn out on to a floured surface and knead for a few minutes only, until it is smooth. Then either put into a greased and floured 2 lb. (900 g.) loaf tin, or shape into two round cakes which should be flattened by hand. Make a deep incision on top to allow it to rise evenly and bake in a pre-heated oven, 375°F. (190°C.) or gas mark 5, for 35–40 minutes. Take out and brush the top lightly with milk and put back for a further 10 minutes.

The mixture can be shaped into small scones if preferred and cooking time will then be 15–20 minutes.

VARIATION: add 3 tablespoons raisins or sultanas to the dry ingredients.

ABERDEEN CRULLAS

Traditional Aberdeen small, plaited fried cakes. The name is thought to have come from the Gaelic *kril*, a small cake or bannock.

4 oz. (125 g.) butter or
  margarine
4 oz. (125 g.) sugar
4 eggs
1 lb. (450 g.) flour
1 teaspoon bicarbonate
  soda

½ teaspoon cream of tartar
pinch of nutmeg or ginger
½ teaspoon salt
¼ pint (150 ml.) approx.
  buttermilk or sour milk
deep oil for frying
castor sugar for garnish

Cream the butter and sugar, then add the beaten eggs, flour, soda, ginger or nutmeg, cream of tartar and salt. The dry ingredients should be well mixed before adding. Pour in the buttermilk, slowly, mixing well, so that the dough is firm. You might need slightly more or less buttermilk according to the size of the eggs. Put out on a floured surface and roll into long strips. Cut into 1 inch (2·5 cm.) ribbons leaving the top joined. Then plait the strips, damping the ends so they stick.

Have the oil very hot, but not smoking (365°F., 185°C.) and fry until they are golden brown. Drain on kitchen paper and sprinkle with castor sugar. Makes about 24 crullas.

BUTTERY ROWIES

These are traditional Aberdeen yeasted butter rolls. They are also called Aberdeen Butteries.

See that all ingredients and utensils are at room temperature before starting to cook.

1 lb. (450 g.) sifted flour
½ teaspoon salt
1 oz. (25 g.) yeast or ½ oz.
  (12 g.) dried yeast

¾ pint (450 ml.) tepid
  water
8 oz. (225 g.) butter
4 oz. (125 g.) lard

Mix the sifted flour and salt in a mixing bowl, then cream the yeast with the sugar in a smaller bowl. When it has bubbled up add the water which should be at blood heat. Add to the flour, mix very well, cover and set to rise in a warm place for about half an hour or until almost doubled in bulk. Cream the butter and lard, then divide into three.

Turn the dough out on to a floured surface and roll out into a long strip. Put the first third of the fats in dots on the top third of the pastry and fold over like an envelope, as if making puff or flaky pastry. Then let it rest for 30 minutes. Roll out, and do this twice more until all the fats are used up and well amalgamated. Then roll out and cut into small ovals or rounds and put on to a floured baking sheet with about 2 inches (5 cm.) between each one to allow for spreading. Cover and leave to rise for almost an hour. Then take off the cover and bake in a moderate to hot oven, 375°F. (190°C.) or gas mark 5 – 400°F. (200°C.) or gas mark 6, for 20–25 minutes. Makes about 15.

Scones

The Scots are famous for the variety of scones (from the Gaelic, *sgoon*, and it should rhyme with 'gone'): some of the most popular ones are given below. Some scones are cooked on a griddle, but can also be cooked in the oven.

SODA SCONES

8 oz. (225 g.) flour
½ teaspoon bicarbonate soda
¼ teaspoon cream of tartar

pinch of salt
¼ pint (150 ml.) approx. buttermilk or clotted sour milk

If using a griddle put it on to heat just before you start to make the scones. For the oven, pre-heat to 425°F. (220°C.) or gas mark 7.

Sift the dry ingredients in a basin and mix to a soft dough with the milk, adding a little more if it is too dry. Put on to a lightly floured surface and roll out to half an inch (1·2 cm.) thickness. Cut into rounds or large bannocks using a dinner plate, and cut into four farls if preferred. Cook for 10 minutes on a fairly hot griddle which has been lightly floured, turning over after 5 minutes and reducing the heat slightly.

If using the oven, then put on to a lightly floured baking sheet and bake in the pre-heated oven for 10–15 minutes. Eat hot, split in half and buttered. Jam or honey can also be served with them.

VARIATION: use half brown wholemeal flour or half barley-meal and cook as above.

WHOLEMEAL SCONES

This is a different recipe from the Scottish Women's Rural Institutes.

6 oz. (175 g.) wholemeal flour	2 oz. (50 g.) butter or margarine
6 oz. (175 g.) white flour	2 teaspoons syrup, warmed
2 teaspoons baking powder	¼ pint (150 ml.) approx. milk
pinch of salt	

Mix the flours, salt and baking powder in a mixing bowl, then rub in the fat until it is like coarse breadcrumbs. Stir in the slightly melted syrup and then the milk to make a soft dough, adding a little more if needed. Turn out on to a floured surface and roll out quite thinly. Cut into rounds with a cutter about 1½ inches (3·8 cm.) in diameter. Put on to a floured baking sheet and cook in a moderate to hot oven, 375°F. (190°C.) or gas mark 5, for 10–15 minutes. Serve hot, spread with butter.

RICH WHITE SCONES

½ lb. (225 g.) flour
1 teaspoon baking
  powder
pinch of salt

1 oz. (25 g.) butter or
  margarine
¼ pint (150 ml.) sour cream
1 beaten egg

Sift the dry ingredients, then rub in the butter. Make a well in the centre and pour in the cream and the beaten egg. Mix to a soft dough and turn out on to a floured surface. Roll out, or pat to a half an inch (1·2 cm.) thickness, prick over with a fork, cut into rounds or shape into large cake and either cook on the heated griddle on both sides or in a hot oven, 400°F. (200°C.) or gas mark 6, for 10–15 minutes. Serve warm.

TREACLE SCONES

1½ oz. (38 g.) butter or
  margarine
½ lb. (225 g.) white flour
½ teaspoon each:
  bicarbonate of soda and
  cream of tartar
pinch of salt

½ teaspoon each: ground
  cinnamon and ginger
1 teaspoon sugar
1 tablespoon treacle
  (molasses)
¼ pint (150 ml.) approx.
  buttermilk

Rub the butter into the flour, then add all the other dry ingredients and mix thoroughly. Heat the treacle and mix with a spoonful or so of the buttermilk, then add this gradually to the flour mixture, adding enough to make a stiff dough. Knead very lightly, then roll out on a floured surface to ¾ inch (1·9 cm.) thick, shape into a round and cut into 8 triangular slices. Put on to a greased baking sheet and bake at 400°F. (200°C.) or gas mark 6 for 10–15 minutes. Serve warm with butter etc.

POTATO SCONES

See *Potato Scones*, page 179.

BALLATER SCONES

Recipe of Mrs. Macnab, Aberdeenshire, *c.* 1880s.

½ lb. (225 g.) flour
½ teaspoon salt
½ teaspoon bicarbonate of soda

1 teaspoon cream of tartar
1 oz. (25 g.) butter
¼ pint (150 ml.) approx. buttermilk

Mix the dry ingredients, then rub in the butter and mix to a soft dough with the buttermilk. Put on to a floured surface and flatten with the hand, do not roll. Shape into a round, then cut into farls (quarters) and prick all over lightly with a fork. Cook in quick oven 425°F. (220°C.) or gas mark 7 for 10–15 minutes. Serve warm with butter, jam, etc.

DROP SCONES

These are traditional griddle scones, looking more like a pancake than the conventional scone. Some recipes use baking powder, but this recipe from Miss Kitty Forbes is excellent.

1 lb. (450 g.) self-raising flour
3 oz. (75 g.) sugar
½ teaspoon salt
2 tablespoons golden syrup (this gives the scones a smooth surface)

½ pint (300 ml.) approx. milk or buttermilk
2 eggs, beaten

Put the dry ingredients and the warmed syrup into a mixing

bowl. Beat the milk with the eggs, then add to the mixture and beat until it is of dropping consistency like a thick cream. Heat up the griddle or a heavy pan and grease it very lightly. Drop by tablespoons in rounds, seeing that.they are spaced apart and have even edges like a pancake. (If you are not used to making them, then cook them singly to begin with.) Turn over when little bubbles appear on top and the bottom is golden brown, then cook the other side.

Cool in a clean tea-towel keeping them wrapped, unless they are to be eaten hot from the pan. Serve warm with butter, honey, jam, etc. They will keep for some time in an airtight tin and can be heated up in a warm oven or under a slow grill. Makes about 24 scones.

Biscuits

ABERNETHY BISCUITS

Abernethy biscuits are named after Dr John Abernethy (1764–1831) who was chief surgeon at Bart's Hospital, London. He suggested to a nearby baker that he add sugar and caraway to a plain biscuit and the baker gave the new biscuit the patron's name.

½ lb. (225 g.) sifted flour
1 level teaspoon baking
  powder
3 oz. (75 g.) butter or
  margarine

3 oz. (75 g.) castor sugar
1 teaspoon caraway seeds
1 beaten egg and approx.
  1 tablespoon milk

Mix the flour and baking powder in a mixing bowl, then rub in the fat until it is like coarse breadcrumbs. Add the sugar, caraway seeds, mixing well, then gradually add the beaten egg and milk until it makes a stiff dough. Put out on a floured surface and roll out thinly, then cut into rounds about 3 inches (7·6 cm.) across. Put on to a lightly greased baking sheet leaving enough room for expansion, then prick the centres with a fork and cook at 375°F. (190°C.) or gas mark 5 for 10–15 minutes. Cool on a rack before storing.

FLY CAKES OR BISCUITS

Children are fond of these biscuit-like cakes and often call them 'squashed fly biscuits'. There are several recipes, some richer than others.

½ lb. (225 g.) flour
1 oz. (25 g.) sugar
pinch of salt
4 oz. (125 g.) butter
1 tablespoon grated lemon rind
3–4 tablespoons ice water

For the filling
5 oz. (150 g.) currants
4 tablespoons redcurrant jelly
2 tablespoons melted butter
sugar

Mix the flour, the sugar and the salt in a mixing bowl, then rub in the butter thoroughly. Add the finely grated lemon rind and enough iced water to make a soft but dry dough. Knead the dough to distribute the fat evenly, then roll into a ball and chill for 1 hour.

Meanwhile mix the currants with the redcurrant jelly and reserve, then heat the butter. Cut the pastry into two, and roll out the two pieces in a rectangular shape on a floured surface to ¼ inch (0·6 cm.) thick. Brush one half of the dough over with the melted butter, lightly, then cover with the currant mixture seeing that a space is left all around the edges. Dampen the edges, then lay the other piece of pastry on top, pressing down the edges well and then cutting into 2 × 1 inch (5 × 2·5 cm.) pieces or into 2 inch (5 cm.) squares. Brush with the remaining melted butter lightly and sprinkle lightly with sugar. Transfer to a greased baking sheet and bake them in a pre-heated oven at 450°F. (230°C.) or gas mark 7 for about 10–15 minutes or until they are golden brown. Cool on a rack. Makes about 30 small cakes.

VARIATION: for special occasions soak the currants in 2–3 tablespoons of whisky overnight.

OATMEAL BISCUITS

3 oz. (75 g.) sugar
4 oz. (125 g.) butter or margarine
½ teaspoon baking powder
4 oz. (125 g.) porridge oatmeal
3 oz. (75 g.) flour
1 beaten egg

Cream the sugar and butter, then add the dry ingredients, and finally mix in the well-beaten egg, mixing thoroughly. Grease a baking sheet and drop spoonfuls on to it spacing them apart to allow for spreading. Bake in a moderate oven, 350°F. (180°C.) or gas mark 4, for about 15 minutes.

RATAFIA BISCUITS

Recipe from Lady Forbes, *c.* 1900.

These little biscuits are used a lot in Scottish cookery, particularly in trifles, see page 221. Ratafia is an old flavouring for cakes and biscuits. It is made from bitter almonds or from the kernels of peaches or apricots.

2 stiffly beaten egg whites
6 oz. (175 g.) castor sugar
1 oz. (25 g.) butter
1 tablespoon flour
4 oz. (125 g.) ground almonds
4 drops of ratafia essence
rice paper

Beat the egg whites until stiff, then cream the butter and sugar, add the flour and the ground almonds and mix well. Then fold into the egg whites and beat to a smooth paste. When it begins to get stiff put into an icing bag with a plain pipe, and pipe drops (about ½ inch 1·2 cm.) on to the rice paper about 2 inches (5 cm.) apart. Bake at 350°F. (180°C.) or gas mark 4 for about 15–20 minutes. Makes about 24–30 ratafias.

Cakes

BLACK BUN

Black Bun is a traditional Scottish cake formerly eaten on Twelfth Night, but nowadays at Hogmanay. Like Christmas cake it is rich with fruit and should be made several weeks before it is wanted so that it can mature. See also *Het Pint*, page 269, and *Haggis*, page 140.

For the casing
12 oz. (350 g.) flour
1 level teaspoon baking powder
6 oz. (175 g.) butter or margarine
approx. 4–5 tablespoons water
1 beaten egg for glazing

For the filling
1 lb. (450 g.) raisins
1½ lb. (700 g.) currants
4 oz. (125 g.) chopped, blanched almonds

6 oz. (175 g.) flour
4 oz. (125 g.) brown sugar
1 teaspoon ground allspice
½ teaspoon ground ginger
1 teaspoon ground cinnamon
¼ teaspoon black pepper
½ teaspoon each: baking powder and cream of tartar
1 tablespoon whisky, brandy or rum
2–3 tablespoons milk

First make the casing by sifting the flour with the baking powder, then rub the butter into it well, and mix to a stiff paste with the water. Roll out to a thin sheet, and line a 9-inch (22·8-cm.) tin with two-thirds of it, keeping back enough for the lid.

To make the filling, mix all the ingredients together except the milk. Then add just enough to moisten the mixture. Put into the lined tin, dampen the edge and lay the pastry lid on top and pressing down the edges. Prick all over with a fork and with a small skewer make 4 holes right down to the bottom. Brush with beaten egg and bake at 300°F. (150°C.) or gas mark 2 for about 3 hours. When cool it will keep for a year in an airtight tin.

BRIDES CAKE

From the Scottish Women's Rural Institutes.

12 oz. (350 g.) flour
6 oz. (175 g.) sugar
1 lb. (450 g.) currants
1 level teaspoon baking powder
2 tablespoons syrup, warmed
3 eggs
2 tablespoons milk

For the icing
4 oz. (125 g.) ground almonds
3 oz. (75 g.) castor sugar
2–3 drops vanilla essence
squeeze of lemon juice
1 beaten egg

Mix all the dry cake ingredients together, then add the eggs, syrup and milk and beat thoroughly. Pour into a greased and lined tin and cook in a slow oven, 300°F. (150°C.) or gas mark 2, for about 3 hours. Cool in the tin, then on a wire rack.

To do the icing turn the cake upside down and brush over with either some warmed apricot jam or a little beaten egg. Mix all the icing ingredients together until smooth, then roll out and put over the cake. It can be iced with sugar icing later (after about 5 days when the paste is dry) if liked.

To ice, use 4 egg whites beaten lightly with a fork, then add sifted icing sugar gradually, about 2 lb. (900 g.), then add the juice of 1 lemon and about 2 teaspoons glycerine which prevents it becoming too hard. Beat until there are no tiny air bubbles, then spread over the cake, the top first and then the sides.

BROONIE

Broonie comes from the Norse word *Bruni* meaning a thick bannock. It is traditional to Orkney and is like an oatmeal gingerbread.

6 oz. (175 g.) each: medium oatmeal and white flour
2 heaped tablespoons butter
4 oz. (125 g.) sugar
pinch of salt
1 heaped teaspoon ground ginger

1 level teaspoon baking powder
2 tablespoons black treacle, warmed
1 beaten egg
½ pint (300 ml.) approx. buttermilk

Mix the oatmeal and flour together in a mixing bowl, then rub in the butter, and add the sugar, salt, ginger and baking powder, mixing very well. Heat the treacle a little, then add to the beaten egg and half the buttermilk. Stir this into the oatmeal mixture, adding the remaining buttermilk gradually until the mixture is soft enough to drop from a spoon. You may need more or less buttermilk according to the size of the egg.

Well grease a tin 8 inches (20·3 cm.) by 4 inches (10 cm.) wide, pour the mixture in and bake in a moderate oven, 350°F. (180°C.) or gas mark 4, for about 1–1½ hours or until it is risen and cooked in the centre if a thin skewer is put in. Leave to cool for about 20 minutes before taking from the tin and cooling on a rack. It is better to leave it for a day before cutting to make it set.

VARIATION: the mixture can be put on to a greased baking sheet in small balls with an almond pressed into each. Do not put them too close to allow for spreading and the cooking time is about 20 minutes.

CADDISTON CAKE

This is a traditional fruit cake which keeps well in an airtight tin.

7 oz. (200 g.) butter
8 oz. (225 g.) castor sugar
5 eggs
¼ pint (150 ml.) milk or half milk and half whisky
pinch of salt
6 tablespoons golden syrup

1 lb. (450 g.) plain flour
1 teaspoon baking powder
8 oz. (225 g.) each:
- raisins or sultanas and currants
4 oz. (125 g.) chopped mixed peel

Cream the butter and sugar very thoroughly, then add the beaten eggs gradually. Mix the sifted flour with the baking powder and salt and heat up the syrup and milk together until warm but not hot. Add the syrup to the creamed butter mixture with a little of the flour, then add the remaining flour, the dried fruit and peel. Mix very well and put the mixture into an 8-inch (20·3-cm.) cake tin which has been greased and lined. Cook in a moderate oven, 325°F. (170°C.) or gas mark 3, for about 3 hours, covering with greaseproof paper if the top is getting too brown. Test with a thin skewer in the centre before taking from the oven. Leave to cool a little in the tin and then on a wire rack.

DIET LOAF

This is not a loaf at all but a very light Scottish traditional sponge.

½ lb. (225 g.) butter
1 lb. (450 g.) castor sugar
6 eggs
grated rind of 1 lemon

½ teaspoon ground cinnamon
12 oz. (350 g.) sifted flour
icing sugar for garnish

Cream the butter and sugar, beat the eggs very well, then add them to the butter mixture and beat for about 15 minutes. (Today, this can be done in a blender.) Add the lemon peel and cinnamon, then gradually stir in the flour, beating well after each addition, until it is very smooth.

Line a tin with greaseproof paper, buttered and pour in the mixture. Bake in a pre-heated oven at 400°F. (200°C.) or gas mark 6 for about 30–35 minutes or until it is risen and golden brown. Five minutes before it is cooked sprinkle with icing sugar and put back to finish cooking. It will curl slightly from the edges when it is done. Leave for a few minutes before taking from the tin and cooling on a rack.

DROP SCONES

See page 234.

DUNDEE CAKE

This is a traditional cake which can be kept and served for Christmas and other special occasions.

6 oz. (175 g.) butter
6 oz. (175 g.) sugar
4 eggs
8 oz. (225 g.) flour
1 level teaspoon baking powder
1 oz. (25 g.) ground almonds
6 oz. (175 g.) each: sultanas, currants and raisins
3 oz. (75 g.) chopped mixed peel

grated rind and juice of $\frac{1}{2}$ lemon
pinch of salt
2 tablespoons whisky, brandy or rum
1 oz. (25 g.) blanched, split almonds
2 tablespoons milk boiled with 1 tablespoon sugar for glaze

Cream the butter well, then work in the sugar and when white and creamy add the eggs, one at a time with a little flour, beating well after each addition. Stir in the ground almonds, the dried fruits, rind and juice of the lemon and the salt. Add the remaining flour, sifted with the baking powder and then the whisky or other spirit. If it seems very stiff add about a tablespoon of milk. Turn into an 8-inch (20·3 cm.) greased and lined cake tin, cover with foil or buttered greaseproof paper and bake at 325°F. (170°C.) or gas mark 3 for 2 hours. Half way through cooking time take off the foil and arrange the split almonds over the top, then continue cooking for half an hour. Test with a skewer before taking from the oven, but 5 minutes before it is cooked brush the top with the sweetened milk and put back for 5 minutes to dry and glaze. Leave in the tin to cool.

GINGERBREAD

2 oz. (50 g.) butter or margarine
2 tablespoons black treacle
2 oz. (50 g.) brown sugar
6 oz. (175 g.) flour
1 level teaspoon bicarbonate of soda

pinch of salt
2–3 tablespoons milk
1 egg, beaten
1½ oz. (40 g.) sultanas
¼ teaspoon ground ginger
½ oz. (15 g.) candied peel, chopped
1½ oz. (40 g.) preserved ginger, chopped

Melt the butter slowly in the treacle and the sugar. Mix the flour, ginger, bicarbonate of soda and salt well together. Add a little milk to the mixture of butter, treacle and sugar, stir well and pour it slowly into the middle of the flour mixture, stirring thoroughly. When it has amalgamated, beat it well with the spoon, adding a little more milk if the mixture is too stiff and pour into a shallow 8 inch (20·3 cm.) greased and lined tin. Bake at 350°F. (180°C.) or gas mark 4 for 1 hour. Turn out on to a damp cloth and cut into squares.

INVERNESS GINGERBREAD

12 oz. (340 g.) plain flour
1 teaspoon bicarbonate of
  soda
4 oz. (115 g.) fine oatmeal
8 oz. (225 g.) butter or
  margarine
4 tablespoons top of
  milk

12 oz. (340 g.) black
  treacle
4 oz. (115 g.) candied
  lemon peel
1 oz. (25 g.) finely
  shredded green ginger

Mix together the flour, bicarbonate of soda and the oatmeal. Cream the butter or margarine and beat in the flour mixture alternately with the milk. Stir in the warmed treacle, then add the finely chopped peel and ginger. Beat into a light dough, turn out on to a well-greased tin 9 inches square (22·8 cm.) and bake at 350°F. (180°C.) or gas mark 4 for about ¾–1 hour, or until firm to the touch. Leave in the tin to cool.

SEE ALSO: *Broonie*, page 240.

GINGER SHORTBREAD, ICED

4 oz. (125 g.) butter or
  margarine
2 oz. (50 g.) castor sugar
10 oz. (275 g.) plain flour
1 level teaspoon ginger,
  ground
1 teaspoon baking powder

2 oz. (50 g.) butter or
  margarine
2 tablespoons golden
  syrup
¾ teaspoon ginger,
  ground
1 oz. (25 g.) crystallized
  ginger (optional)

For the icing:
4 tablespoons icing sugar

Cream the butter or margarine with the sugar and mix in the flour, ginger and baking powder. Put into a greased 7-inch

(18-cm.) tin and bake at 325°F. (170°C.) or gas mark 3 for 40
minutes or until testing with a skewer shows it to be done. In a
small saucepan, over a low light, melt together the ingredients
for the icing except for the preserved ginger. When they are
completely blended together, pour over the still hot shortbread
and when it has cooled a little decorate the top with pieces of
crystallized ginger cut into shapes. Cool completely before removing from the tin.

HONEY CAKE

4 oz. (125 g.) self-raising
flour
4 oz. (125 g.) castor sugar
4 oz. (125 g.) butter or
margarine

4 oz. (125 g.) ground
almonds
5 fl. oz. (150 ml.) clear
honey
2 eggs, well beaten

Mix together the flour and half the ground almonds. Cream the
butter or margarine and sugar together and gradually add, in
small alternating amounts, the well-beaten eggs and the flour.
Beat the mixture thoroughly and pour into 2 × 7-inch (17·8-
cm.) sandwich tins, well greased. Bake at 350°F. (180°C.) or
gas mark 4 until firm and well risen, do not allow to become too
dark on top. Blend the honey and the remaining ground almonds
together and when the cakes are completely cold, spread the top
of one with the mixture and place the other on top.

MELTING MOMENTS

6 oz. (175 g.) butter or
margarine
3 oz. (75 g.) castor sugar
1 heaped teaspoon zest of
lemon

2 eggs, well beaten
8 oz. (225 g.) cornflour
1 teaspoon baking powder

Cream the butter or margarine and the sugar, adding the zest of lemon. Add the eggs in small amounts alternately with the corn-flour, into the last spoonful of which has been mixed the baking powder. Put a teaspoonful of the mixture into a greased patty-tin (you should need 2 dozen) and bake at 350°F. (180°C.) or gas mark 4 for 10–12 minutes but do not let the tops go beyond the golden stage.

MONTROSE CAKES

4 oz. (125 g.) flour
3 oz. (75 g.) currants
3 eggs, well beaten
4 oz. (125 g.) butter or margarine

4 oz. (125 g.) castor sugar
pinch of grated nutmeg
2 teaspoons brandy
1 teaspoon rose water

Sift the flour and wash, strain and dry the currants, then beat the eggs. Cream the butter or margarine and the sugar and gradually mix in the beaten eggs, flour and nutmeg, finally adding the brandy and the rose water. Beat the mixture thoroughly and half fill well-greased patty-tins. Bake for ¼ hour at 400°F. (200°C.) or gas mark 6, but do not let the tops become too brown.

PAISLEY ALMOND CAKES

2 oz. (50 g.) cornflour
2 oz. (50 g.) rice flour
1 level teaspoon baking powder
3 oz. (75 g.) butter or margarine

3 oz. (75 g.) castor sugar
1½ oz. (40 g.) ground almonds
2 eggs, well beaten

Sieve the flours and the baking powder together into a separate bowl. Cream the butter or margarine and the sugar in the mixing bowl and then alternately add the beaten eggs and the flours, beating well with the spoon. When thoroughly mixed and creamy add the ground almonds and mix well. Half fill 12 greased patty-tins and bake at 350°F. (180°C.) or gas mark 4 for 10–15 minutes until they have risen well and are golden on top. Turn out on to a wire tray while hot.

PARLIES

These ginger biscuits take their name from the tradition that they were eaten by members of the Scottish Parliament. In the last century they were sold on stalls in the streets of Edinburgh. Very good they are too.

1 lb. (450 g.) flour, sifted and dried	½ lb. (225 g.) brown sugar
4 teaspoons ground ginger, sifted	½ lb. (225 g.) butter or margarine
	½ lb. (225 g.) black treacle

Mix the flour, ginger and sugar well together. Melt the butter in a saucepan, add the treacle to it and bring to the boil stirring all the time. Pour into the dry ingredients while mixing vigorously. Work the paste with your hands as soon as it is cool enough to be bearable and roll out on a slab until it is very thin, hardly more than ⅛ inch (0·3 cm.). Cut into squares with a knife and bake at 300°F. (150°C.) or gas mark 2 for 15–20 minutes. Allow to cool completely before serving and keep them in an airtight jar or tin in a cool place to preserve their crispness.

PETTICOAT TAILS

Some say that the name comes from the French *petites gatelles*, little cakes, but in *The Cook and Housewife's Manual* of 1826 by

'Meg Dods' (Christian Isobel Johnstone) the author says: 'It may be so: in Scottish culinary terms there are many corruptions, though we rather think the name petticoat tails has its origin in the shape of the cakes, which is exactly that of the bell-hoop petticoats of our ancient Court ladies.' Mary Queen of Scots is said to have been fond of these biscuits.

1 heaped teaspoon caraway seeds (optional) 12 oz. (350 g.) flour, sifted and dried	3 heaped tablespoons castor sugar 4 tablespoons milk

If you are using them, mix the caraway seeds with the sifted flour and put the milk and the butter into a small saucepan over a low light to melt and warm up but do not allow to boil. Making a well in the centre of the flour, pour in the milk and melted butter, then add the sugar. Mix thoroughly and knead it a little to ensure thorough amalgamation, but do not knead it too long or the texture will be spoiled. Put it on to a lightly floured slab or board and roll out until it is $\frac{1}{4}$ inch (0·6 cm.) thick. Put an inverted dinner plate on top and cut around the edge to secure a large circle, and, with a wine glass, cut out a small circle in the centre, reserving the piece so removed to be baked with the rest. Transfer to greased paper on a baking sheet (together with the circular piece from the centre). With a knife make 8 deep radial cuts in the paste, evenly spaced and bake at 350°F. (180°C.) or gas mark 4 until golden and crisp (about 20 minutes). Cool completely on a wire rack, dust with castor sugar and arrange so that the small circular cake is in the centre, surrounded by the separated petticoat tails. Keep in an airtight jar or tin to preserve their crispness.

PITCAITHLY BANNOCK

8 oz. (225 g.) butter or
  margarine
4 oz. (125 g.) castor sugar
2 oz. (50 g.) rice flour
13 oz. (375 g.) flour,
  sifted and dried

2 oz. (50 g.) almonds,
  blanched and chopped
2 oz. (50 g.) candied
  orange peel, chopped

Work together by hand the butter or margarine and the sugar on a slab or pastry board, then work in the rice flour and finally the sifted wheat flour. Flatten out and strew with the blanched, chopped almonds and chopped peel, working them well in so that they are evenly distributed, but do not continue kneading for too long or the texture will be spoiled. Put into a polythene bag and leave overnight in the refrigerator (the warmest part). The following day press out by hand into a round cake ¾ inch (1·9 cm.) thick and decorate the edge by pinching with the thumb or using a pastry wheel. Prick the top all over with a fork, place on a sheet of greased grease-proof paper on a baking sheet and bake at 425°F. (220°C.) or gas mark 7 for the first 10 minutes, then lowering the heat to 375°F. (190°C.) or gas mark 5 and continuing until the top is golden brown all over. If you find that, in your oven, the edge tends to become too deeply coloured, this can be overcome by surrounding the edge with a strip of doubled grease-proof paper held in position with a paper clip.

SEED CAKE

8 oz. (225 g.) butter or
  margarine
8 oz. (225 g.) castor
  sugar

4 large eggs, separated,
  whites beaten stiff
8 oz. (225 g.) flour, sifted
  and dried

3 oz. (75 g.) candied
   orange peel
¼ level teaspoon nutmeg,
   grated
1 level teaspoon caraway
   seeds

2 tablespoons brandy
½ oz. (15 g.) caraway
   comfits

Cream the butter and sugar well and beat in a teaspoon of flour followed by an egg yolk, repeating until all the yolks have been beaten in, then add the candied peel, the grated nutmeg and the caraway seeds. Gently fold in the stiffly beaten white of the eggs and the rest of the flour and then add the brandy. Put the mixture into a well-greased and lined cake tin 8 inches (20·3 cm.) size and scatter the caraway comfits on the top. Bake at 350°F. (180°C.) or gas mark 4 for 1 hour, but keep a watch towards the end that the top does not become too brown. Test with a knitting needle to confirm that the middle is cooked and lower the heat if the top shows signs of passing beyond the golden stage, or cover loosely with grease-proof paper.

SELKIRK BANNOCK

This bannock is a yeasted fruit not at all like the oatcake bannock, page 225, and it was first made by Robbie Douglas, a baker of Selkirk in 1859. It was originally made only with the best Turkish sultanas, but nowadays a little candied orange peel is also added and this gives a very pleasant flavour.

4 oz. (125 g.) butter
4 oz. (125 g.) lard
½ pint (300 ml.) milk,
   tepid
1 oz. (25 g.) fresh yeast or
   ½ oz. (12 g.) dried
½ teaspoon sugar
2 lb. (900 g.) sifted flour

1 lb. (450 g.)
   sultanas
½ lb (225 g.) sugar } slightly warmed
4 oz. (125 g.) candied
   orange peel, chopped,
   optional
a little milk mixed with
   sugar for glazing

Heat the butter and lard until soft, but do not let it oil. Add the milk, warmed to blood heat and reserve. Cream the yeast with the ½ teaspoon sugar, add the milk and butter mixture and let the yeast work.

Meanwhile sift the flour, make a well in the middle and pour in the liquid, then sprinkle the flour from the sides lightly over the top, so that it bubbles through and makes a batter. Cover with a cloth and leave in a warm place for about 1 hour or until it has almost doubled in size. Knead well by punching it down, add the fruit with the remaining sugar and the peel. Knead again for about 5 minutes, then shape into a round flattish shape (or put into a loaf tin if preferred, but the dough should only come to two-thirds of the way up) and put again, covered in a warm place to rise for about 45 minutes. It can be enclosed and secured in a large polythene bag if preferred.

Then bake in a moderate oven, 350°F. (180°C.) or gas mark 4, for 1¼ hours, take out and brush over the top with the milk which has had a little sugar dissolved in it and put back in the oven to cook for a further 15 minutes. Test with a skewer before taking from the oven and the bottom will sound hollow when tapped if it is properly cooked.

SHORTBREAD

This traditional cake is special to Scotland and is eaten all the year round, but especially at Christmas and for the New Year. It is made only from the finest ingredients and will not have the proper flavour if butter is not used (although margarine makes a pleasant enough cake). Originally it was made with oatmeal, but nowadays the finest sifted flour and rice flour are used. The Hogmanay shortbread is often larger and a little thicker and decorated with candied citron peel and some almond comfits.

In Shetland and Orkney islands it is called the Bride's Bonn and has a few caraway seeds in it. The edges are traditionally notched by pinching with the finger and thumb and this is thought to symbolize the sun's rays, from the early days of sun-worship.

The ingredients should be warm and dry.

1 lb. (450 g.) butter	1 lb. (450 g.) sifted flour
8 oz. (225 g.) castor sugar	8 oz. (225 g.) rice flour
pinch of salt	

Cream the butter and sugar together very well. Mix the flours and salt, sift them, then incorporate them gradually but thoroughly until the dough is like a shortcrust pastry texture. Do not knead or roll out as this only toughens it. Press with the hand into 2 round cakes and if you don't have a wooden short-bread mould, then put on to an ungreased baking sheet covered with baking-paper. The usual thickness is about ¾ inch (1·9 cm.) for an 8-inch (20·3-cm.) shortbread.

Pinch the edges regularly with the finger and thumb and prick all over, lightly with a fork. Cook in a pre-heated oven at 375°F. (190°C.) or gas mark 5 for about 1 hour, and after 20 minutes reduce the heat to 350°F. (180°C.) or gas mark 4 to let it crisp up and get a pale fawn colour. Leave to cool before putting on to a rack.

NOTE: if rice flour is not available then all wheat flour can be used, but reduce to 1 lb. (450 g.) in all.

SEE ALSO: *Ginger Shortbread*, page 244, and *Pitcaithly Bannock*, page 249.

SNOW CAKE

This is a very light Scots cake made only with arrowroot: butter only should be used.

8 oz. (225 g.) butter	flavouring, such as almond
4 oz. (125 g.) castor sugar	essence, ½ grated lemon
8 oz. (225 g.) arrowroot	rind or use vanilla sugar
3 stiffly beaten egg whites	

Beat the butter until it is creamy and light. Mix the arrowroot with the sugar and if using grated lemon rind then add it now; reserve the other flavourings if using. Gradually add the arrowroot to the butter, beating well after each addition. Beat the egg whites until stiff but not too firm, then add to the cake mixture and beat well for about 15 minutes and when finished add the almond or other flavouring if using.

Butter an 8-inch (20·3 cm.) cake tin, pour the mixture in and bake in a moderate oven, 350°F. (180°C.) or gas mark 4, for about 1 hour, or until the cake is well risen, and is firm and springy to the touch. Test with a very thin skewer if in doubt.

TANTALLON CAKES

These little cakes are possibly named after Tantallon Castle, North Berwick, formerly owned by Earl Fife. They are popular all over, but this recipe comes from Edinburgh in the nineteenth century. They are light and delicious.

8 oz. (225 g.) sifted flour	8 oz. (225 g.) castor sugar
8 oz. (225 g.) rice flour	2 eggs, beaten
1 teaspoon bicarbonate of soda	finely grated rind of 1 lemon
8 oz. (225 g.) butter	castor sugar for garnish

Mix the two flours and the bicarbonate of soda, then sift them well. Cream the butter and sugar, beat the eggs, then add them alternately with the flours beating well after each addition. Add the finely grated lemon rind and mix it in thoroughly.

It should be a stiff dough: then put out on to a lightly floured surface and roll out thinly and cut into small shapes if possible with a scallop edge. Put on to a lightly greased baking sheet about 2 inches (5 cm.) apart and bake at 400°F. (200°C.) or gas mark 6 for about half an hour.

When cool, dust them lightly with the castor sugar. Makes about 15–20 small cakes.

TEA LOAF

There are a great many varieties of these to be found all over Scotland.

4 oz. (125 g.) butter or margarine	½ level teaspoon ground caraway seeds
12 oz. (350 g.) flour, sifted and dried	1 teaspoon powdered cinnamon
8 oz. (225 g.) sugar	2 eggs, well beaten
8 oz. (225 g.) sultanas	1 level teaspoon bicarbonate of soda
1 teaspoon ground cloves	

Rub the butter into the flour until it is flaky, then add the sugar, sultanas and spices, mixing thoroughly. Dissolve the bicarbonate of soda in the beaten eggs and mix well into the dry ingredients. Put into a greased loaf tin, 2 lb. (900 g.) size, and bake at 425°F. (220°C.) or gas mark 7 for 10 minutes, after which lower the heat to 375°F. (190°C.) or gas mark 5 for 1 hour and 20 minutes. Test with a knitting needle to make sure that the inside is done and turn out on to a wire tray to cool.

VINEGAR CAKE

This is an excellent 'no-egg' cake for the family.

6 oz. (175 g.) butter or margarine	4 oz. (125 g.) raisins, stoned and washed
1 lb. (450 g.) flour, sifted	3 tablespoons vinegar
½ lb. (225 g.) sugar	6 fl. oz. (175 ml.) milk
½ lb. (225 g.) currants, washed	1 teaspoon bicarbonate of soda

Rub the butter or margarine well into the flour until it is flaky, then add the sugar and fruit. Put the vinegar into a jug of at least 1½ pints (850 ml.) capacity, add 5 fl. oz. (150 ml.) of the milk and stir well. Warm the remaining milk slightly and dissolve the bicarbonate of soda in it, then add to the milk and vinegar in the jug, holding it over the mixing bowl, as the milk will froth up vigorously. Add it to the mixture, stirring it in quickly and, without delay, put the cake mixture into a greased cake tin, 9-inch (22·8-cm.) size, and bake at 350°F. (180°C.) or gas mark 4 for 20–25 minutes until it has risen well, then lower the heat to 325°F. (170°C.) or gas mark 3 and continue baking for another 40–50 minutes. Test with a knitting needle to be sure that the inside is done and turn out on to a wire tray to cool.

MISCELLANEOUS

Preserves

AVERN JELLY

Avern is a Scottish regional name for wild strawberries.

3 lb. (1·4 kg.) wild strawberries	2 pints (1 litre) cold water
juice of 2 lemons	white sugar as required

Put the wild strawberries into a preserving-pan or large saucepan and add the lemon juice and the cold water. Bring slowly to the boil and simmer very gently until the fruit is cooked and all the juice is liberated from it. Drip the juice through a jelly bag or muslin overnight and next day measure the quantity. To every pint (600 ml.) of juice add 1 lb. (450 g.) of white sugar. Bring all the juice and sugar to the boil and stir to ensure that all the sugar is dissolved and continue boiling at between 220° and 222°F. (104·5° and 105·5°C.), removing any scum that may rise to the top and from time to time testing a few drops on a cold plate until it shows signs of setting into a jelly. Then pour it into sterilized and warmed pots and seal at once.

Makes about 6 lb. jelly.

BLAEBERRY JAM

7 lb. (3·2 kg.) blaeberries   5 lb. (2·3 kg.) preserving
1 lb. (450 g.) rhubarb   sugar

Make sure that the blaeberries are well cleaned and without fragments of leaf or stalk. Swill out a preserving-pan or large saucepan with cold water to moisten it, then put the rhubarb into it and cover with the sugar. Maintain over a low heat stirring continuously until the rhubarb gives up its juices and the sugar dissolves. When all the sugar is dissolved, boil rapidly for 10 minutes and add the blaeberries. When the mixture has come back to boiling, simmer gently, skimming periodically, until the jam, when tested on a cold plate, shows sufficient signs of setting, about 15–20 minutes, then pour into sterilized and heated pots and seal.

Makes about 10–12 lb. jam.

DAMSON CHEESE

washed ripe damsons   white sugar

Put the damsons into the inner part of a large double boiler and bring the water in the outer part to the boil, cooking the damsons until they are a pulp. Pass them through the fine sieve appliance of a food processor or rub the pulp through a fine sieve. Discard the stones and skins. Measure the resultant damson pulp and for every pint (600 ml.) allow 1 lb. (450 g.) white sugar. Put the pulp and sugar into a preserving-pan or large saucepan and stir continuously over a low heat until the sugar is all dissolved and continue at a higher heat until the mixture reaches boiling point. Boil for 30 to 40 minutes until the cheese sets when tested on a cold plate. It is particularly important to keep stirring continuously in the last stages of boiling as the cheese has a tendency to catch and burn if this is not done. Fill into sterilized and heated pots and seal. Damson cheese is not only very good at breakfast and tea but is excellent in many kinds of puddings. Apples and plums can also be used.

DUNDEE MARMALADE

3 lb. bitter Seville oranges (1·35 kg.)	6 pints (3·4 litres) water
3 lemons	6 lb. (2·7 kg.) preserving sugar

Wash the oranges and lemons and put them, whole, into a large saucepan with the water. Cover and bring to the boil, simmer gently for around 1½ hours until the skins are tender when pricked with a skewer, then lift out with a draining spoon, leaving the juice in the saucepan. When the fruit has cooled enough to handle cut it into quarters and remove the pips and add them to the juices in the saucepan, boiling it up again for ten minutes. Meanwhile, slice the fruit to the thickness you prefer (a traditional Dundee marmalade has quite a coarse texture). Strain the juice in the saucepan to remove the pips and return the cut fruit to it and add the sugar, stirring until the sugar dissolves and the whole returns to the boil. Boil rapidly without stirring for about ½ hour until the temperature reaches 220°F. (104·5°C.) or a few drops 'wrinkle' on a cold plate. Pour into sterilized and heated jars and seal.

Makes around 8 lb. (3·6 kg.)

RED CURRANT JELLY

See *Avern Jelly* (page 256), but omit lemons.

Cleaned and washed redcurrants	water white sugar

Put the cleaned and washed redcurrants (there is no need to destalk them) into a large saucepan and barely cover with water. Bring to boil and boil until soft but not longer. Turn into a jelly-bag or muslin and drip overnight without squeezing. The next day measure the juice and to very pint (600 ml.) of juice allow 1 lb. (450 g.) of white sugar. Put the juice and sugar into a preserving-pan or large saucepan and bring to the boil, stirring to ensure that all the sugar is dissolved. Boil briskly until the temperature reaches 220°F. (104·5°C.) or until a few drops tested on a cold plate jelly. Pour at once into sterilized and heated pots and seal.

ROWANBERRY JELLY

Rowanberries are known as Rodden in Scotland.

3 lb. (1·4 kg.) rowanberries	water
2 large apples, chopped	white sugar

Put the rowanberries and the chopped apples (no need to peel or core the latter) into a large saucepan, cover with the water and boil for 40 minutes. Turn into a jelly-bag or muslin and drip overnight. Next day measure the amount of juice and allow 1 lb. (450 g.) white sugar for every pint ($\frac{1}{2}$ litre) of juice. Bring the juice and sugar to the boil in a preserving-pan or large saucepan, stirring to ensure that the sugar is completely dissolved and continue boiling briskly until the temperature reaches 220°F. (104·5°C.) or until a few drops tested on a cold plate jelly. Pour into sterilized and heated pots and seal.

Sweetmeats

BUTTERSCOTCH

2 lb. (900 g.) brown sugar   1 tablespoon lemon juice or
¼ pint (150 ml.) milk   1 heaped teaspoon
¼ pint (150 ml.) water   ground ginger
8 oz. (225 g.) butter, creamed

Put the sugar, milk and water into a saucepan and bring to the boil while stirring continuously to ensure that the sugar dissolves completely, then add the creamed butter, allow to come to the boil again and keep the mixture boiling gently while stirring all the while until it has been boiling for about 20 minutes. Test it from time to time by dropping a little into ice-cold water and when it forms a hard lump in the water, beat it very well for about 5 minutes and pour it on to a buttered slab or into a buttered tin. While still a little warm, mark it into squares on the top with a knife. When it is fully cold and set, remove it, turn it upside down and tap it with the heavy handle of a knife to break it up into squares. Store it in an airtight tin or it will turn soft and sticky.

EDINBURGH ROCK

Traditionally made since the eighteenth century by the Edinburgh firm of Ferguson.

> Quelle est cette odeur agréable
> That's wafted on the air?
> The perfumes of Arabia
> Cannot with it compare.
> What makes the crowds to Melbourne Place
> With wide-stretched nostrils flock?
> It's Ferguson who's boiling up
> His Edinburgh rock.
>
>   John W. Oliver

1 lb. (450 g.) crushed lump sugar

½ teaspoon cream of tartar

8 fl. oz. (225 ml.) water

a pinch or a few drops of each:

flavours and colours to taste as below:

ginger – fawn, raspberry – pink, orange – orange, lemon – yellow, peppermint – green, vanilla – white.

Heat the sugar and the water stirring the while to ensure that the sugar is completely dissolved. Just before the solution begins to boil, add the cream of tartar and boil without stirring until the temperature reaches 250°F. (130°C.). Remove from the heat and stir in whatever colouring and flavouring you wish (always remembering that the colour should be brighter than the final colour you want as it will fade as the rock is 'pulled'). If you do not have a sugar thermometer, test by dropping a few drops into ice-cold water; it is ready when it forms a hard ball. Pour on to 'candy bars' (available at shops selling confectioner's equipment) or on to a buttered slab. Cool slightly and turn the edges to the centre with a buttered spatula or knife. When it is cool enough to handle, dust it with icing sugar, top and bottom, and 'pull' it quickly and evenly, taking care not to twist it while doing so. It is best to do this in a warm room, or near a stove or fire, or the candy will cool too quickly in the process and become stiff and brittle. Finally, draw the candy out into strips and cut it into pieces about 1 inch (2·5 cm.) in length with a pair of well-oiled scissors. Leave the pieces on greaseproof paper in a warm room for 24 hours and store them in an airtight tin.

GLESSIE

A traditional toffee.

1 teaspoon cream of tartar

2 tablespoons cold water

½ lb. (225 g.) moist brown sugar

½ oz. (15 g.) butter or margarine

1½ lb. (700 g.) golden syrup

Put the cream of tartar, water, sugar and butter or margarine into a non-stick saucepan and bring slowly to the boil, stirring the while to ensure that the ingredients are thoroughly mixed and dissolved. After boiling for five minutes add the golden syrup and continue stirring until the candy comes to the boil again, then boil without stirring for 30 minutes, until a few drops dropped into ice-cold water form a hard ball. It is now ready to be poured out on to a greased slab or tin. Mark into sections with a greased knife and break by tapping when cold. It can also be 'pulled' and cut like rock.

GUNDY

Another old sweetmeat; in Sir Walter Scott's boyhood it was sold by Mrs Flockhart in Potter Row, Edinburgh.

1 lb. (450 g.) brown sugar
1 tablespoon golden
  syrup
2 oz. (50 g.) butter or
  margarine

a few drops of oil of
  aniseed or cinnamon

Put the sugar, syrup and butter into a saucepan and heat on a low flame, stirring continuously to avoid the mixture catching. When all is dissolved and has come to the boil, continue boiling until a little dropped into ice-cold water becomes at once brittle. Flavour with oil of niseed or cinnamon to taste, stirring well to mix the flavouring evenly and pour out on to a buttered slab. When nearly cool mark the top into squares with a knife and when quite cold, remove from the slab and break into squares by tapping the bottom with the handle of a knife. Glessie is another traditional toffee similar to Gundy but without the flavouring.

HELENSBURG TOFFEE

From the town of the same name, across the water from Green-
ock, the town of sugar refineries.

2 lb. (900 g.) crushed
  lump sugar
1 tin of sweetened
  condensed milk

4 oz. (125 g.) salted butter
7 fl. oz. (200 ml.) water
½ vanilla pod

Put the sugar, the condensed milk, the butter and the water into
a preserving-pan or large non-stick saucepan and bring gently to
the boil, stirring continuously. Boil for 45 minutes, stirring all
the while to avoid sticking. In the last five minutes add the
½ vanilla pod, but remove it before pouring the toffee out on to a
buttered slab or tin. When nearly cool, mark the top into squares
with a knife and when completely cold, remove from slab and
break up into squares by tapping the bottom with a knife handle.
Halved walnuts placed on the top of the toffee just after it has
been poured out make a pleasant addition, or chopped walnuts
may be stirred in immediately after the vanilla pod has been
removed.

MEALY CANDY

An old farmhouse and cottage sweetmeat.

3½ lb. (1·6 kilos) crushed
  lump sugar
1 lb. (450 g.) treacle
1¼ pints (750 ml.) water

½ lb. (225 g.) toasted
  oatmeal
2 oz. (50 g.) ground
  ginger

Put the sugar, treacle and water into a large non-stick saucepan
and bring to the boil, stirring continuously with a wooden
spoon. After it has boiled for 10 minutes, remove from the heat
and beat vigorously with the spoon until the whole becomes

creamy, then stir in the oatmeal and the ginger. Pour into tins lined with oiled greaseproof paper to a depth of half an inch (1·3 cm.). When it has become firm enough, cut it into cubes and when cold, remove the greaseproof paper. Store in an airtight tin or jar.

BLACK MAN

A traditional cottage and farmhouse toffee.

2 lb. (900 g.) treacle
1 teaspoon vinegar
a few drops of almond,
  lemon or peppermint
  flavour

$\frac{1}{4}$ teaspoon bicarbonate of
  soda

Put the treacle and vinegar into a large non-stick saucepan and bring gently to the boil, stirring continuously to avoid the treacle sticking. Let it boil very gently for 10 minutes, stirring the while and then test it by dropping a few drops into ice-cold water; if it becomes brittle, it is done. Add the flavouring to taste and then the bicarbonate of soda, stirring the latter in vigorously. Pour over greased candy bars or on to a greased slab. When it has cooled slightly turn the edges in to the centre with a buttered spatula or knife. Oil the hands well and when the candy is cool enough not to burn the skin 'pull' it energetically until it has become light in colour and cut into lengths of around six inches (15·2 cm.) with a well-oiled pair of scissors. Keep in an airtight jar or tin.

TABLET OR TAIBLET

Traditional toffee recipe.

½ lb. (225 g.) butter or
  margarine
1 pint (½ litre) water
4 lb. (1·8 kg.) castor
  sugar

1 lb. (450 g.) sweetened
  condensed milk

Put the butter and water into a non-stick saucepan and melt on a low heat. When the butter is melted add the sugar and bring to the boil stirring all the time to avoid the sugar catching. When boiling add the condensed milk and simmer for 20 minutes, stirring to prevent sticking, then take off the heat and beat vigorously for 5 minutes adding the flavouring of your choice. Pour into a greased tin and, when partly cooled, divide into bars about 5 inches long by 1½ inches wide (12·5 cm. × 3·8 cm.). When cold, wrap each bar in waxed paper and store in an airtight jar or tin. Makes about 4 lb. (1·8 kg.) of toffee.

Oatmeal

BROSE

3 oz. (75 g.) oatmeal
salt, to taste

½ oz. (15 g.) butter
boiling water, to cover

Put the oatmeal into a wooden, preferably birchwood, bowl, add the salt to taste and the butter. Pour on enough boiling water to well cover the oatmeal and stir it with a spirtle or a wooden spoon, allowing lumps to form. It is good eaten with either sweet milk or buttermilk. See also *Kail Brose*, page 15.

PORRIDGE

2½ oz. (65 g.) medium oatmeal	1 pint (½ litre) water salt to taste

Bring the water to the boil in a non-stick saucepan and, when it is bubbling vigorously, add the oatmeal in a thin stream with the left hand while stirring briskly (tradition says *always* clockwise) with the right hand. When it has returned to a brisk boil, reduce the heat, cover and simmer very gently for 15 minutes, then add the salt to taste and stir well. Cover again and simmer gently for a further 5–10 minutes depending upon the quality of the oatmeal. Serve piping hot in wooden bowls. Silver porringers, while elegant in appearance, are not satisfactory in performance as they are not only at first burningly hot (if you must use them supply each guest with an additional napkin to hold them with) but quickly allow the porridge to become too cold. Wooden bowls are best but, failing them, use china soup plates. The tradition still continues that porridge is always eaten standing.

Serves 2.

Savouries

NUN'S BEADS

Adapted from a recipe of Mrs Dalgairns, c. 1829.

4 oz. (125 g.) cheese, Dunlop for preference salt to taste 3 egg yolks, well beaten	1 oz. (25 g.) breadcrumbs 6 oz. (175 g.) puff pastry, see page 218 cooking oil for deep-frying

Grate the cheese finely and blend it with the beaten egg yolks adding the salt to taste. Some naturally salty cheeses will not need the addition of salt. Next blend the breadcrumbs into the mixture and form the whole into balls the size of walnuts. Cover each ball with a thin layer of puff pastry and deep-fry them in cooking oil that is really hot but not smoking until they are a golden brown. Drain them well and serve in a dish lined with absorbent paper. This makes a delicious savoury to serve with drinks. A very tiny pinch of marjoram or curry powder added to the mixture before the breadcrumbs, while not traditional, makes a stimulating variation.

SCOTS EGGS

10 eggs (8 hard-boiled)
1 tablespoon cold water
1½ lb. (700 g.) pork
  sausage-meat
a pinch of mace
salt and freshly ground
  black pepper

4 oz. (125 g.) approx.
  breadcrumbs, toasted
cooking oil for deep-frying
watercress, well washed

Boil 8 of the eggs for 10 minutes in salted boiling water, then take them out, cool them under the cold tap and shell them. Beat up 1 of the remaining eggs with 1 tablespoon of cold water. Season the sausage-meat with the mace, salt and freshly ground black pepper. Dip a hard-boiled egg into the beaten egg and cover it all over with sausage-meat, pressing it firmly on with the hands. Repeat with the other hard-boiled eggs. Beat up the last egg and carefully roll the sausage-meat covered eggs in this and then in the breadcrumbs, pressing the breadcrumbs into the sausage-meat. Then deep-fry them one by one in the hot but not smoking cooking oil until they are a golden brown, drain well and serve on a very hot dish garnished with watercress and accompanied with mustard. They may also be served cold with a salad of chopped celery and apple dressed with olive oil and vinegar to taste.

Serves 4.

SCOTS WOODCOCK

4 slices of bread, crust
  removed
½ oz. (15 g.) butter or
  margarine
8 anchovy fillets, chopped

4 egg yolks
½ pint (¼ litre) thin cream
pinch of cayenne pepper
1 tablespoon parsley,
  finely chopped

Toast the bread on both sides, spread thinly with the butter
and make 2 sandwiches with the chopped anchovies, reserving
each upon a hot plate. Well beat the egg yolks with the cream
and cayenne pepper and, continuously stirring, heat in a double
boiler until the sauce thickens, then pour over the toasted sandwiches and scatter with the finely chopped parsley. Serve piping
hot.

Serves 2.

Beverages and Punch

ATHOL BROSE

The Duke of Atholl's recipe (the 8th duke).

3 oz. (75 g.) oatmeal
2 tablespoons liquid
  heather honey

whisky to make up 1 quart
¾ pint (450 ml.) cold water

Put the oatmeal into a bowl and mix it with the water until it is a
thick paste, then let it stand for ½ hour, after which pass it
through a fine strainer, pressing down with a wooden spoon to
expel the last of the liquid. Throw away the dry oatmeal and mix
the liquid with the clear heather honey, stirring with a silver
spoon until it is well blended. Pour the mixture into a quart
bottle and fill up with whisky, cork it well and always shake the
bottle before pouring. It can also be used as a dessert by putting
8 tablespoonsful into four tall glasses, topping up with whipped

cream and sprinkling over a little lightly toasted oatmeal.

Serves 4.

AULD MAN'S MILK

Meg Dods's recipe, *c.* 1826, is no doubt the origin of egg-nog.

6 eggs, separated
4 pints (2 litres) milk or thin cream

1 pint ($\frac{1}{2}$ litre) whisky
pinch of ground nutmeg

Beat the egg yolks with the milk or thin cream and stir in the whisky, then whip the whites stiffly and fold them into the mixture. Serve in a punch bowl with the top scattered with the ground nutmeg.

HET PINT

A traditional drink at Hogmanay.

4 pints (2·3 litres) mild ale
1 teaspoon ground nutmeg
4 oz. (125 g.) castor sugar

3 eggs
$\frac{1}{2}$ pint (275 ml.) whisky

Put the ale into a large, thick-bottomed saucepan, add the nutmeg and bring to just under boiling-point. Then add the sugar and stir until it is dissolved. Beat the eggs, and making sure that the mixture is not boiling, add them very gradually to the mixture stirring vigorously to ensure that they do not curdle into lumps, next add the whisky, mixing well and allow the whole to become really hot but just a little under boiling. Serve in warmed tankards, pouring back and forth to give a head. If the mixture is allowed to boil, it will curdle so care should be taken.

PIRR

A recipe from the Shetland Islands.

2 tablespoons oatmeal	$\frac{1}{4}$ pint (150 ml.) milk, warm
1 teaspoon sugar	$\frac{1}{2}$ pint ($\frac{1}{4}$ litre) water, boiling
$\frac{1}{4}$ teaspoon cream of tartar	

Mix the oatmeal, sugar, cream of tartar and the warm milk in a warmed jug until it is a smooth paste, then pour on the boiling water stirring vigorously. Serve hot.

TODDY

'Sit roun' the table well content
An' steer aboot the toddy.'

3–4 lumps sugar	whisky, hot but not boiling
slice of lemon	

Warm a toddy glass or tumbler, put the sugar and the lemon into it and pour over them enough boiling water so that the sugar dissolves easily when stirred (with a silver spoon), then add the same amount of hot whisky. It is well to put the silver spoon into the glass before pouring in the boiling water as silver, being an exceptionally good conductor of heat, will prevent the glass from cracking.

WHISKY PUNCH, HOT

2 pints (1·1 litres) freshly made milkless tea, strained	1 lemon, thinly sliced
1 lb. (450 g.) lump sugar	1 bottle of whisky, hot but not boiling

Pour the hot tea over the sugar and lemon in a large bowl, stirring with a silver spoon until the sugar has dissolved, then add the hot, but not boiling whisky, flame and serve.

VARIATION: with a very sharp vegetable knife carefully pare the thin yellow outer rind from two lemons, having first cut a few slices from one of them. Squeeze the lemons and put the juice, together with the thin rind and the pound of sugar, into the bowl and proceed as in the first recipe. Before flaming add the thin lemon slices. This variation avoids the quantities of lemon pith and fibre that tend to spoil the appearance of the punch if the first recipe is followed. The lemon rind may be removed before serving.

WHISKY PUNCH, COLD

3 lemons	$\frac{1}{2}$ lb. (225 g.) lump sugar
2 pints (1·1 litres) water, boiling	1 bottle whisky
	a few leaves of mint

With a sharp vegetable or other small knife take the outer rind (the yellow part only, not the pith) from the lemons and squeeze the juice from them. Put the lemon peel, juice, mint and sugar into a large jug, add the boiling water stirring well to ensure that the sugar fully dissolves and allow to grow cold. When cold, remove the lemon peel and chill before serving. A garnish of thinly sliced soft fruit can be added just before serving if liked.

Cheeses

DUNLOP cheese was first made by Barbara Gilmour in Ayrshire in 1688 after she had travelled to Ireland to learn the art of cheese-making. It was named after the town she lived in and is Scotland's earliest hard cheese. It is similar to Cheddar in flavour, but is slightly softer and has a high water content so does not travel well. However, it has a mellow flavour and can be used both for eating plain or for cooking. Formerly it was very white in colour, but nowadays it is also made in a red variety.

ORKNEY is a cheese from the Orkney Islands which is a creamy cow's milk cheese, not unlike a cheddar but more flaky. It began as a farmhouse cheese, but is now commercially produced in red, white and also smoked. It is an interesting cheese and worth trying.

STEWART cheeses are made in two varieties: one white and the other blue. The latter is a mild cheese, pleasant to taste, but the white Stewart cheese is inclined to be salty and an acquired taste.

CABOC is an unusual cheese which deserves to be better known. It is a cream cheese shaped like a thick sausage and rolled in coarse oatmeal. It is good for eating with oatcakes or cheese biscuits. It is fairly bland and is improved if served with a little freshly ground black pepper.

HRAMSA cheese is made with cream and flavoured with wild garlic. It is soft in texture and needs to be eaten freshly. It is good for canapés or for making a cheese spread or dip.

CROWDIE is a soft cottage cheese, best made with fresh milk from a farmhouse. It has many uses, some of which will be found in this book. Cream is sometimes added to the commercial variety, but in the writer's opinion does not improve it.

SCOTTISH CHEDDAR is only one of the several cheeses made which are not traditional to Scotland but imitations of foreign cheeses. They are quite pleasant, but do not come up to the original cheeses made in the country of origin.

INDEX